Accents of English is about the way English is pronounced by different people in different places. Volume 1 provides a synthesizing introduction, which shows how accents vary not only geographically, but also with social class, formality, sex and age; and in volumes 2 and 3 the author examines in greater depth the various accents used by people who speak English as their mother tongue: the accents of the regions of England, Wales, Scotland and Ireland (volume 2), and of the USA, Canada, the West Indies, Australia, New Zealand, South Africa, India, Black Africa and the Far East (volume 3). Each volume can be read independently, and together they form a major scholarly survey of considerable originality, which not only includes descriptions of hitherto neglected accents, but also examines the implications for phonological theory.

Readers will find the answers to many questions: Who makes 'good' rhyme with 'mood'? Which accents have no voiced sibilants? How is a Canadian accent different from an American one, a New Zealand one from an Australian one, a Jamaican one from a Barbadian one? What are the historical reasons for British–American pronunciation differences? What sound changes are currently in progress in New York, in London, in Edinburgh? Dr Wells has written principally for students of linguistics, phonetics and English language, but the motivated general reader will also find the study both fascinating and rewarding.

An illustrative cassette accompanies volume 1.

The author is Professor of Phonetics, University College London

Cover design by Jan van de Watering

The depth of shading on the world map indicates those areas where English is to a greater or lesser degree the mother tongue of the population.

Accents of English I

Accents of English   I

An Introduction

J. C. WELLS

CAMBRIDGE
UNIVERSITY PRESS

Published by the Press Syndicate of the University of Cambridge
The Pitt Building, Trumpington Street, Cambridge CB2 1RP
40 West 20th Street, New York, NY 10011-4211, USA
10 Stamford Road, Oakleigh, Melbourne 3166, Australia

First published 1982
Reprinted 1985, 1988, 1992, 1995, 1996, 1998

Library of Congress catalogue card number: 81-10127

British Library cataloguing in publication data

Wells, J. C.
Accents of English
I: An introduction
I. English language – Pronunciation
I. Title
421.5'2   PE1137

ISBN 0 521 29719 2 paperback Volume 1
ISBN 0 521 24224 X hardback Volume 2
ISBN 0 521 28540 2 paperback Volume 2
ISBN 0 521 24225 8 hardback Volume 3
ISBN 0 521 28541 0 paperback Volume 3

Transferred to digital printing 1999

Contents

Volume 1: An Introduction

Contents

Contents

Volume 2: The British Isles

Contents

Volume 3: Beyond the British Isles

Contents

To the memory of my father,
Philip Wells (1909–1974),
who encouraged me

Preface

I believe that the three volumes of *Accents of English* represent the first attempt ever to offer a reasonably comprehensive account of the pronunciation of English in all its native-speaker varieties.

I have of course exploited my own familiarity with the various accents – such as it is, varying in depth in accordance with the varying exposure to them which life has happened to give me. These biases will no doubt be apparent. But I have also endeavoured to make appropriate use of all kinds of scholarly treatments of particular regional forms of speech, wherever they have been available to me and to whatever tradition they belong (philological, dialectological, structuralist, 'speech', generativist, sociolinguistic, variationist). My aim has been to bring together their principal findings within a unified and integrated framework.

My own descriptive standpoint, as will be seen, lies within the University College London 'phonetic' tradition of Daniel Jones, A. C. Gimson, and J. D. O'Connor. I am fortunate to have been their pupil. This standpoint could be said to involve an eclectic amalgam of what seems valuable from both older and newer theoretical approaches.

Where surveys based on substantial fieldwork exist, I have made use of their findings. Where they do not, I have had to rely partly on my own impressions. The reader must bear in mind that some of the statements I make are for this reason necessarily tentative.

Inevitably I may be laying myself open to the charge of rushing in where angels fear to tread. Many readers will know more about the socially sensitive pronunciation variables of their home areas than I can hope to. The Rotherham native will look here in vain for a discussion of the features which distinguish his speech from that of Sheffield a few miles away – features obvious to the native, but opaque to the outsider (1.1.4 below). There is a great deal of descriptive work remaining to be done.

I see the original contribution of these volumes as lying principally in the following areas: (i) the description of certain neglected accents, including certain accents of the British Isles and the West Indies; (ii) the identification and naming of a number of phonological processes, both historical and synchronic; (iii) the bringing together into a single descriptive framework of accounts by scholars working in many different places and in many different traditions.

Many people have helped me through discussion or correspondence, and in some instances by reading parts of the manuscript. In this regard I would mention particularly D. Abercrombie, K. Albrow, C.-J. N. Bailey, A. Bliss, N. Copeland, R. Easton, A. C. Gimson, T. Hackman, J. Harris, S. Hutcheson, L. Lanham, R. Lass, F. MacEinrí, J. D. McClure, J. Milroy, J. D. O'Connor, H. Paddock, S. M. Ramsaran, H.-H. Speitel, P. Trudgill and J. Windsor Lewis. Our views do not always coincide, nor have I accepted all their suggestions; responsibility for the facts and opinions here presented remains mine. I am aware that these are far from the last word on the subject. For any shortcomings I beg indulgence on the grounds that something, however inadequate, is better than nothing.

I am also grateful to J. L. M. Trim for first suggesting that I write this work, and to G. F. Arnold and O. M. Tooley – not to mention Cambridge University Press – for enquiring so assiduously after its tardy progress.

London, January 1981   JOHN WELLS

Typographical conventions
and phonetic symbols

Examples of pronunciation are set in *italics* if in ordinary spelling, otherwise in / / or [ ]. Sometimes methods are combined, thus *disapp*[ɪə]*rance* (which draws attention to the quality of the diphthong corresponding to orthographic *ea* in this word).

/ / is used for **phonemic** transcriptions: for representations believed to be analogous to the way pronunciations are stored in the mental lexicon (= underlying phonological representations); for transcriptions in which only significant sound units (phonemes) are notated.

[ ] is used for **allophonic** transcriptions: for representations believed to include more phonetic detail than is stored mentally (= surface phonetic representations); for transcriptions involving the notation of certain non-significant phoneme variants (allophones); also for **general-phonetic** or **impressionistic** notation of unanalysed data.

Note that symbols enclosed in [ ] are only selectively 'narrowed'. Thus on occasion [r] is used to stand for the ordinary English voiced post-alveolar approximant, more precisely written as [ɹ]; similarly [i] or [iː] may sometimes stand for [ɹi], etc. But where the quality of /r/ or /i(ː)/ is the topic under discussion, then the precise symbols are employed.

Phonetic symbols are taken from the International Phonetic Alphabet (see chart, p. xx). The following additional symbols are employed:

ɝ   r-coloured ɜ
ω   unrounded ʊ
ʟ   voiced velar lateral
C˺ unreleased C
C͇ unaspirated C
C   any consonant

Typographical conventions and phonetic symbols

V   any vowel
→   goes to, becomes, is realized as
~   or
$ ⎤
  ⎥ syllable boundary (indicated only when relevant)
. ⎦
stem boundary, word boundary
‖   sentence boundary, end of utterance
Ø   zero
/   in the environment:
     X → Y / A __ B   X becomes Y in the environment of a preced-
                      ing A and a following B, i.e. AXB → AYB.

Words written in capitals

Throughout the work, use is made of the concept of **standard
lexical sets**. These enable one to refer concisely to large groups of
words which tend to share the same vowel, and to the vowel which
they share. They are based on the vowel correspondences which
apply between British Received Pronunciation and (a variety of)
General American, and make use of **keywords** intended to be
unmistakable no matter what accent one says them in. Thus 'the
KIT words' refers to 'ship, bridge, milk . . .'; 'the KIT vowel' refers to
the vowel these words have (in most accents, /ɪ/); both may just be
referred to as KIT.

RP	GenAm			
ɪ	ɪ	1. KIT	ship, sick, bridge, milk, myth, busy . . .
e	ɛ	2. DRESS	step, neck, edge, shelf, friend, ready . . .
æ	æ	3. TRAP	tap, back, badge, scalp, hand, cancel . . .
ɒ	ɑ	4. LOT	stop, sock, dodge, romp, possible, quality . . .
ʌ	ʌ	5. STRUT	cup, suck, budge, pulse, trunk, blood . . .
ʊ	ʊ	6. FOOT	put, bush, full, good, look, wolf . . .
ɑː	æ	7. BATH	staff, brass, ask, dance, sample, calf . . .
ɒ	ɔ	8. CLOTH	cough, broth, cross, long, Boston . . .

ɜː	ɜr	9. NURSE	hurt, lurk, urge, burst, jerk, term ...
iː	i	10. FLEECE	creep, speak, leave, feel, key, people ...
eɪ	eɪ	11. FACE	tape, cake, raid, veil, steak, day ...
ɑː	ɑ	12. PALM	psalm, father, bra, spa, lager ...
ɔː	ɔ	13. THOUGHT	taught, sauce, hawk, jaw, broad ...
əʊ	o	14. GOAT	soap, joke, home, know, so, roll ...
uː	u	15. GOOSE	loop, shoot, tomb, mute, huge, view ...
aɪ	aɪ	16. PRICE	ripe, write, arrive, high, try, buy ...
ɔɪ	ɔɪ	17. CHOICE	adroit, noise, join, toy, royal ...
aʊ	aʊ	18. MOUTH	out, house, loud, count, crowd, cow ...
ɪə	ɪ(r	19. NEAR	beer, sincere, fear, beard, serum ...
ɛə	ɛ(r	20. SQUARE	care, fair, pear, where, scarce, vary ...
ɑː	ɑ(r	21. START	far, sharp, bark, carve, farm, heart ...
ɔː	ɔ(r	22. NORTH	for, war, short, scorch, born, warm ...
ɔː	o(r	23. FORCE	four, wore, sport, porch, borne, story ...
ʊə	ʊ(r	24. CURE	poor, tourist, pure, plural, jury ...

THE INTERNATIONAL PHONETIC ALPHABET

(Revised to 1979)

CONSONANTS		*Bilabial*	*Labiodental*	*Dental, Alveolar, or Post-alveolar*	*Retroflex*	*Palato-alveolar*	*Palatal*	*Velar*	*Uvular*	*Labial-Palatal*	*Labial-Velar*	*Pharyngeal*	*Glottal*
(pulmonic air-stream mechanism)	*Nasal*	m	ɱ	n	ɳ		ɲ	ŋ	ɴ				
	Plosive	p b		t d	ʈ ɖ		c ɟ	k g	q ɢ		k͡p g͡b		ʔ
	(Median) Fricative	ɸ β	f v	θ ð s z	ʂ ʐ	ʃ ʒ	ç ʝ	x ɣ	χ ʁ		ʍ	ħ ʕ	h ɦ
	(Median) Approximant		ʋ	ɹ	ɻ		j	ɰ		ɥ	w		
	Lateral Fricative			ɬ ɮ									
	Lateral (Approximant)			l	ɭ		ʎ						
	Trill			r					ʀ				
	Tap or Flap			ɾ	ɽ				ʀ				
(non-pulmonic air-stream)	*Ejective*	p'		t'				k'					
	Implosive	ɓ		ɗ				ɠ					
	(Median) Click	ʘ		ʇ ʗ									
	Lateral Click			ʖ									

DIACRITICS

- ˳ Voiceless n̥ d̥
- ˬ Voiced s̬ t̬
- ʰ Aspirated tʰ
- ̤ Breathy-voiced b̤ a̤
- ̪ Dental t̪
- ̫ Labialized t̫
- ʲ Palatalized tʲ
- ~ Velarized or Pharyngealized ɫ, ɫ
- ̩ Syllabic n̩ l̩
- ͡ or ͜ Simultaneous s͡f (but see also under the heading Affricates)
- ˔ or ̝ Raised e˔, e̝, e̝ w̝
- ˕ or ̞ Lowered e˕, e̞, e̞ ʁ̞
- ̟ Advanced u+, u̟
- - or ̠ Retracted i̠, i-, t̠
- ̈ Centralized ë
- ̃ Nasalized ã
- ˞, ʴ, ʁ r-coloured ɑ˞
- ː Long ɑː
- ˑ Half-long ɑˑ
- ̆ Non-syllabic ŭ
- ̹ More rounded ɔ̹
- ̜ Less rounded y̜

OTHER SYMBOLS

- ɕ, ʑ Alveolo-palatal fricatives
- ʆ, ʓ Palatalized ʃ, ʒ
- ɼ Alveolar fricative trill
- ɺ Alveolar lateral flap
- ɧ Simultaneous ʃ and x
- ʃˢ Variety of ʃ resembling s, etc.
- ɪ = ɩ
- ʊ = ɷ
- ɜ = Variety of ə
- ɚ = r-coloured ə

VOWELS

	Front		Back	*VOWELS*	Front		Back
	i ɩ	ɨ	ɯ	*Close*	y ʏ	ʉ	ɷ u
	e	ə	ɤ	*Half-close*	ø	ɵ	o
	ɛ		ʌ	*Half-open*	œ		ɔ
	æ	ɐ					
	a		ɑ	*Open*	ɶ		ɒ
		Unrounded				*Rounded*	

STRESS, TONE (PITCH)

ˈ stress, placed at beginning of stressed syllable: ˌ secondary stress: ¯ high level pitch, high tone: ˍ low level: ˊ high rising: ˏ low rising: ˋ high falling: ˎ low falling: ˆ rise-fall: ˇ fall-rise.

AFFRICATES can be written as digraphs, as ligatures, or with slur marks; thus ts, tʃ, dʒ: ʦ ʧ ʤ: t͡s t͡ʃ d͡ʒ.

I

Aspects of accent

1.1 Linguistic and social variability

1.1.1 Introduction

These three volumes are about **accents** of English. By the term 'accent', in this sense, I mean a pattern of pronunciation used by a speaker for whom English is the native language or, more generally, by the community or social grouping to which he or she belongs. More specifically, I refer to the use of particular vowel or consonant sounds and particular rhythmic, intonational, and other prosodic features; to the syntagmatic (structural) and paradigmatic (systemic) interrelationships between these, and to the more abstract (phonological) representations which can be seen as underlying the actual (phonetic) articulations, together with the rules which relate the one to the other; and to the relationship between all of these and the individual words or other items which constitute the speaker's mental lexicon or vocabulary.

An accent, in this sense, is something every speaker has. To some small extent it will be special to him or her as an individual: it is part of one **idiolect**. To a very much greater degree it is characteristic of people belonging to some geographical region and/or social class; and it may well be typical of the speaker's sex, age group, or level of education.

In this book I shall therefore avoid using the term 'accent' in its other sense, that is as a synonym of 'stress' or as a term referring to a complex of stress and tonal features. There will also be very little on the subject of 'foreign accents', that is of pronunciation patterns seen as typical of the speech of those for who English is not the native language, patterns which may be expected to reflect many of the phonological and phonetic characteristics of their mother tongue.

I shall also in these volumes leave out of account the various non-phonetic differences between different forms of the language – differences of morphology and syntax, of vocabulary, of idiom and usage. Together with the pronunciation differences which constitute the subject-matter of these volumes, these add up to the kind of variation within a language which is usually termed 'dialectal'. But one must be circumspect in using the term 'dialect' with reference to English – as discussed in the next few sections, where I shall argue the thesis that dialect exists, but dialects do not.

1.1.2 Dialect and accent

Joseph Wright, author of *The English dialect grammar*, describes a conversation he had one day in a Westmoreland village, 'A man said to me: [ðə roːdz ə dɜːtɪ], and I said to him: [dʊənt jə seː ʊp ɪər ət t rɪadz əz mʊkɪ]? With a bright smile on his face he replied: [wɪ dɪʊ], and forthwith he began to speak the dialect in its pure form.' (Wright 1905: vii. I have brought the phonetic transcription into line with that used in this work.)

The sentence *the roads are dirty* is a sentence belonging to what we may call **General English** (a range of forms of English which includes Standard English but is wider than it: see below). This first utterance by the villager is addressed to a stranger, and is therefore appropriately couched in the form of English used to communicate with outsiders, namely General English. Even so, it has certain local characteristics of pronunciation, such as the monophthong in [roːdz]: a pronunciation not localizable within England would of course have a diphthong, [roʊdz ∼ rəʊdz]. So the villager's first utterance is an instance of English spoken with a **local accent**.

The sentence which Wright then supplied has the same meaning, but sounds quite different: [t rɪadz əz mʊkɪ]. It is not a part of General English, and we have no agreed way of spelling it: perhaps *t' reeads is mucky*. It differs from the first sentence in various ways. There are some differences in vocabulary and syntax, which happen in this case to be minor: *mucky* rather than *dirty* (though *mucky* is a word which has a place in General English too, with a more restricted meaning), and *is* rather than *are* in the syntactic environment NP$_{pl}$ — Adj. The pronunciation differences are more striking:

the definite article appears as [t] rather than as [ðə], while the word for *road* is [rɪad], with a front and opening diphthong such as is found in no local accent of English. In fact Wright's alternative formulation is not a sentence of General English, but of what is known (locally, at least) as **dialect**. The Westmoreland villager is, as it were, bilingual (bidialectal). He controls not only a form of General English (which he pronounces with a local accent), but also this other tongue.

The term 'dialect' in the sense just described can be a mass noun: we use expressions such as *to speak dialect*, or *there's not much dialect nowadays around these parts*. The term is – confusingly – also used in various other senses, but in all such other senses it is a count noun (*to speak a dialect*).

In linguistics the term is applied, often in a rather vague way, to any speech variety which is more than an idiolect but less than a language. It is in this sense that one can claim that 'languages normally consist of dialects', and it is in this sense that the author whose claim I am quoting entitled his book *Dialects of American English* (Reed 1967: 2).

To avoid confusion, I shall avoid the bare term 'dialect'. The northern villager's other tongue I shall call **traditional-dialect** (resisting the urge to coin some such neologism as *paleolect* or *boreolect*). Otherwise I shall generally use the neutral term **variety**, and speak of the several varieties of General English. (An alternative terminology, which may well come to be preferred, uses **lect** rather than 'variety', with derivatives such as *isolect, sociolect*: Bailey 1973a.)

A difference between varieties, then, may involve any or all of syntax, morphology, lexicon, and pronunciation. Within General English, for instance, there are non-standard varieties in which one says *I couldn't see no one* and *Peter done it* rather than the standard *I couldn't see anyone* and *Peter did it*; and the same type of vehicle is variously called a *lorry*, a *truck*, and a *waggon*. A difference of **accent**, on the other hand, is a difference between varieties of General English which involves only pronunciation. (It seems to me that Wakelin (1972) is guilty of a regrettable misconception when he uses the expression 'local accents' as the title of a chapter devoted mainly to the phonetics of traditional-dialect.)

Thus (1a, b) are different ways of pronouncing the Standard

English sentence *you must eat it up*. They exemplify a north-of-England and a West Indies accent respectively; they differ from one another, and from the same sentence in other accents, in several phonetic or phonological details. Non-standard varieties of General English are illustrated by (2a, b), in which characteristic local lexico-syntactic usage is added to the accent details of (1). Versions (3a, b) fall outside General English: (3a) is from north-of-England traditional-dialect, and (3b) from 'basilectal' Jamaican Creole.

(1a) jə məst 'i:t ɪt 'ʊp
(1b) jʊ mɔ̃s 'i:t ɪt 'ɔ̃p

(2a) jə məs 'gɛr ɪt 'i:tṇ   *You must get it eaten*
(2b) jʊ mɔ̃s 'i:t ɪt 'ɑ:f   *You must eat it off*

(3a) ða mʊŋ 'gɛr ɪt 'ɛtṇ
(3b) jʊ mɔ̃s 'njam ɪ 'a:f

1.1.3 Traditional-dialect

As a coherent alternative language variety, traditional-dialect is restricted to a small area of the geographical territory where English is spoken as first language. It is found in eastern, central, and southern Scotland and in a part of Northern Ireland: in these places it is generally known as Scots, and its boundaries can be fairly accurately delimited. It is also found in various parts of England which are well removed from London, particularly the north and the rural west. In England it is usually referred to as '*x* dialect', where *x* is the name of a traditional county, as Lancashire dialect, Devon dialect.

With the possible exception of Newfoundland and the Appalachians, traditional-dialect is not found in English-speaking countries outside the British Isles. Popular West Indian English and (in one view) American Black English Vernacular constitute a special case: it is true that they do not altogether belong within General English, being creoles (or more exactly 'post-creoles' in the course of decreolization), but they are not traditional-dialect such as we are now discussing.

Some years ago I wrote that 'dialects involve grammar and vocabulary as well as pronunciation; accents involve only the latter'

(Wells 1970: 231). I feel now that this is by no means the whole story. The distinction between variety differences in general and accent differences in particular is indeed that varieties may involve everything, accents only pronunciation. Paradoxically, though, I should suggest that one important distinction between speaking traditional-dialect and speaking General English with a given accent is in fact phonological. More exactly, it is a matter of the phonological specifications of lexical items, that is of the lexical incidence of particular phonemes in particular words.

Consider the data recorded in *Survey of English Dialects* (hereafter referred to as *SED*) for the word *bridge*, elicited in response to the question 'What do you call the thing built across a river to help you get from one side to the other?' (Orton *et al.* 1962–71: IV.1.2). Throughout southern and central England the answer [brɪdʒ] was received (with certain minor phonetic differences that are not relevant at this moment). This was also the answer recorded for southern Lancashire, villages near industrial Tyneside, and the Isle of Man. Elsewhere, north of a line from Lancashire to Lincolnshire, the form was [brɪg]. In some localities both forms were recorded, and several informants are reported as saying that [brɪg] was 'older' or 'better dialect' than [brɪdʒ].

It is also known that *brig* is the Scots form. It is in fact the traditional-dialect term for *bridge* throughout the north of England and Scotland, where it co-exists with the General English word. Exactly comparable are *rigg* (*ridge*), [kaf] (*chaff*), etc.

It seems clear to me that people who use the form [brɪg] must have two parallel phonological specifications for this item in their mental lexicon, /brɪg/ and /brɪdʒ/, in rather the same way as French–English bilinguals have the two specifications /brɪdʒ/ and /pɔnt/ (if that is indeed the correct phonological formula for what underlies the pronunciation [pɔ̃]). And the crucial point is that traditional-dialect speakers, all of whom nowadays also control a variety falling within General English, possess paired parallel specifications of this kind for a substantial proportion of their vocabulary. For it does not seem plausible to postulate a phonological rule in order to derive [brɪdʒ] from /brɪg/, given that the traditional-dialect *big* [bɪg], for example, has no corresponding General English equivalent *[bɪdʒ]. (Even if we were to invoke some 'minor rule' to deal with this case and a few others, we should come up against the law of diminishing returns long before we had succeeded in accounting for all the data. That this is so is clear from Speitel 1968, and implicit in the *SED* material. Any sceptics are welcome to take up the challenge.).

It is safe to say that every speaker of General English has a vowel of the type [e ~ ɛ] used in words such as *red* and *second*. The *SED* data shows that *second* (VII.2.3) also has this vowel in all traditional-dialects. But with *red* (V.10.7) things are different. In the northern-most part of England it has the [iː] of *sheep* rather than the [ɛ] of *second*, presumably making it a homophone of *reed*. In Somerset and part of Devon it shows the result of a historical metathesis, and appears as [(h)ɜ·ːd], which may well make it a homophone of *herd*. Again, it is not plausible to derive General English [rɛd] from these traditional-dialect forms by synchronic phonological rule, nor for that matter vice versa. (I believe that similar considerations apply to the other types recorded in *SED*, namely [rəd] in a small part of Cumbria and North Yorkshire, [rɪəd] also in part of North Yorkshire, and [rɪd] on the North Yorkshire–Humberside border and in patches along the south and west coast.)

The bulk of a thesis by Speitel (1968) comprises a careful com-parison of traditional-dialect (Scots) and General English pro-nunciations of the same words by the same informants in Midlothian, the area around Edinburgh. He reports that of nearly five thousand lexical items investigated, between a third and a half have a Scots form differing (in an unpredictable way) from the same speakers' General English form. It is to be supposed that in rural areas away from Edinburgh the proportion would be even higher.

Nevertheless it is true that traditional-dialect is recessive every-where that it persists at all. Its speakers, who are as we have seen normally bilingual – in the sense of controlling two distinct and permanent language varieties – are a steadily decreasing minority. Nowadays traditional-dialect seems to be heard most often from children under the age of ten and from elderly people. Social pressure to use General English forms rather than those of traditional-dialect starts in the primary school, if not before. On the basis of his research in Scotland, Speitel suggests that by the age of ten most children with a traditional-dialect background abandon it for ever in favour of General English; a second group likewise abandon it, but return to it upon retirement; and a third group retain and use both traditional-dialect and General English through-out their life. Only the latter two groups are linguistically resistant; only they can pass traditional-dialect on to further generations.

A Derbyshire village with which I am familiar is probably fairly typical. Forms such as ['watə] *water*, [wɒm] *home* are now nothing but a memory of how the grandparents of people born in the 1940s used to speak. They have been replaced by the General English equivalents ['wɔːtə] and [hʌʊm ~ ʌʊm].

The replacement of traditional-dialect forms by those of General English is a matter of **relexification**, that is an alteration of the underlying phonological representation of the lexical items in ques-tion. (Trudgill & Foxcroft 1978 refer to the process as 'transfer', i.e. the transfer of lexical items from one lexical set to another.) Differences between accents, on the other hand, quite often involve only differences in phonological/phonetic rules applied to what may be assumed to be an identical underlying representation: see discussion below, 1.3.2.

As the bulk of traditional-dialect pronunciations are replaced, a small residue may well remain to give colouring to the basically General English that results. Pronunciations such as [riːt ~ rɛɪt] for *right* (compare [raɪt] *write*) typically persist in urban working-class north-of-England speech from which things like [riːd] *red* or ['feːðə ~ 'faðə] *father* have long disappeared. Forms such as *gawp* or *hoik* (*to gawp at someone, to hoik something out*) are etymologically traditional-dialect doublets of *gape* and *hook* respectively; they are commonly used by English people who could in no sense be called speakers of traditional-dialect, always with a sharply restricted meaning or in set phrases; so also *kirk* alongside *church*. In the rural United States there are folk pronunciations such as [pæm] *palm*, [dif ~ dɪf] *deaf*, (*The Pronunciation of English in the Atlantic States* (*PEAS*) ch. 5) which may similarly be viewed as relics of traditional-dialect imported from Britain by early settlers. The same is true of non-standard pronunciations such as [kɛtʃ] *catch* (with the vowel of DRESS rather than that of TRAP) which are very widely distributed everywhere that English is spoken.

The distinction between areas where we recognize the persis-tence of traditional-dialect and those where we do not is thus perhaps a matter of degree rather than an absolute one.

German dialectologists have drawn a distinction between **pri-**

mary and **secondary** dialect features (Schirmunski 1930, quoted by Speitel 1968). Primary dialect features are those of which a speaker is aware in a 'bilingual' situation, and which he can control and replace at will; secondary dialect features are those which are carried over into standard forms of speech. This distinction appears to correspond to the distinction I draw between traditional-dialect and accent. A speaker of traditional-dialect has conscious control over the choice between [brɪg] and [brɪdʒ] or between [riːd] and [rɛd] ('primary dialect features'); he characteristically has much less awareness of, or control over, such local-accent matters as saying ['mʊkɪ] rather than ['mʌkɪ] or [rɛd] rather than [rẹd] ('secondary dialect features').

1.1.4 Geographical variation

One of the most obvious things we notice about a person's speech is that it tells us something about where he comes from: where he grew up and, in some cases, where he lives now. Accents are thus powerful indicators of geographical identity.

In everyday terms, some people are regarded as not having an accent at all. In the Ira Levin novel *A kiss before dying* there is a character – very much a social climber – who 'had been dismayed to hear the word "accent" used in relation to himself, having always thought of it as something someone else had'. Indeed, many people think of an accent as being essentially a pronunciation different from their own. It may be socially distinct, whether perceived as inferior ('a vulgar accent') or superior ('a posh accent', 'an affected accent'). But most often it is **geographically** distinct. We speak of 'a Scottish accent', 'an Australian accent', 'a southern accent' (which means something different according to whether we live in England, Ireland, or the United States), 'a Brooklyn accent', and indeed of 'an American accent' (if we are not American) or 'a British accent' (if we are not British).

From a linguistic point of view it is sensible to consider every speaker of the language as speaking it with some accent or other; this accent, as we have seen, may be regarded as the phonetic/ phonological component of the variety he speaks. And one of the social factors with which a person's accent correlates most closely is his geographical provenance or **regionality**.

At the very least, a native speaker's accent usually indicates whether he is from North America or from what we may call the British-oriented countries. Within the latter group it is usually possible to say whether the speaker is from England or Wales, from Scotland or Ireland, from the West Indies, or from the southern hemisphere (Australia and New Zealand, southern Africa). How much further we can go in recognizing regionality from accent depends upon how much familiarity we have with the speech of the area concerned. To any American, an accent characteristic of the deep south or of New York City is immediately recognizable; to an Englishman or an Australian they may or may not be. To any Englishman, an accent characteristic of the north or of the west country is easy to identify as such, and probably most people in England could confidently identify the accents associated with the individual cities of London, Birmingham, Liverpool, and Newcastle-upon-Tyne. But it would be an exceptional American who could do this. The English are frequently embarrassed by confusing Canadians with Americans, or New Zealanders with Australians, on the basis of their accent; for the relevant locals, mistakes are more easily avoided.

On a much finer scale, someone from Sheffield may insist that Rotherham speech is clearly distinguishable from Sheffield speech, and Barnsley speech absolutely different. He may well be right as far as concerns the ability of Sheffield people to perceive these distinctions, in spite of geographical proximity (four miles to Rotherham, thirteen to Barnsley) – though this sort of claim has not been tested objectively. But to outsiders all three will probably just be identified as South Yorkshire or, in increasing order of vagueness, Yorkshire, north-of-England, English, or British.

Just how finely a local accent can be localized is not known. Bernard Shaw represents Professor Higgins, the phonetician in *Pygmalion*, as able to identify people's origins with a precision that is astounding:

The Bystander. He aint a tec. He's a blooming busybody: thats what he is. I tell you, look at his be-oots.

The Note Taker (i.e. Higgins) [*turning on him genially*]. And how are all your people down at Selsey?

The Bystander [*suspiciously*]. Who told you my people come from Selsey?

The Note Taker. Never you mind. They did. [*To the girl*] How do you come to be up so far east? You were born in Lisson Grove.　　(Act I)

A moment later he correctly sums up another bystander, a gentleman, as 'Cheltenham, Harrow, Cambridge, and India'. Of course it is doubtful whether anyone, even Henry Sweet (or more recently Henry Lee Smith Jr), has been able to achieve this degree of skill, or whether it is in principle possible – at least on the basis of the sentence or two which is all the Higgins character has to go on. But there are people, amateurs as well as professionals, who can achieve remarkable accuracy.

Placing someone by their accent in this way to within a hundred miles or so is something very many laymen can do – provided that both the speaker and the identifier are English and that the speaker has a local accent. But success would be less likely if they were American, and almost certainly due to pure chance if they were Australian. It is clear that geographical differentiation of local accents is densest in those places that have long been settled by English-speaking populations, and coarsest in those that have been settled, or English-speaking, for only a century or two. Thus the finest distinctions can be made in England and in those parts of Wales, Scotland, and Ireland which have been anglicized for several hundred years. The territories which are geographically most homogeneous in their accent are Australia, New Zealand, South Africa, and the American far west, with an English-speaking settlement history not yet two centuries old.

In England, though, there are some speakers who do not have a local accent. One can tell from their speech that they are British (and very probably English) but nothing else. This non-localizable accent of England is what phoneticians refer to as **Received Pronunciation** (RP). It is characteristic of the upper class and (to an extent) of the upper-middle class. An Old Etonian sounds much the same whether he grew up in Cornwall or Northumberland. The phonetic and social characteristics of this accent are discussed further below: 1.1.5, 2.1.1–2, vol. 2, 4.1.1–9.

In the United States, it is true not just of a small minority, but of the majority, that their accent reveals little or nothing of their geographical origins. They are the speakers of **General American** (GenAm). This is a convenient name for the range of United States accents that have neither an eastern nor a southern colouring; dialectologically, though, it is of questionable status. The phonetic and social characteristics of this accent, or range of accents, are discussed further below: 2.1.1, 3, vol. 3, 6.1.1–7.

Quite apart from the accent differences associated with the transition from one town, county, state, province, island, country, etc., to another, it seems likely that there are certain characteristics common to all urban accents as against rural ones. In an Australian experiment (Jernudd 1969) university students were considerably more successful in saying whether a speaker whose recorded voice they heard was from the city or from the countryside than they were in saying whether he was from Sydney, Brisbane, or Adelaide. In Britain, the accents of large cities such as London, Birmingham, Liverpool, or Glasgow are widely regarded as 'harsh' or 'ugly', while rural accents are 'charming' or 'quaint'. It is perhaps universally true that rural accents tend to be slower in tempo, reflecting the unhurried life of the countryside: compare a New York and a hillbilly accent, or Cockney and Wiltshire. Urban accents tend to be not only faster, but also more up-to-date in terms of sound changes in current progress.

Having discovered the geographical distribution of some particular linguistic variable, one can plot it on a map. In some instances it turns out that a sharp boundary line – an **isogloss** – is revealed (some scholars adopt the more logical but less usual term **heterogloss**). Fig. 1 exhibits just such an isogloss setting off the areas of England with rhotic accents (according to the data collected in *SED*) from those with non-rhotic accents (see 1.3.3, 3.2.2 below). The linguistic atlases compiled by dialectologists over the past century consist of just such mappings of geographical variation.

Often, however, the data do not show a sharp isogloss. Instead, there appears a gradual and fuzzy transition from one of the forms in question to the other. There may be a considerable overlap area where both forms are current. (See discussion in Chambers & Trudgill 1980: ch. 8.)

Another difficulty is the increased geographical mobility of the population. In many of the English-speaking countries today, people do not typically remain in one place throughout their lives. They move around, from country to city, or from one city to another, often from one country to another. In consequence the speech of those living in a given area at a given time is inevitably heterogeneous. Restricting the choice of informants to those who have spent their whole lives in the area whose speech is being

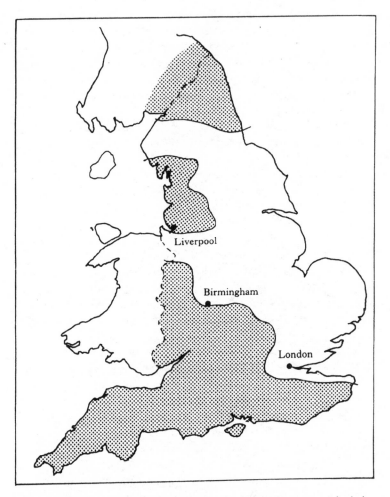

Fig. 1. Isogloss dividing areas of England with rhotic accents (shaded areas) from those with non-rhotic accents. This map is based on *SED*, which largely ignores urban speech (from Chambers & Trudgill 1980)

investigated biases the sample against the many who have moved around.

We are far from understanding just how regional variation in speech arises – how the geographical diffusion we observe in this or that word, usage, or pronunciation is to be accounted for. The classical model to account for it is the **wave-theory** put forward by Schmidt (1872), who visualized linguistic changes spreading across the country like waves or meteorological fronts. Different innovations spread at different rates and perhaps in different directions, so that the areas covered by different innovations do not coincide. The result of successive waves is a network of isoglosses.

It has recently been claimed (Trudgill 1974c) that geographical diffusion may not be like this. Instead, innovations are seen as typically spreading from cities to towns, and from larger towns to smaller towns, leaping over the intervening countryside, which is the last to be affected. Thus H Dropping (3.4.1 below) has spread from London to Norwich and then from Norwich to other East Anglian towns, while the Norfolk countryside remains /h/-pronouncing. Since geographical considerations are clearly among the most salient factors in variation within English, it has seemed sensible to organize volumes 2 and 3 of this work on a geographical basis, with chapters 4–9 dealing each in turn with a particular area.

1.1.5 Socio-economic class

In probably all English-speaking countries there exists a close and obvious connection between language and social class. Speech stratification correlates with social stratification.

Both non-phonetic factors (morphology, syntax, perhaps vocabulary) and phonetic factors (accent) may be involved in this correlation. A person's social position is reflected in the words and constructions he uses, as well as in the way he pronounces them. It seems fair to say, though, that in England the phonetic factors assume a predominating role which they do not generally have in, say, North America. A lower-class British Columbian has the same vowel system as an upper-middle-class British Columbian, with much the same phonetic realizations of the vowel phonemes; this is quite evidently not true of a lower-class Londoner or Mancunian compared with a member of the London or Manchester upper middle class.

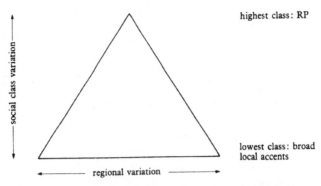

Fig. 2   Relation between social and regional accents in England

It has long been pointed out that in England the accent situation can be compared to a triangle or pyramid (see fig. 2). The horizontal dimension represents geographical variation (regionality), the vertical dimension social variation. The pyramid is broad at the base, since working-class accents exhibit a great deal of regional variation. It rises to a narrow point at the apex, since upper-class accents exhibit no regional variation within England – such variation within RP as does exist depends on other factors than geographical ones. Among the lower middle classes the geographical variation is greater than in the upper middle class, but less than in the working class – or so this model implies, and all the evidence suggests that it is on the whole correct.

Thus at any given locality in England there is to be found a range of accents extending from RP (at the top of the social scale) down through mildly regional accents to a broad local accent (at the bottom). Any regional accent is by definition not an upper-class accent, and hardly an upper-middle-class accent: because in those social classes such accent differences as do exist are not regional. The more localizable (and hence non-upper-class) characteristics an accent has, the 'broader' we say it is. A maximally **broad** accent reflects (i) regionally, the highest degree of local distinctiveness, (ii) socially, the lowest social class, and (iii) linguistically, the maximal degree of difference from RP.

An important and defining characteristic of RP is thus its non-localizability within England. And it is to be noted that all labels for accents in England tend to have social connotations as well as (except for RP) regional ones.

We may extend this model to cover Wales as well as England without serious modification. But we cannot extend it to Scotland or Ireland, or of course to outside the British Isles. In Scotland and Ireland RP is generally seen as a foreign (English) accent; these countries have their own higher-class accents which differ in many important respects from RP.

North America, too, is different inasmuch as it has no non-localizable accent at the apex of a pyramid. An upper-class New England accent is quite different from an upper-class Virginian or Chicago accent. That is, regional variation characterizes American accents of all social classes; although, as we have seen, regional variation is very minor away from the east and south.

Elsewhere, the pyramid model tends to fail because of the absence of local geographical variation within each country. Thus in Australia there is quite a high degree of social variation in accent, but very little regional variation whether at the top or at the bottom of the social scale. The same appears to be true on the whole for New Zealand and South Africa.

That there are speech differences associated with social class differences is something well-known to every member of the speech community. In 1972 a survey carried out by National Opinion Polls included the question 'Which two of these [eleven specified factors] would you say are most important in being able to tell which class a person is?'. The respondents were a random sample of the British public. The factor which scored highest overall was 'The way they speak'; next in order came 'Where they live', 'The friends they have', 'Their job', 'The sort of school they went to', 'The way they spend their money', and only then 'The amount of money they have' and various other factors (Reid 1977: 27). Hence speech was regarded as more indicative of social class than occupation, education, and income; and the likelihood is that by 'the way they speak' respondents meant, above all, 'accent'.

Yet it is only comparatively recently that there has been any precise investigation of the social stratification of speech. Until the 1970s, dialectologists in Britain concentrated on the broadest local accents (or, indeed, traditional-dialect), while phoneticians described RP (or, in the case of Scottish writers, an educated Scottish accent). In the United States, the Linguistic Atlas workers (from the 1930s onwards) did divide their respondents into three categories (cultivated, middle-class, and folk), mainly by educational criteria. But it was not until William Labov's *The social stratification of English in New York City* (1966) that an investigator succeeded in coming fully to grips with the social dimension of accent variation. The **sociolinguistic** approach of Labov and his followers depends upon a large random sample of the population of an urban area, rather than upon a handful of informants who might be friends or personal contacts.

A brief outline of Labov's research methodology is given below (1.1.12). What he succeeded in demonstrating quite clearly is that variability in a New York accent is socially stratified. There exist in the speech of a given community linguistic variables (in this case more specifically phonological variables), such that the score recorded for a given group of speakers on a variable bears a consistent relationship to the same group's position in terms of non-linguistic parameters such as socio-economic class and ethnicity. For example, among Labov's New York phonological variables were two labelled (r) and (dh). The score for (r) represents the number of non-prevocalic /r/s pronounced, as a percentage of those that would be present in a fully rhotic accent; for (dh), the realization of /ð/ was scored in such a way that 100 would imply consistent use of a plosive (as in the stereotype of a Brooklynese accent, e.g. [dæt] for *that*), 50 an affricate, [dðæt], and 0 a standard-type fricative, [ðæt]. In a style identified as 'careful speech', different socio-economic classes scored as tabulated in (4).

(4)	(r)	(dh)
Middle class	25	17
Working class	13	45
Lower class	11	56

(Derived from Labov 1966: 221)

Thus as one passes down the social-class scale from the 'middle class' (the wealthiest and best educated, in highest-status jobs) through the 'working class' to the 'lower class' (poorest, least educated, lowest-status jobs or none), one sees a steady decrease in the percentage of non-prevocalic /r/s and a steady increase in the proportion of non-standard realizations of /ð/. (There is no 'upper class' in the table. In the Lower East Side of New York, where Labov's survey was done, it is either entirely unrepresented or else so small as to be negligible in a random-sample survey. The same is true of many other places.)

Labov followed a common sociological procedure in using a mathematical formula based on occupation, education, and income as the way to define a person's socio-economic class. Other investigators have sometimes used other ways of calculating it, some simpler, some more elaborate. In a survey of the speech of Jamaicans resident in London I used only the very simple criterion of manual vs. non-manual occupation (Wells 1973); for his study of Norwich, on the other hand, Trudgill (1974a) used not only occupation, education, and income, but also housing, locality, and father's occupation. In both cases the social stratification of speech was clearly revealed.

In (5) I tabulate the London Jamaicans' scores by occupational class on five phonological variables: (θ) is the use of [θ] as against [t] in words where the standard pronunciation has [θ], e.g. *mouth*; (ð) is the same for [ð] and [d], e.g. *breathe*; (t) is the presence vs. absence of postconsonantal final [t] in words such as *first*; (d) is the presence vs. absence of postconsonantal final [d] in words such as *wild*; and (h) is H Dropping, i.e. the presence vs. absence of [h] in words where standard accents have it, as *horse*. A consistently standard pronunciation would lead to a score of 100 each time, a consistently non-standard one to a score of zero. In (6) are shown some of the Norwich findings: (ng) is the use of [n] as against [ŋ] in the *-ing* unstressed ending; (t) is the percentage of [ʔ] as against [t] for syllable-final /t/, as in *butter* and *bet*; and (h) is again H Dropping. For the Norwich data a consistently standard pronunciation would score zero, a consistently non-standard one 100 – the reverse of what applies in (5).

(5)

	(θ)	(ð)	(t)	(d)	(h)
Non-manual occupation	99	99	100	93	100
Manual occupation	67	85	70	58	75

(Derived from Wells 1973: 86–92)

(6)

	(ng)	(t)	(h)
Middle middle class	31	41	6
Lower-middle class	42	62	14
Upper working class	87	89	40
Middle working class	95	92	59
Lower working class	100	94	61

(Trudgill 1974b: 48)

For situations where a clear social stratification of language varieties (lects) exists, a convenient terminology has been proposed whereby the standard, the prestige norm, the idealization of the variety associated with the highest social stratum is called the **acrolect**, while the idealization of the variety which deviates most extensively from the acrolect is called the **basilect**. With reference to accents, then, 'basilectal' is a synonym of 'maximally broad' – the variety associated with the lowest social class. Intermediate varieties – the vast majority in practice – can be referred to as the **mesolect** (Bickerton 1972, 1973, 1975).

By all accounts, society was much more sharply stratified in England at the end of the nineteenth century than it is today. Since then there has been a blurring of the once sharp divisions between different social classes, so that we are faced – in England as elsewhere – with a continuum of phonetic variation as we pass along the continuum of social-class gradation. The finer we make our socio-economic classification, the finer the sociolinguistic stratification we may expect to be able to reveal. But it must always be remembered that we cannot make firm predictions about a given person's accent just on the basis of his social and regional characteristics: human beings are individuals. All we can say is that, given these or those social and regional characteristics, it is statistically probable that his score on stated linguistic variables will tend to average such-and-such. (Findings of this nature are reported and summarized in the course of the discussion on the accents of the relevant localities in volumes 2 and 3.)

1.1.6 Sex, ethnicity

We have a certain degree of choice over our socio-economic class: it depends, in some part at least, on what we make of our lives. It would be a very determinist view to insist that our ultimate level of education, income, and occupation are all fixed immutably at the moment of our birth. Our sex and our ethnic identity, on the other hand, are so fixed.

What is not fixed is the extent to which our sex or our ethnic identity influences our behaviour. Apart from obvious biological differences in mean pitch and voice quality, there is no law which prescribes that men must talk differently from women; there is no biological reason for blacks to have to talk differently from whites, or Scots from Welshmen, or Jewish New Yorkers from Italian New Yorkers. And yet there are observable pronunciation differences which correlate with these differences in sexual or ethnic identity.

In some languages very sharp differences have been reported between men's speech and women's speech, as in the American Indian language Koasati, where the sentence meaning 'He will lift it' is pronounced /lakauwa:s/ if the speaker is male, but /lakauwà:/ if female. In English gross differences of this kind do not exist, at least not at the level of phonetics/phonology (in semantics it may be a different story – consider the meaning of the statement 'I'm a professional' as uttered by a man or by a woman). The sex differences in accent that have been claimed to exist are often so subtle that people are not aware of them. What has been revealed by sociolinguistic surveys is not absolute differences between men's and women's pronunciation (apart from obvious biological differences in mean pitch and voice quality), but differences of a kind which come to light only when we consider the average scores recorded for men and women respectively on particular pronunciation variables. Holding other factors constant, it has repeatedly been found that women achieve a score significantly closer to the prestige norm than men.

In a pioneering study, Fischer (1958) found that among children in a New England village boys tended to [n] in *-ing*, while girls tended to [ŋ]. Among English adults in Norwich the same pattern appeared within each social class: the percentage of non-RP [n] forms found by Trudgill (1974a: 94) was as (7):

(7)
Class	Middle middle	Lower middle	Upper working	Middle working	Lower working
Men	4	27	81	91	100
Women	0	3	68	81	97

In the speech of blacks in Detroit, the difference between men's and women's scores for 'postvocalic /r/' (3.2.2 below) was again evident within each social class (Wolfram 1969: 117); in (8), 'percentage of r absence', the higher scores are those deviating more from the midwestern prestige norm of full rhoticity:

(8)

Class	Upper middle	Lower middle	Upper working	Lower working
Men	33	47	80	75
Women	10	30	56	68

A similar pattern was found in a study of the speech of some children attending London secondary schools. The percentages of omitted /h/s, by social class and sex, were as in (9), which also shows the proportion of vocalized non-prevocalic /l/s. Both H Dropping (vol. 2, 4.2.9) and L Vocalization (vol. 2, 4.2.7) are matters to which low prestige is attached.

(9)

	H Dropping		L Vocalization	
	Middle class	Working class	Middle class	Working class
Boys	14	81	18	71
Girls	6	18	12	51

(Derived from Hudson & Holloway 1977: 27)

On the other hand it must be confessed that by no means all the phonological variables in this last-mentioned survey gave the same neat pattern. And there are communities where it is the males, not the females, who show the greater tendency towards the prestige norm, e.g. St Lucia (Le Page 1977: 124).

Usually, though, the tendency is indeed for women's average scores on phonological variables to differ from men's average scores in the same direction (higher or lower) as the middle class average scores differ from those of the working class. The usual explanation for this fact runs as follows. First, women in western society are usually more status-conscious than men. This is because a woman's social position is less secure than a man's: a man defines his own social position through his occupation, his property, or his power, while a woman typically derives hers through her husband. The result is that women may be more insecure socially, and therefore tend to emphasize and display indications of (high) status, both material and linguistic. Secondly, the roughness and toughness perceived as characterizing working-class culture are also seen as having connotations of masculinity. Roughness and toughness (and the working-class pronunciations which share that image) are thus felt to be appropriate for men in a way they are not for women. It is the sexist character of our society that is responsible for both these factors. If recent advances towards a sexually more equal society continue, there may well be a diminution in the extent to which women's scores tend to differ from men's in the higher-class direction.

Other differences between men's and women's pronunciation may depend on prosodic features like intonation and tempo. Here it is not a question of the two sexes having different linguistic repertoires, because as far as is known all members of a speech community have the same repertoire of intonation patterns and tempos at their disposal. Rather, it is a matter of the use the different sexes make of the repertoire. It is generally supposed that women tend to use more animation in their voices than men – i.e. use greater variation in intonation, perhaps divide the chain of speech into shorter tone units, use a wider pitch range. It has also been claimed that women tend to use more 'tentative' intonation patterns (typically, rising tones) than men, so reflecting their relative powerlessness and inferior status (Lakoff 1975: 197). It is known that there are many comparable differences between men's and women's speech which lie outside phonology – for example, in the use of question tags, in vocabulary, and in willingness to interrupt the other person or people in a conversation.

This leads us to the question of the pronunciation characteristics associated with sexual minorities. As far as I am aware, no study of the possible correlation of linguistic variables with sexual orientation has yet been attempted, so that what follows is inevitably speculative; but it is certainly popularly believed that some homosexuals can be recognized as such by their speech. It should be emphasized that the vast majority of gay people (both men and women) cannot be so recognized, any more than they can be by their appearance or their general behaviour. It is only a minority within a minority who choose to conform to the stereotype of the effeminate man or the butch woman. Further, there are some apparently effeminate men and butch women who are heterosexual in their orientation. This said, it is of interest to ask what speech characteristics are perceived as effeminate or mannish, respectively. I suspect that many of them are prosodic matters – intonation, pitch range rhythm, tempo – such as were mentioned above in connection with men's and women's speech. All of those discussed by Tripp (1975: ch. 9) are of this kind, or else non-phonological matters like choice of words. Many gay men can certainly switch 'camp' voice quality and vocal mannerisms on and off at will. More subtly, it is conceivable that gender/sex-rôle hang-ups have led some gay people to use the kind of pronunciation which on Labov-style phonological variables would score in a way characteristic of someone of their own social class and age but of the opposite sex. More crudely, there are the extremes of 'camp' pronunciation such as lisping, i.e. using [θ] or [s̺] in place of [s], and so on. Here, again, one must remember that some people lisp not because of effeminacy but because of a speech defect. Further, it may frequently happen that a pronunciation which would be entirely usual in one locality may sound effeminate in another. This appears to be the case, for example, with the use of a voiceless intervocalic [t] in words such as *better, party* – normal in England, but in America widely perceived as unmasculine. The same applies, I suspect, to the use of [ɑː] in BATH words.

Turning now to the question of the relationship between accent and ethnic group, we must perhaps first reiterate that there is no necessary connection between language (dialect, accent) and racial or ethnic origin. A speaker's language is determined by the linguistic environment in which he is raised or to which he subsequently becomes exposed, and so is his pronunciation of it.

Many of the accent characteristics often thought of as ethnic are in fact geographical. If a Scotsman living in London seems to his English neighbours to have a typically Scottish accent, the reason in all likelihood is that he grew up in Scotland and so acquired a Scottish regional accent. The crucial period for acquiring one's native language finishes well before puberty, and although in later life we may modify our accent as a result of moving away (geographically or socially) from our original milieu we are unlikely to efface all traces of the accent we had acquired by the age of, say, eleven.

A child's parents are obviously important as models: their speech is likely to be constantly available for imitation. So we might expect that the London-born child of parents with a Scottish accent would acquire from them some degree of Scottish accent. Everyday experience shows that this does not happen: the London-born and London-raised child ends up sounding like other Londoners (of the appropriate social class), whatever his parentage. The accent model is not that of his parents, but that of his peer group. At most, the parental model may equip the child with an additional accent, a Scottish one, which he can turn on when appropriate for some special purpose (which, however, is as likely as not to be a humorous purpose).

How far this applies when a group from outside moves into a locality in such large numbers as to become the majority is something that has not really been investigated. Anecdotal evidence suggests that the local accent of the steel town of Corby, Northamptonshire (in the heart of England), sounds typically Scottish as a result of the overwhelmingly Scottish origin of the work-force.

Labov's researches in New York City revealed interesting findings in this connection. Taken as a group, there were small but apparently important differences between Jewish and Italian New Yorkers, as well as between both of these groups and Blacks: these differences were a matter of slight differences in average score on certain phonological variables. For instance, the pronunciation of the vowel of TRAP as a close vowel of the [ɪə] type is found among most New Yorkers alongside opener qualities such as [ɛə, æ]. But it is used by speakers of Italian origin rather more than by other New Yorkers. Labov hypothesizes that this is the result of a subconscious desire to avoid the very open, [a]-type vowel used by the first-generation immigrants from Italy, for whom [æ] was a difficult foreign sound. Similarly, Jewish New Yorkers, more than others, tend to favour very close, [ʊə]-type vowels in CLOTH, THOUGHT, NORTH, FORCE: this is seen as a reaction against the tendency of Yiddish-speaking immigrants to confuse the /ɔ/ of these words with the /ʌ/ of STRUT.

1.1.7 Age: the time dimension

The speech of young people is different from the speech of older people. Partly this is just an effect of growing older. As a boy grows into a man, his vocal tract size increases and his voice deepens, so that he comes to sound like an adult instead of a child. As an adult ages, other physiological changes occur, making him or her sound in due course like an old person. All of this is an automatic consequence of bodily changes.

But there are other ways in which the speech patterns of different generations differ. Old people do, literally, speak in an old-fashioned way; young people's speech is rightly judged 'new-fangled'. On the whole speakers do not alter their accents much once they are past puberty: thus the constant flux or alteration and development which occurs in all local or social accents as they change over time results overwhelmingly from innovations in the speech of children and adolescents. It is they who launch and spread new fashions in pronunciation.

As children acquire the grammar of their native language (including the appropriate accent), they proceed by making inferences and hypotheses on the basis of the language they hear around them, from their parents at first, and then, increasingly, from their peer group. As three-year-olds we typically create *mouses* as the plural of *mouse* – not because we have heard other people say *mouses*, but because that is the form regularly created according to our internalized grammar at that stage. Later we learn that this noun is irregular, and we respond to the pressure of everyone around us by replacing *mouses* with *mice*. Similarly with pronunciation: innovations may begin as children's errors, e.g. *thin* with [f] instead of [θ]. Later we usually learn to use the adult form; but in some cases peer-group pressures may prevail, e.g. in a large group of children all saying [fɪn] for *thin*, in which case an innovation will have occurred, a sound change will have taken place, as the [f]-pronouncing children grow up to be adults. This is what may be surmised to have happened in London and other English cities where [f] for standard [θ] is frequently encountered as an adult working-class characteristic.

Other sound changes are not persistent infantilisms, but nevertheless can be shown to have originated in pre-adolescent or adolescent speech. If at the present time we find a particular pronunciation to be used by everyone in a given locality under the age of forty-five, by some of those between forty-five and fifty-five, and by none of those or fifty-five or older, we conclude that the innovation was made or adopted by those now aged around fifty, who successfully set the fashion for the age cohorts of children who followed them. Instances of **age grading** as dramatic as this are rare, but any sound change currently in progress can be demonstrated to be in progress by examination of the speech of different age groups.

In his New York study (1966: 339), Labov found that the use of the [ɜɪ] variant in NURSE words varied by age as (10):

(10)   Age   Percentage of speakers
                       using [ɜɪ]
        8–19   04
        20–39   24
        40–49   33
        50–59   59
        60 and over   100

Thus what used to be an unremarkable characteristic of a New York accent had, by the 1960s, become a rare variant (restricted, in fact, in the eight–nineteen age group of Labov's sample, to the lowest socio-economic class). An innovation, namely the boycotting of [ɜɪ] in favour of a GenAm-type [ɝ], started among the generation who were in their fifties at the time of the study. Remarkably quickly it became the usual pronunciation for those whose speech patterns were not already set, so that it is now used by all later generations of speakers.

Young people's accents are not just physiologically different from those of older people. They also reflect the successful linguistic innovations adopted by intervening generations.

1.1.8 Styles and rôles

It has long been known that an individual will use different pronunciation patterns (as well as other grammatical and lexical differences) in different circumstances. In particular, there is often a considerable difference between our casual style of pronunciation, when we are relaxed and not monitoring our speech, and a more formal style when we are giving attention to how we behave and speak. It is the achievement of Labov and his followers to have quantified and measured this kind of variation.

Casual and formal styles of speech reflect differences in the **social context** – the social situation in which a speaker finds himself interacting at a given time. **Casual** speech – unmonitored, informal everyday speech – is difficult for an interviewer to elicit from an informant, since his very presence, with tape-recorder, tends to call forth a style characterized by a considerable degree of formality. But casual speech will tend to occur outside the framework of the interview, with some member of the family who bursts in, for example. And Labov found that certain questions by the fieldworker were successful in triggering an emotionally-involved response in casual-style speech (in particular the question 'Have you ever been in a situation where you thought you were in serious danger of being killed?').

Formal speech is the style which an interviewer will most usually elicit in a field interview. It is the style we use when speaking to strangers or in public situations. It is not, however, the most formal style possible. **Reading aloud** is an activity which calls forth an even more formal style, while reading aloud a **list of words** (in particular if it includes potential minimal pairs relating to socially sensitive pronunciation variables) calls forth the most monitored, most formal style of all.

In the case of many linguistic variables researchers have found a pattern of steady increase (or steady decrease) in the value of a particular variable as the speaker moves from casual style (CS) through formal style (FS) and reading-passage style (RPS) to word-list style (WLS). In Norwich, Trudgill found the following percentages for [n] as against [ŋ] in the -*ing* variable: CS 70 per cent of [n], FS 56 per cent, RPS 27 per cent, WLS 11 per cent (Trudgill 1974a: table 7.1, crudely averaged over social class). That is, the [n] pronunciation was nearly seven times more likely to occur in casual speech than when reading word lists.

Style differences usually operate along the same scales as socioeconomic class differences in speech. That is, the formal style of a speaker in a relatively low class will tend to resemble the casual style of a speaker in a relatively high class. Taking these class differences into account, the Norwich figures for -*ing* are as (11):

(11)		WLS	RPS	FS	CS
	Middle middle class	0	0	3	28
	Lower middle class	0	10	15	42
	Upper working class	5	15	74	87
	Middle working class	23	44	88	95
	Lower working class	29	66	98	100

Thus a pronunciation with consistent [ŋ] (0 per cent [n]) was achieved by the middle middle class in both reading styles; in the formal speech of the interview situation they were very nearly consistent (and no doubt many individuals were wholly so), whereas in casual style they used [n] over a quarter of the time, which is what the lower working class achieved only in the word-list style. But although the casual speech of the highest class is like the most

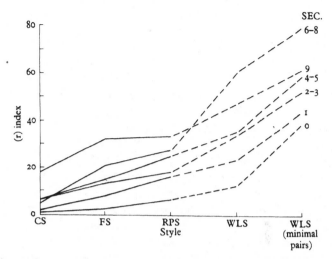

Fig. 3 Class stratification of the (r) variable in New York City. Socio-economic class is analysed on a ten-point scale from 0 (lowest) to 9 (highest) (after Labov 1972a)

formal speech of the lowest class in this respect, the direction of the style shift along the formality scale is the same in all social classes.

It sometimes happens that the style shift of a lower social class as it moves into the most formal style is so great that it overtakes the social class above it. In his study of the New York (r) variable, Labov found a crossover of this kind between the lower middle and upper middle class when RPS was compared with WLS. In CS, only the upper middle class shows a significant amount of rhoticity (just under 20 per cent, with the lower middle class scoring well under 10 per cent). But in the most formal style, the lower middle class gets over 60 per cent (and for minimal pairs like *god* vs. *guard* 80 per cent) or possible /r/s, while the upper middle class is content with just under 50 per cent (minimal pairs, just under 65 per cent). (See fig. 3.)

This kind of crossing over has been found to be typical of the lower middle class. Labov refers to it as 'hypercorrection', perhaps an unfortunate application of a term needed for another linguistic phenomenon (see 1.4.7 below). We could perhaps, for clarity, call it **Labov-hypercorrection**. In Labov's view it constitutes one of the important factors in linguistic change, since the lower middle

class's tendency to adopt the formal-style pronunciation characteristics of younger upper-middle-class speakers provides a vital
link for new pronunciation fashions to percolate down the class
strata.

The kind of London speech characterized as 'refayned' belongs
here. It is associated with a type of lower-middle-class speaker so
anxious to escape from the negative connotations of [ɒɪ] in PRICE
words that he or she overshoots RP [aɪ] and lands in [ɛɪ], a phonetic
area more associated with FACE.

Not quite identical with the stylistic variation attributable to the
degree of formality of the social context is the assumption of particular pronunciation patterns as an accompaniment of particular
social rôles. Certain professions and occupations are popularly
associated with particular accents – in England this applies to
Anglican clergymen, headmasters, barristers, army officers, Ox-
bridge academics, and also to pop singers and male hairdressers. Of
course the proportion of Anglican clergymen who actually conform
to the stereotype of a 'clergyman's accent' may in reality be quite
small; but the stereotype exists, and the old-fashioned pronunciation and particular voice quality involved may have some indexical
value (see 1.1.9 below), proclaiming the speaker's clerical status in
the same way as clerical dress does.

Temporary rôles, too, may have their particular accents. Many
people have a special 'telephone voice', extremely formal in style
and slower in rate of delivery than the non-telephone version.
Speaking over the telephone is different from face-to-face interaction in that no visual cues are available to assist in conveying
attitudes and other important non-verbal information; so it is not
surprising that the voice may then take on special indexical
functions.

1.1.9 Perceiving a stereotype

Human beings are too many and too various for us to be able to
build up an accurate individual picture of every single person with
whom we come into contact. There are indeed some people we
know well – friends and relatives – and of them we can form and
hold an individual picture. But we deal with many other, casual or
transient, contacts by slotting them into preconceived **stereo-**

types. These stereotypes are simplified and standardized conceptions of kinds of people, conceptions which we share with other
members of our community. Few people in Britain have ever met a
genuine working cowboy: but we have our stereotyped view of what
a cowboy is like. We know what we wears, the way he behaves, the
kind of food he is likely to eat, and the way he talks. And if we came
across someone dressed as a cowboy, hitching his horse to the
wooden rail outside the saloon, then swaggering in and up to the bar
to order a whisky in a U-RP accent (vol. 2, 4.1.2), we should notice
that something was odd. Accents constitute an important part of
many stereotypes.

We use the indexical information we collect from listening to a
person speak in order to slot him into an appropriate stereotype.
Not only historical or quasi-mythical figures like cowboys are seen
as stereotypes, but all kinds of categories of people: occupational
groups (plumbers, piano-tuners, oil tycoons, hairdressers, nurses,
reporters, advertizing executives, builders/construction workers),
national, local, or ethnic groups (Irishmen, Americans, Australians, Englishmen, New Yorkers, Glaswegians, Italians, West
Indians, Chinese, Poles, Arabs), political groups (conservatives,
communists, liberals and so on, depending on the political make-up
of the community in question), age and sex groups (old women,
boys, middle-aged men, teenage girls), socio-economic groups
('lazy' workers, 'exploiting' bosses, 'respectable' people you would
be proud to be associated with, 'rough' people you would not be
proud to be associated with, 'stand-offish' middle-class people who
give themselves airs, nouveaux riches, aristocrats, jet-setters,
ordinary decent working men and women), and many others. And
in most cases the stereotype includes an appropriate accent.

To that extent a general notion of the kind of sociolinguistic
variation we have been discussing is common knowledge. This
knowledge may not always be very accurate, but it is a significant
part of the community's shared set of attitudes. And we use it to
make judgements about people we meet or hear (e.g. on radio or
television). In Britain in particular, we are accustomed to make
instant and unconscious judgements about a stranger's class
affiliation on the basis of his or her accent. As we saw in 1.1.5, the
way a person speaks was held to be the most important single factor
one uses to determine a person's class affiliation.

An English journalist and television reporter, well-known for her strong Cockney accent, has recounted how difficult it is for her to keep a domestic cleaning lady. 'They'd work happily for a woman with a Kensington voice [sc. RP], but, because they sound the same [themselves] as I do, they say to themselves, "Blinkin' cheek. Why should I clean up while she goes out to work?". I've had six in a year' (Janet Street-Porter, *Daily Express*, 10 October 1973). A Cockney accent signals working-class status and conflicts disturbingly with the stereotype of the kind of wealthy upper-middle-class woman who would employ domestic help in the home.

The point here is that a hearer, having made a stereotype identification of a speaker on the basis of his or her accent, then attributes to him or her all kinds of other qualities that are popularly associated with the stereotype in question. Thus we may (often quite unconsciously) use a person's speech as grounds for forming an opinion about their political opinion, their general intelligence, their reliability, even (for someone the hearer cannot see) their handsomeness or beauty. And we may find their arguments more persuasive, or less persuasive, depending on the qualities we implicitly attribute to them on the basis of their accent.

Social psychologists have found that in England RP speakers, judged purely on the basis of their pronunciation, were adjudged to be more ambitious, more intelligent, more self-confident, more determined, and harder-working than speakers with a regional accent. On the other hand they were thought to be less serious, less talkative, less good-natured and with less of a sense of humour than non-RP speakers (Giles 1970, 1971). Thus not all positive qualities are associated with one stereotype. In other experiments a regional accent was found to be more persuasive than RP: listeners were more readily swayed by an argument presented in their own regional accent.

An interesting point about the rural stereotype has been made by Trudgill (1974b: 20).

It is quite common in heavily urbanized Britain for rural accents, such as those of Devonshire, Northumberland or the Scottish Highlands, to be considered pleasant, charming, quaint or amusing. Urban accents, on the other hand, such as those of Birmingham, Newcastle or London, are often thought to be ugly, careless or unpleasant. This type of attitude towards rural speech is not so widespread in the United States, and this difference may well reflect the way in which rural life is evaluated in the two countries.

The **indexical** function of a speaker's accent is the way in which it leads the hearer to stereotyped judgements of this kind. A phonetic characteristic (e.g. a particular voice quality, or a typical value of some phonologic variable) which is associated with some social stereotype leads the hearer to ascribe the character of the stereotype in question to the speaker in whose speech it is heard. This may well vary from one place to another. Thus if a speaker's accent is variably rhotic (some non-prevocalic /r/s pronounced, others absent), different conclusions will be drawn in England and in the United States respectively. In an accent of England it is the occasional presence of rhoticity that attracts attention, since non-prevocalic /r/ immediately signals a west-of-England or Lancashire accent (vol. 2, 4.3.5, 4.4.8). In an American accent, however, it is the absence of rhoticity that is noticed, since it signals an eastern or southern accent (vol. 3, 6.4.2, 6.5.7).

A common allophone of /t/ in a London accent is a heavily affricated [ts], thus [tsɑɪʔ ~ tsɑɪts] *tight*, ['pʰɑːtsi] *party*. To an American ear, as mentioned above, this evokes the stereotype of effeminacy, if the speaker is a man; but in London it has absolutely no such connotations, being quite ordinary. In the United States the pronunciation /ɛt/ for *ate*, past tense of *eat*, is perceived as rustic and uneducated; in Britain it is entirely unremarkable (it is the pronunciation I use myself, although the standard American form /eɪt/ is also widely found in Britain).

1.1.10 Projecting an image

While the hearer hears, the speaker speaks. He, too, is concerned with the way he will be judged by hearers. Willy-nilly, he projects an **image** of himself; and, if he chooses, he has considerable discretion over the nature of that image. He can consciously endeavour to project an image of himself full of favourable qualities: to seem efficient, intelligent, sexy, trustworthy, or modest. But without any kind of acting or pretending to be what he is not, he will tend to wish to project an image of himself which agrees with his own self-image. To do otherwise would mean being dishonest with himself.

One of my best Cockney informants in London happens also to be an excellent mimic. For telling a joke involving an upper-class figure he can put on a quite faultless U-RP accent. But his everyday speech is rather broad Cockney. Clearly he has within his competence not only the local working-class accent but also the local upper-class accent. He could, if he chose, pass himself off as a member of the élite, the establishment. (He would, I think, be rather better at this than Eliza Doolittle was.) Why does he not seize the advantages which would undoubtedly flow from such a course? Because that is not how he sees himself. He thinks of himself as an honest working-class man. Speaking RP would make him sound more competent, but also perhaps less reliable.

It seems likely that most speakers, perhaps all except younger children, have the ability to 'raise' or 'lower' the apparent social-class characteristics of their speech in this way. Making one's speech more like that of one's interlocutor (**convergence**) is a way of showing solidarity, sympathy, or approval; making it less like the interlocutor's (**divergence**) shows the opposite.

The self-image which speakers have of themselves may not objectively be a very accurate one. The impression they have of their own speech is often erroneous: they often believe they pronounce things differently from the way they actually do, as any teacher of first-year phonetics can vouch. Sociolinguists have now documented the extent of some of these false impressions.

'In the conscious report of their own usage, New York respondents are very inaccurate,' claims Labov (1966: 455), going on to conclude that 'when the average New Yorker reports his own usage, he is simply giving us his norm of correctness. No conscious deceit plays a part in this process.' Of his subjects whose speech was judged rhotic (actually, with 30 per cent or more of the relevant /r/s present), 79 per cent reported that they used /r/ in the word *card*, 21 per cent that they did not; but of the far larger number whose speech was essentially non-rhotic (less than 30 per cent /r/s pronounced), as many as 62 per cent reported themselves as using /r/ (Labov 1966: 459, table 2).

In Norwich, Trudgill (1972) found similar inaccuracy in self-reporting. He discovered the interesting fact that whereas women tend to report themselves as using a more prestigious pronunciation than they really do, men tended to report their own speech as less prestigious than in reality. He explains this finding by reference to the covert prestige, particularly among men, of non-standard working-class speech (see further 1.4.4 below).

Informants can also be very inaccurate when introspecting about whether they pronounce two words identically or differently, or whether they pronounce words so as to rhyme or not. It was long ago pointed out by Kenyon (1958: 261n; first edition 1924), 'the consciousness of making a distinction between *mourning* and *morning*, etc., is not a condition of making it. I have repeatedly found individuals who declared they made no distinction, when in fact they did so.'

People also have rather inaccurate perceptions of accents other than those of their own locality. English hearers, exposed to a New York accent, hear it primarily as being American, and only secondarily, if at all, as being associated specifically with New York. They are quite deaf to the sociolinguistic information contained, say, in the prevalence of [beəd] over [bæːd] for *bad* or vice versa. A Philadelphian, though, will perceive the same accent primarily as being a New York accent; its Americanness he takes for granted. A New Yorker is very alive to the indexical sociolinguistic information it conveys. Similarly, a Liverpool working-class accent will strike a Chicagoan primarily as being British, a Glaswegian as being English, an English southerner as being northern, an English northerner as being Liverpudlian, and a Liverpudlian as being working-class. The closer we get to home, the more refined are our perceptions.

Actors can exploit this. For a non-New Yorker to assume a New York working-class accent which will be fully convincing to a native New Yorker is very difficult. Only the most talented actor from London can achieve a Scouse (Liverpool working-class) accent which will convince native Liverpudlians. But unless the audience consists of native New Yorkers or Liverpudlians respectively, they will be satisfied with something that is not authentic in every detail, providing only that it conforms to the mental stereotype which they have already formed about the accent in question. Scots often complain about the hopelessness of the Scottish accents put on by English actors in films or television plays; but the largely non-Scottish audience notices nothing wrong. If I want to play the part of an American, a British audience will on the whole be quite satisfied with pronunciations such as [dɔrn] for *dawn* or ['soʊfər] for *sofa*: this is what many British people believe Americans say (since they do after all say [θorn] for *thorn* and ['loʊfər] for *loafer*, and most English people rhyme *dawn*–*thorn* and *sofa–loafer*). But a Chicago audience will not for a moment believe in the authenticity of such an accent – at the very least it will convey overtones of an easterner or southerner who has been messing about with his speech.

Most people, though, are not actors. And to the ordinary native speaker of English his accent is closely bound up with his personality and his perception of it. Our pronunciation reflects our self-image. This is why it can be so devastating for a school-teacher to criticize a pupil's accent by calling it slovenly or ugly – such criticism is seen as attributing these qualities to the pupil himself, not just to his speech. One's accent is a part of one's personal identity.

1.1.11 Standards

Certain accents have a special position in that they are regarded, whether tacitly or explicitly, as **standard**. In England it is RP which enjoys this status, in the United States the range of accents known collectively as GenAm. A standard accent is the one which, at a given time and place, is generally considered correct: it is held up as a model of how one ought to speak, it is encouraged in the classroom, it is widely regarded as the most desirable accent for a person in a high-status profession to have.

Any non-standard accent, on the other hand, will tend to have associations of provinciality and/or lower status. While many will defend such an accent on grounds of local patriotism or democratic egalitarianism, others will not hesitate to condemn it as incorrect. It may well also be seen as corrupt or slovenly. If urban, it is likely to be considered ugly; if rural, perhaps merely as quaint and picturesque.

Two points must be reiterated: first, that a standard accent is regarded as a standard (or 'norm') not because of any intrinsic qualities it may possess, but because of an arbitrary attitude adopted towards it by society, and reflecting the attitude the community implicitly holds towards its speakers; and secondly, that particular phonetic characteristics can be, and often are, prized as standard at one time and in one place but stigmatized as non-standard or substandard at another time or in another place.

Contrary to the first claim, it is widely believed by the general public that the reason a standard accent enjoys its position of prestige is that it is inherently the most pleasing, the most beautiful variety of pronunciation. This view has been labelled the 'inherent value' hypothesis, as opposed to the 'imposed norm' hypothesis, which holds that the prestige of a standard accent is essentially a cultural accident (Giles *et al*. 1974). There is a body of experimental evidence in favour of the imposed norm hypothesis and against the inherent value hypothesis. Speakers of Canadian French regard their own French as aesthetically less pleasing than European French; but when both varieties were played to non-French-speaking Welsh listeners, the listeners could not distinguish them aesthetically. And whereas French Canadians perceive speakers of European-style French to be more intelligent, ambitious, and likeable than speakers of Canadian French, the Welsh listeners could not make any such judgement. In another experiment British undergraduates failed to distinguish aesthetically between Athenian Greek (which Greeks consider standard and beautiful) and Cretan Greek (non-standard and supposedly ugly).

The fact that English has more than one standard accent means that some absurdities of the inherent value hypothesis are easily exposed. Within an American cultural framework, a non-rhotic pronunciation ('dropping ones *r*s') is readily perceived as slovenly or ugly – particularly so in the many parts of the Unites States where the only locals who use such an accent are black. In England such a claim would not for one moment be entertained, since to English ears the non-rhotic pronunciation is the norm, while non-prevocalic [r] is readily perceived as rustic, even comic. In one place [stɑrt] and [nɔrθ] are prized, [stɑːt] and [nɔːθ] stigmatized; in another place it is the other way round.

Nor are people's views on the qualities of particular sound types consistent. In Britain a glottal stop is widely regarded as ugly and also as a lazy sound; but in Farsi (Persian) glottal stops are a characteristic of careful, standard styles of speech, so that [ʔ] is adjudged a beautiful sound and its omission as slovenly. It has been pointed out by Gimson (1980: 90) that the phonetic sequence [paɪnt] is considered ugly as the Cockney pronunciation of *paint*, but perfectly acceptable as the RP form of *pint*.

How many standard accents of English are there? It is perhaps only since the convulsions of the Second World War that GenAm has entirely ceased to look over its shoulder at RP, i.e. that Americans have resolved that Americans, not the British, set the pronunciation standard for America. RP retains very high prestige among some American circles at least, though it is also quite commonly perceived as almost comic. It seems probable that Australia is now undergoing a similar development; perhaps New Zealand and South Africa are too, although hitherto RP has been implicitly treated as a standard in all these countries. There are various other English-speaking territories where the local accent of the upper social echelons has most of the attributes of a standard: this is true of Scotland, Ireland, and the West Indies, places which are exposed to RP in a way in which the United States and Canada are not.

1.1.12 What are the facts?

Some speakers, particularly if helped by sound training in phonetics, can achieve a reasonably objective insight into their own pronunciation. Most cannot. It follows that accurate information about accents and their variability within the community can only be gathered through systematic research.

Before Labov, dialectological research in England typically proceeded as follows. The fieldworker would select a village of suitable size, i.e. about 500 inhabitants. There he would seek out old people who were natives of the village, with local-born parents. The ideal would be a man of about seventy, retired but still mentally alert, with a good memory for the days of his youth, speaking broad dialect. The fieldworker would work through a questionnaire with him – a questionnaire designed to elicit, usually as one-word responses, the items of interest. ('The animal which gives us milk is a …' *Cow*.) In a given locality, perhaps some three or four such informants would be interviewed. This is the procedure employed by the *SED* fieldworkers, who would spend a week or a fortnight in each locality investigated before moving on to the next. There were also many studies involving much longer periods of contact with one single locality, in which case the fieldworker might base his findings on the speech of a much larger number of informants, and collect his data in a more unstructured manner, not relying on a questionnaire but perhaps conducting an in-depth phonetic/ phonological investigation of selected helpful informants.

The material would be recorded in an appropriately narrow form of phonetic transcription. In the early days this would sometimes be backed up by gramophone recordings, although there were great difficulties in making these in the field; latterly tape-recordings could be made. Since the advent of cheap portable tape-recorders, their use has of course been very general. They have, however, two disadvantages: the presence of a running tape-recorder may make the informant self-conscious and inhibit his use of casual style; and they tempt the fieldworker to rely on the recording rather than on direct observation. A tape-recording is almost always less clear than listening to someone direct; and it fails to record the visual cues (e.g. of lip position) which are available in face-to-face observation.

American dialectologists operated in a generally similar way, except that they were much more aware of the influence of age and social class on speech, and disinclined to restrict their investigations to the older members of the rural working class. The Linguistic Atlas fieldworkers accordingly included in their sample 'cultured' informants, 'representatives of a group comprising the social and cultural élite and the upper middle class' (*PEAS*: 11).

Labov was the first to devise a procedure for building up a picture of linguistic variability throughout a given speech community by interviewing a statistically selected sample of the whole population of a locality. Some of his smaller studies have involved telephone calls to names chosen from the telephone directory, or contrived encounters with sales staff in department stores of known social status. But his best-known study, in New York City, involved face-to-face interviews in the homes of 122 native-born informants, who together constituted 63 per cent of a random quota target sample drawn from the inhabitants of one selected area, the Lower East Side. This gave satisfactory numbers of informants for each social class, age group, and ethnic group.

Rather than study all the many varied characteristics of an informant's accent, Labov restricted his investigation to a small number of linguistic variables. For the main part of his New York study he chose five such variables, knowing (as a native New Yorker) that they were likely to be those of greatest interest. They were as follows: (r), the presence vs. absence of a phonetically realized /r/ in non-prevocalic position (but excluding NURSE and *lett*ER words) – i.e. rhoticity vs. non-rhoticity; (eh), the height of the vowel in words of the TRAP-BATH set in which the vowel is followed by a voiced plosive, a voiceless fricative, /m/ or /n/ (vol. 3, 6.1.4, 6.3.5); (oh), the height and rounding of the vowel in THOUGHT-CLOTH words; (th), the realization of /θ/, as fricative vs. affricate vs. plosive; and (dh), the realization of /ð/, likewise. For each of these variables he calculated scores for each speaker's performance in each of the various contextual styles he recognized. From these, scores for given social classes, age groups and so on were derived and compared.

Concentrating on a small number of variables in this way enables the investigator to keep a research project within bounds while going deeply enough to reveal significant patterns of correlation between the linguistic variables and the non-linguistic parameters (socio-economic class, contextual style, age, sex, etc.). But only an investigator with a good hunch about what is likely to turn out as an important variable will be able to select suitable variables for investigation from the hundreds potentially available. There is probably no substitute for being a native of the locality under investigation, or at least having advice from one who is.

Labov's general methodology has been followed by many other investigators. Trudgill's research in Norwich, England, for example (reported most fully in 1974a), was obviously inspired by and based on Labov's work in New York. It is, by the way, very much easier to select a random sample of the adult population in a British town than in an American one: all one has to do is to extract every *n*th name from the published Register of Electors, which lists the name and address of every citizen entitled to vote.

Before Labov, most linguistic and dialectological surveys were based on informants chosen either because they were elderly natives (see above), or else because they happened to be conveniently available. Such a sample of the population is not representative, and does not furnish grounds for making valid statements concerning the speech of the locality as a whole. Statements applying to the whole population of a locality can only be validly made, Labov and his followers would claim, if the informants constitute a genuine representative sample selected in accordance with accepted statistical methods.

Disagreement with this view has come latterly mainly from investigators who set great store by the establishment of really close links between the fieldworker and the community whose speech is under study. Only a fieldworker really integrated into a group of family or friends, they would claim, is in a position to witness genuine face-to-face casual speech undistorted by the interview situation.

Ebenso ist der Kontakt mit Informanten über eine repräsentative Stichprobe und ohne jegliche persönlichen Beziehungen eine äußerst spezielle soziale Situation, von der zu erwarten ist, daß sie das sprachliche Verhalten des Informanten beeinflußt. Er wird kaum umhin können, sich als Testperson zu fühlen und entsprechend zu reagieren.
[In the same way, contact with informants through a representative random sample and without any personal relationship is an extremely exceptional social situation, of which it is to be expected that it would influence the linguistic behaviour of the informant. He will scarcely be able to help feeling like an experimental subject and reacting correspondingly.]

(Bertz 1975: 24)

1.2 Accent phonology

1.2.1 Why phonology?

Phonology can be defined as the linguistic aspect of phonetics: that is, as the study of the linguistically relevant patterning of phonetic events. It deals not so much with the physical nature of speech sounds – their acoustic, auditory, or articulatory qualities – as with their use in language, their functions and their interrelations.

Looked at from a different standpoint, phonology can be defined as the phonetic aspect of grammar: that is, as the study of the way words and sentences are pronounced. The knowledge of how to pronounce is part of the speaker's competence, his ability to speak his language. The phonologist's task is to attempt to model this part of his competence.

The patterns revealed and described in phonology lie between a detailed phonetic description, on the one hand, and the more abstract, meaning-related patterns of morphology, syntax, semantics and pragmatics, on the other. An unfamiliar language sounds like a confused babble. Yet to one who knows it it is meaningful and patterned. In seeking phonological systems or rules we are investigating the first level of patterning which actually underlies the apparent confusion. From this angle of approach, 'from the bottom up', phonology involves the segmentation of the mass of speech sound and the identification within it of relevant features of sound patterning. We aim to analyse the material so that the phonetically essential is separated out from the phonetically redundant or irrelevant.

Looked at from the other side, 'from the top down', phonology gives an insightful answer to the question 'How is this language pronounced?'. It enables us to predict how such-and-such a morpheme, in such-and-such a word, in such-and-such a sentence, is likely to be pronounced by such-and-such a speaker. The answers it gives should not only be concise and economical, but also such that they enable us to epitomize the differences between different accents of the language, whether separated by geographical or social space or by time.

There are some dialectologists who take a stand against all phonology. They consider the detailed phonetic record made by the fieldworker as complete in itself, and any phonologizing as likely only to interpose the phonologist's whims and prejudices between the genuine facts and the reader. Other such dialectologists may simply be unaware of notions such as the phoneme or of any phonological theory. In either case, no attempt is made to seek out deeper patterns lying behind the pronunciations used by the informant. This approach characterizes the *SED* (Orton *et al.* 1962–71) and the *Linguistic Atlas of England* (*LAE*) based on it (Orton *et al.* 1978) (although the data they present has actually been subjected to some tacit and unacknowledged phonologizing). Many monographs on the speech of particular localities take the same line: thus for example Lediard (1977) treats the vowels used in a suburb of Cardiff, south Wales, simply by listing the ninety-six phonetic phonetic vocoids he detects in his material, mentioning a handful of words in which each occurs. Occasional remarks to the effect that vowel [x] is a variant of vowel [y] are as far as he goes down the phonological road; to anyone who believes, as linguists do, that speech sounds can or must be assigned to phonemes, or that they realize or manifest phonemes or other underlying phonological units, this approach inevitably seems wholly lacking in insight.

Perhaps the essential objection to the anti-phonological approach in dialectology is that it is boring. Its end-product is masses of detail and no easily-grasped generalizations. It omits to ask the questions that linguists find interesting. Not only does it fail to see the wood for the trees, it declines to acknowledge that the trees can be seen as a wood.

1.2.2 The taxonomic-phonemic model

Phonetic analysis often shows that certain sets of speech sounds which at first seem to be identical are in fact different. The layman may perceive them as the same; for the native speaker of the language (or accent) in which they occur they **are** the same for linguistic purposes. Yet the phonetically trained investigator can discriminate them; instrumental evidence may demonstrate their non-identity in physical terms. It was the great achievement of phoneticians and linguists in the first sixty years of the twentieth century to develop the concepts of **phoneme** and **allophone** to deal with this apparent paradox. Sounds constituting a set of this kind may indeed differ physically ('phonetically', 'allophonically') from one another, because they are different allophones of the phoneme in question; but they are the same linguistically ('functionally', 'phonemically', 'phonologically'), because they represent the same phoneme.

A well-known example concerns the initial consonants in the words *keep*, *cup*, and *cool* in almost any accent of English one cares to select. Isolation of the first segment in each word shows clearly that in *keep* it is considerably fronted from velar: we may write it [k+]. The initial segment in *cup* is usually a fairly 'average' velar, [k]. That of *cool* is typically somewhat retracted, [k−]; in many accents it also has noticeable lip rounding. Thus physically the three sounds are distinct from one another; the difference on a spectrograph tracing is quite clear. Yet the native speaker is typically unaware of any difference until it is pointed out. Investigation of the phonetic environments in which the three sounds are to be encountered reveals that [k+] regularly appears before relatively high front vowels, [k−] before relatively high back vowels, and [k] (we will assume) elsewhere. (The details differ from accent to accent, although the principle remains the same.) Thus [k+], [k−] and [k] do not contrast with one another. We classify them as llophones of the same phoneme, which we write /k/. Obviously, hey reflect an automatic adjustment of tongue position to facilitate o-articulation with the following vowel. Allophonic alternation of his kind is sometimes termed **accommodatory**, **intrinsic**, or co-.rticulated.

There are numerous examples of accommodatory allophones in English. Another one, in most accents quite striking, relates to the ʃ/ allophones in *sheep* and *shop* respectively.

The [d] in a word such as *adore* has plosive approach and release tages performed by the tongue tip. That of *under*, however, has a asal approach performed by the soft palate, the tongue tip remain-ng in contact with the alveolar ridge (or teeth) without moving as ɹ] gives way to the compression stage of the plosive. That of *kidney* in most accents) has a nasal release, whereby the air pressure built p during the compression stage is released nasally when the soft alate comes down, coverting the [d] into [n], while the tongue tip loes not move away until the end of the [n] segment. In *elder* (as ronounced in an accent which does not have L Vocalization) the d] has a lateral approach; in *badly* a lateral release; and in *mildly* oth approach and release are lateral. But in spite of the differences n the articulatory movements performed, these sounds are clearly ll allophones of the same phoneme /d/.

Vowels, too, often have accommodatory allophones. In many ccents the vowel /uː/ is considerably fronter after /j/ than else-vhere; thus *beauty, few, music*, but *booty, food, moon*. The fronting ɪf /uː/ represents a co-articulatory accommodation to the preceding alatal.

The accommodation can also be to silence. In most kinds of English lenis ('voiced') obstruents (i.e. /b, d, g, dʒ, v, ð, z, ʒ/) are ully voiced only when between voiced segments, e.g. /dʒ/ in *budget, ejoice, a joke, a large one*. Adjacent to a fortis ('voiceless') segment ɪr to the silence surrounding an utterance, they are partly or en-irely devoiced, e.g. /dʒ/ in *James!*, *Miss Gerrard, vengeful, ledge*. They typically remain distinct from their fortis counterparts by heir lenis quality, their failure to shorten a preceding sonorant, heir lack of possible glottalization, and their lack of possible ɪspiration.)

It may be that many or all accommodatory allophones are auto-natic in the sense that they do not involve distinct neural commands to the muscles controlling the organs of speech. Perhaps the brain sends the same command for the /ʃ/ of *sheep* as for the /ʃ/ of *shop* and it is neuromuscular interaction with the command for /i/ that makes first /ʃ/ different from the second.

Much accommodatory variation is so obviously non-distinctive that even the most anti-phonological dialectological records make the appropriate generalizations (e.g. by writing [ʃ] both in *sheep* and in *shop*). Nevertheless there are also many cases of allophonic variation which cannot be explained as accommodatory. It is here that phonological theorizing begins in earnest.

The distribution of clear and dark (velarized) /l/ in RP and some other accents is a good example. Inspection shows that the clear variety, with its front or central resonance, occurs before a vowel or /j/ (as *let, blow, valley, million, fall off*), while the dark variety, with its back resonance, occurs elsewhere, i.e. before a consonant, /w/, or pause (as *milk, meals, always, feel*‖). The alternation cannot be accommodatory, since accommodatory alternation would obviously involve a clear lateral, not a dark one, in a word such as *meals*, where a front vowel precedes. Yet the variation is entirely determined by phonetic environment, that is by the nature of the surrounding segments. The two allophones [l] and [ɫ] never contrast, since they never occur in the same environment. In recognizing them as allophones of one phoneme, /l/, we may refer to them as **non-accommodatory** (extrinsic) allophones.

Another example of non-accommodatory allophonic variation is the aspiration of fortis plosives which most accents show in the environment of a following stressed vowel, as [pʰ] in *pin*; compare the reduced or absent aspiration when the following vowel is unstressed, as *happy*, and the lack of aspiration when /s/ precedes, as *spin*.

In Scouse, the local accent of Liverpool in the north of England, /r/ has two distinct allophones. One is [ɹ], a post-alveolar approximant, used in words such as *red, bright, arrive*; the other is [ɾ], an alveolar tap, heard typically in words such as *marry, story, stir it*. The variation is non-accommodatory, but predictable: the tap occurs immediately after a stressed vowel, the approximant elsewhere. Both can be assigned to, or regarded as realizations of, the phoneme /r/.

In classical phonemics, as developed up to the end of the 1950s, the analyst's concern is to classify the speech sounds of a given language, dialect, accent or idiolect into phonemes, assigning each such 'phone' to a particular phoneme as one of its allophones. To be so assigned to the same phoneme, a pair or group of sound types have to satisfy two criteria: **phonetic similarity** and **non-contrastive distribution**.

1.2.3. Phonetic similarity

Phonetic similarity is not a well-defined notion. There are languages where phonetically rather different sound types have clearly to be assigned to the same phoneme, for instance [m] and [w] in Hidatsa, [t] and [k] in Niihau, [t] and [s] in Daga; and yet in English the [tʷ] of *twin* and the [d̥ʷ] of postpausal *dwell*, both phonetically voiceless labialized alveolar plosives, and differing only as voiceless (fortis) vs. devoiced (lenis), must belong to different phonemes, /t/ and /d/ respectively.

In English there is usually not a great deal of difficulty in deciding whether sound types are sufficiently phonetically similar to be allowed as co-allophones of one phoneme. There is, for example, the notorious case of [h] and [ŋ], which in most accents are in complementary distribution – [h] only syllable-initially, [ŋ] only syllable-finally – but which it would be absurd to regard as belonging to the same phoneme. They differ in almost all their phonetic features, and this is the justification for refusing them the status of co-allophones. (Irish English is a special case, since Irish characteristically admits [h] in final position, as in the name *McGrath* [mə'grah]; compare *meringue* [mə'raŋ] to establish the opposition in syllable-final position.)

Of all putative co-allophones in accents of English, the phonetically most dissimilar – at least from the articulatory point of view – are the alveolar [t] and the glottal [ʔ], which in many British accents are presumably to be analysed as co-allophones of one phoneme, /t/. The gross difference in their place of articulation is all the more striking in that they straddle the place of [k] (and variants), which belong to the different phoneme /k/. Yet apart from this the grounds for grouping [t] and [ʔ] together are strong, since they do not contrast in syllable-final position, and in many cases alternate freely, as when people pronounce *right* sometimes as [raɪʔ] and sometimes as [raɪt].

Other problems of phonetic similarity arise from the processes of Pre-R Breaking, R Dropping and L Vocalization (3.2.1–2, 3.4.4 below). Faced with pronunciation such as *dare* [dɛɜ̆], *weir* [wɪɜ̆], the analyst may well consider the possibility of regarding the non-syllabic [ɜ̆] as assignable to the phoneme /r/ (i.e. as the realization of 'underlying' /r/), even though there is considerable phonetic dis-similarity between the consonantal [ɹ] of *red* and the [ɜ̆] of *dare* and *weir*. In some cases this is a perfectly satisfactory analysis, though in many accents (including RP) the existence of further forms such as *dairy* ['dɛɜ̆ɹɪ], *weary* ['wɪɜ̆ɹɪ] makes it preferable to apply a different analysis on the grounds that it is unacceptable to posit doubled /rr/ in such words, which would be the consequence of assigning both [ɜ̆] and [ɹ] to /r/. The same type of problem arises with the non-syllabic [ɜ̆], [ɤ̆], or [ŭ] resulting from the vocalization of [ɫ] (= /l/) in accents such as American southern and Cockney.

Another phonemicization once in vogue but now generally re-jected, partly on grounds of failing to satisfy the criterion of phonet-ic similarity, was the grouping of syllable-initial [h] with syllable-final [ɜ̆] as /h/, thus *here* [hɪɜ̆] /hih/ etc. (Trager & Smith 1951).

Recent (post-1960) phonological theories generally abandon the requirement of phonetic similarity among the realizations of under-lying phonological units.

1.2.4. Non-contrastive distribution

There are two types of non-contrastive distribution: **complemen-tary distribution** and **free variation**. A given pair of sound types are said to be complementarily distributed if it is possible to state a rule specifying which of the pair is found in any particular environ-ment. The same applies, mutandis mutatis, to a set of three, four, or more sound types, always provided that each can be slotted into an appropriate environment. Several examples of complementary dis-tribution were given in 1.2.2 above. Thus in RP clear [l] and dark [ɫ] are in complementary distribution, the rule being that the former occurs before a vowel or /j/, the latter elsewhere. Such variation is **conditioned** in that the choice of allophone is determined by the nature of the following segment.

Two or more sound types are said to be freely variant if the occurrence of one or another is a matter of random chance. Beyond a certain level of articulatory precision, of course, every speech sound is subject to free variation, since no repetitions of the same word are perfectly identical in physical terms. Obviously, therefore, we need consider here only grosser differences. There are some British accents in which tap [ɾ] and approximant [ɹ] are free variants, at least in certain phonetic environments. Speakers of such accents may pronounce *thread* sometimes as [θɾɛd], sometimes as [θɹɛd], apparently without any reason for choosing one rather than the other; furthermore, they will immediately accept [θɾɛd] as an identical repetition of [θɹɛd] and vice versa.

It frequently happens that the distribution of allophones of a given phoneme involves both types of non-contrastive distribution. For example, aspirated [tʰ] may regularly be used before a stressed vowel, and unaspirated [t⁼] elsewhere; except that in absolute final (pre-pause) position [tʰ] and [t⁼] vary freely.

Recent work in sociolinguistics has shown that what at first sight appears to be free variation may actually be conditioned by social or stylistic factors, though perhaps only in a statistical way. Thus a Londoner might use both [t] and [ʔ] for syllable-final /t/, both occurring in the same contextual style apparently at random and equally often; but in a more formal style [t] might rise to, say, 80 per cent of instances and [ʔ] drop to 20 per cent.

Allophonic rules and the grouping of sound types into phonemes differ not only as between different languages, but also between different accents of the same language. For example, most accents of English have alveolar [n] and [ŋ] contrastively distributed, as is proved by minimal pairs such as *run* [rʌn] vs. *rung* [rʌŋ], *win* [wɪn] vs. *wing* [wɪŋ]. The inevitable consequence within a taxonomic-phonemic theory of phonology is that [n] and [ŋ] have to be assigned to distinct phonemes, /n/ and /ŋ/; the phoneme /ŋ/ has to be included in the inventory of consonants for any accent of this type. In a part of the midlands and north of England, however, *rung* and *wing* end not in [ŋ] but in [ŋg]. For these accents it can be shown that [ŋ] occurs only before a velar, as *think* [θɪŋk], *thing* [θɪŋg], a phonetic environment from which alveolar [n] is excluded. Hence [n] and [ŋ] are in complementary distribution and can be assigned to the same phoneme: *wing* is phonemicized /wɪŋ/. These accents have one consonant fewer in their consonant phoneme inventory. And it follows that a phonetically identical [θɪŋk] *think* has to be phonemicized /θɪŋk/ in accents of the first type, but /θɪnk/ in those of the second. (An alternative theoretical account of this accent difference is discussed below, 1.2.11.)

An important consequence for the investigator of accents is that he must elicit sufficient data to enable an adequate phonemicization to be carried out. Suppose that one observes that in a certain accent *put, pull, book, butcher, foot* and *full* are pronounced with [ʊ], but *cut, gull, luck, much, cup* and *dull* with [ʌ]. On the face of it, this could represent complementary distribution of the two vowel types, with [ʊ] occurring after labial obstruents, and [ʌ] elsewhere. If this were so, the variation would be conditioned by the nature of the preceding consonant, and we could regard [ʊ] and [ʌ] as allophones of the same phoneme. To test this hypothesis we require the further evidence of words such as *pun, butter, fumble* and *vulture; sugar, cook, good* and *cushion*. If, as in RP, these turn out to be pronounced with [ʌ] and [ʊ] respectively, then clearly the hypothesis is disconfirmed and the two vowel types cannot after all be assigned to the same phoneme. More complex hypotheses, involving for example the presence or absence of a following /l/, can be tested out in the same way. A pair such as *book* [bʊk] and *buck* [bʌk] clinches the matter, since it shows the two vowel types in contrast in an identical environment. Hence no factor of their phonetic environment can be conditioning the occurrence of one vowel type rather than the other.

This is why taxonomic phonemics has traditionally attached such importance to the discovery of **minimal pairs** – pairs of words distinct in meaning but identical in sound except for the fact that one has one of two sound types under investigation, the other the other. A minimal pair is evidence that sounds should be treated as belonging to different phonemes; the absence of minimal pairs leads one to suspect, at least, that they may belong to the same phoneme.

In most accents of English the pairs *pane–pain, sale–sail, raze–raise* are pronounced identically: they are **homophones**. In a few accents, however, they are distinct (heterophonous), e.g. as [peːn] vs. [pɛin] etc., and thus constitute minimal pairs as evidence for the existence of the phonemic opposition /eː/ vs. /ɛi/ in the accent in question. A fieldworkers' questionnaire which (like that of the *SED*) does not seek to elicit such crucial minimal pairs is seriously deficient from the phonologist's point of view.

The absence (or extreme scarcity) of minimal pairs does not necessarily mean that two sound types belong to the same phoneme. It is nearly impossible to find English minimal pairs for [ʃ] vs. [ʒ]: to succeed, we have resort to rare words, obscure proper names, or minority pronunciations, as *Aleutian–allusion, Asher–azure, ruche–rouge, lunch–lunge.* Yet the contrastiveness of [ʃ] and [ʒ] in most accents is clear not only from our inability to find any plausible rule to account for their distribution as members of one putative phoneme, but also from the existence of near-minimal pairs such as the non-rhyming pairs *pressure–pleasure, mission–vision, solution–delusion, vacation–occasion, ocean–erosion.*

1.2.5 Affricates and diphthongs

An uncertainty sometimes arises in phonology concerning whether some speech sound or sequence of speech sounds should be regarded as the realization of one phoneme or of a sequence of two phonemes. This problem particularly affects phonetic affricates (e.g. [tʃ] in *chain*) and phonetic diphthongs (e.g. [aɪ] in *fly*).

A monophonemic interpretation of [tʃ] regards it as assignable to a phoneme /tʃ/ (by many authors written as /č/, which emphasizes its single-unit status). Under this analysis /tʃ/, together with its lenis counterpart, /dʒ/ (/ǰ/), is included in the inventory of consonant phonemes of the language. A biphonemic interpretation, on the other hand, regards [tʃ] as reflecting an underlying phonemic sequence, /t/ plus /ʃ/, with the phonetic [t] assignable to /t/ and the [ʃ] assignable to /ʃ/.

There are arguments in favour of both possible interpretations. Native speakers usually think of [tʃ] and [dʒ] as single sounds, which supports a monophonemic analysis. The palato-alveolar affricates pattern phonotactically in a different way from other affricates: for example syllable-final [ts] and [dz] virtually always involve a morpheme boundary between the plosive and the fricative (*cats, bids*), whereas syllable-final [tʃ] and [dʒ] (*catch, bridge*) never do. There may be a distinction between the genuine affricate and a sequence of the corresponding plosive plus fricative, e.g. *hatchet* vs. *hat-shop*; though the location of word boundaries or morpheme boundaries complicates the issue here and offers an alternative explanation of the phonetic difference.

One strong argument pointing in the other direction, namely towards a biphonemic analysis, is that there are various other affricates in English which could not reasonably be claimed as monophonemic. Examples include the [ts] and [dz] discussed above, as well as the [pf] in *cupful*, the [bv] in *obvious* (both phonetically often labiodental throughout), and, most importantly, the post-alveolar affricates used in most accents of English in *train* and *drain* (phonetically [tɹ], [dɹ]). If the latter are analysed as /t/ plus /r/ and /d/ plus /r/, as by universal consent they are, why should we refuse a corresponding biphonemic analysis to the phonetically very similar palato-alveolars?

The phonological indeterminacy of affricates is something common to all accents of English and we shall pursue it no further. The question of diphthongs is essentially parallel. But here there is the additional consideration that different accents differ greatly in the extent to which diphthongs occur in them. There are accents where a majority of vowels are diphthongal, and where it may seem quite difficult to discover a word where the vowel is reliably monophthongal – for example, Cockney or American southern accents. There are other accents where monophthongs are the rule, with only a small number of well-defined diphthongs – for example, various Scottish and Irish accents.

Do we analyse the [aɪ] in *fly* as the realization of a single phoneme /aɪ/ ('long I', in old-fashioned dictionary transcription /ī/)? Or do we regard it as reflecting a sequence of some monophthongal vowel plus a glide? If the latter, the glide is readily identified with the /j/ of *yes*; but what is the preceding vowel? Depending on the accent we are investigating, there may be phonetic grounds for identifying it with the vowel of *palm*, that of *strut*, or that of *trap*; but in some cases – in RP, for instance – it is phonetically different from all three of these, occupying an intermediate position. Hence the biphonemic interpretation is faced with the arbitrary choice between /ɑːj/, /ʌj/, and /æj/ as a phonemicization of [aɪ]. Similar difficulties arise with the [ɜʊ ~ oʊ ~ eʊ] of *goat* in RP and similar accents: if the second element of the diphthong is assigned to /w/, is the first element to be identified with the /ə/ of *comma*, the /ʌ/ of *strut*, the /ɜː/ of *nurse*, or even the /ɒ/ of *lot* or the /ɔː/ of *thought*? We are confronted with the difficulty of multiple complementation (see 1.2.7 below).

A biphonemic analysis of diphthongs forces the analyst to make many such difficult – and essentially meaningless – choices. Analyses are determined by considerations of phonetic similarity, which is after all a phonetic rather than a phonological criterion.

It is for this reason that in this work I have followed a monophonemic evaluation of diphthongs, including diphthong phonemes as members of vowel systems. This is further supported by diachronic considerations, in that diphthongs typically undergo a different historical development from that undergone by the phonemes of which, under a biphonemic analysis, they would be regarded as consisting.

There is actually a fair case for going even further than I have down this path and for analysing such items as the r-coloured vowels and r-diphthongs of GenAm *start, short, near, square* as unit phonemes rather than as realizations of a vowel phoneme plus /r/; or for treating the [ɪʊ] of Cockney *milk* as justifying the recognition of a diphthong phoneme /ɪʊ/ rather than as a realization of /ɪ/ plus /l/.

1.2.6 The phonological word

We have seen that minimal pairs are excellent evidence of the contrastiveness of two sound types, and therefore of their belonging to distinct phonemes. The fact that *sleep* differs from *slip* both in sound and meaning (in every native-speaker accent of English) means that the phonological representation of the two words must be different. The fact that London [raɪʔ] *right* differs in sound and meaning from [raɪ] *rye* implies that the glottal stop at the end of *right* cannot be ignored, but must be assigned to some phoneme such that the phonological representation of the two words is different. (The obvious way to achieve this is to treat [ʔ] as an allophone of /t/, which means that in such a pronunciation the /t/ has not been 'omitted', as commonly claimed, but realized in a particular way, namely by a glottal rather than an alveolar stop.)

Do minimal pairs have to be words? And how do we define the notion 'word' in phonology?

There is a difference in pronunciation in most (perhaps all) accents of English between *pea-stalks* and *peace-talks*. Yet prima facie each member of this minimal pair consists of the same sequence of vowel and consonant phonemes as the other. How, then, are they different? One solution might involve recognizing separate long /iː/ in *pea* and short /i/ in *peace*, thus /'piːstɔks/ vs. /'pistɔks/. Another might involve recognizing separate aspirated and unaspirated voiceless plosive phonemes, thus /'pʰistɔks/ vs. /'pʰistʰɔks/. But solutions of this type are uneconomical and counter-intuitive. What we must do instead is recognize that the boundary between *pea* and *stalks* in the one case, and between *peace* and *talks* in the other, has phonological relevance. We can write the minimal pair phonologically as /pi#stɔks/, /pis#tɔks/. (Actually there is also another boundary to be recognized in these examples, the one separating the stem from the plural ending /z/.)

Similarly, *an aim* is phonetically different from *a name* in most (but not all) accents. Phonologically the first is /ən#eɪm/, the second /ə#neɪm/.

In the heyday of taxonomic phonemics, in the 1940s and 1950s, such boundaries were identified as a **juncture phonemes** (and usually symbolized as /+/). The theoretical view then prevailing held that morphological and syntactic considerations must be excluded from phonemics. Nowadays few subscribe to this dogma, and phonologists readily recognize that certain morphological and syntactic boundaries may play an important rôle in phonology. This rôle is typically one of constituting part of the environment which conditions the operation of a phonological rule, for instance the selection of allophones. Thus when we speak of a particular allophone being used in 'word-initial' or 'word-final' position we are tacitly admitting the necessity of word boundaries in phonology. Phonology does depend partly on morphological and syntactic considerations.

The number and type of phonological boundaries which call for recognition is a matter of controversy. Is the boundary (#) which we identify between the *pea* and *stalk* of the compound noun *peastalks* the same as that between successive words in a sentence? Is it the same as that between *talk* and *-s* in *talks*? The answer may well differ according to the accent one is describing; it certainly varies according to the phonological theory one adopts.

Assuming that there exist morphological or syntactic criteria by which 'words' can be delimited, it is clear that we need to be able to take into account at least the following kinds of boundaries: (i) those which separate words from one another in the sentence; (ii) those which separate the elements of a compound word from one another (as in *pea-stalks* above); (iii) those which separate stems from inflectional endings such as *-ed, -es, -ing*.

The importance of the last kind is clearly seen in Scottish accents of English, where there is typically a difference of vowel duration between the shorter [i] of *greed* and the longer [iː] of *agreed*, or the shorter [u] of *brood* and the longer [uː] of *brewed*. It would be uneconomical to infer from these and similar minimal pairs the existence of contrastive phonemes /i/ vs. /iː/, /u/ vs. /uː/. On the contrary, we must represent the words in question phonologically as /grid/, /əˈgri#d/, /brud/, /bru#d/, and treat the presence or absence of an immediately following # as one of the factors determining allophonic vowel duration. In the majority of accents, on the other hand, where *greed* and the second syllable of *agreed* sound identical, and where *brood* is a homophone of *brewed*, the possible presence of # in this environment can be ignored.

1.2.7 Multiple complementation and neutralization

Imagine a case where there are three sound types [a, b, c] which occur only word-initially, and a sound type [d] which occurs only word-finally. There are no environments in which [d] contrasts directly with any of [a, b, c]. It follows that [a] and [d] are in complementary distribution; but the same is true of [b] and [d] and also of [c] and [d]. Suppose, further, that [a, b, c, d] are all phonetically similar to one another, sharing the majority of their phonetic features in common. How do we phonemicize? With which word-initial sound type do we group the word-final [d]?

There are languages where this problem of multiple complementation offers serious difficulties to a taxonomic-phonemic approach. On the whole English is not one of them. We have seen, however, that a problem of this type does arise if the diphthongs are not analysed monophonemically (1.2.5 above). It is also possible, extrapolating from current trends, to envisage an accent of English at some future time in which words such as *pit, tick, kip* would all rhyme as [pɪʔ, tɪʔ, kɪʔ], with *pip–pit–pick* as homophones. Then [p, t, k] might prove to be in multiple complementation with respect to [ʔ], and we should have the awkward problem, in a taxonomic-phonemic phonology, of deciding whether to phonemicize [ʔ] as /p/, as /t/, or as /k/.

Very much more frequent is the situation where a phonemic opposition well established in one phonetic environment fails to apply in some other environment. A well-known case in point is the opposition between /p/ and /b/, which are distinct in *pin* [pʰɪn] /pɪn/ vs. *bin* [bɪn] /bɪn/, but not in *spin* [spɪn]: is the appropriate phonemicization of *spin* /spɪn/ or /sbɪn/? There may sometimes be phonetic grounds for preferring one possibility over the other; evidence from slips of the tongue or psycholinguistic experiments could lead to a preferred solution; native-speaker intuition may be firmly in favour of /spɪn/; the answer may differ in different accents (as when Welsh people seem to tilt towards /sbɪn/, English people towards /spɪn/); but in many cases there may be no non-arbitrary solution. We describe the /p/ vs. /b/ opposition as **neutralized** in the environment #s__.

In RP and similar accents of English there is a well-established opposition between the /uː/ of *pew* /pjuː/ and the /ʊə/ of *pure* /pjʊə/. Before a phonetically present /r/, however, this opposition is neutralized, as in *purity, fury*. In this environment the vocoid used may be virtually identical with the [ʊə] of *pure*, or with the [uː] of *pew*, or it may be, say, [ʊː], phonetically different from both. The traditional phonemicization here is /ʊə/, so that *fury* is analysed as /ˈfjʊərɪ/. Some speakers may feel that /ˈfjuːrɪ/ would be a better reflection of their native intuition. Phonetic considerations may push us one way or the other; morphological considerations push us towards /ʊə/, since only then is the vowel of *purity* analysed as identical with that of *pure*, which simplifies the morphology.

Often the phonetic considerations are so overwhelming that one hardly realizes that a neutralization situation exists. All native accents of English distinguish the vowel of *face* from that of *dress*. But the opposition in question does not operate in 'free' stressed monosyllables (those with no final consonant), i.e. in the environment '__#. The vowel or diphthong of *day* is in complementary not only with that of *face*, but also with that of *dress*. In most accents one identifies the vowels of *day* and *face* with no hesitation. Yet there are accents where the other possibility is more appropriate (e.g. Belfast, or the Leeward Islands, where the phonetic quality of the vowel in *day* is more similar to that of *dress* than to that of *face*).

The limiting case is that of **absolute neutralization**, where two posited phonemes never contrast. This situation does not arise within a taxonomic-phonemic framework, in which one would never posit two such phonemes. But there are cases which approach it: cases where an opposition is restricted to a very small range of phonetic environments. In some varieties of GenAm there is a distinction between the phonetically long [ɑː] of *palm* and the phonetically shorter [ɑ] of *Tom*, so that these words do not form a perfect rhyme. Yet the opposition in question is neutralized everywhere except in the environments __m and __n (*Kahn* vs. *con*): *father* rhymes perfectly with *bother*. It is awkward to have to recognize a phonemic opposition on the basis of such a small number of items.

1.2.8 Further difficulties with taxonomic phonemics

In strict versions of taxonomic-phonemic theory a requirement of **biuniqueness** is established such that every speech sound must be uniquely assignable to a given phoneme and every phoneme realized in any given context in a unique way (excluding free variation). This requirement leads to various absurdities, as critics have not been slow to point out.

Many accents of English include a preconsonantal or syllable-final [ʔ] which common sense suggests should be assigned to /t/, thus one or both of [ˈbʌʔn] *button*, [raɪʔ] *right* etc. Yet these accents, as well as most others, also include a prevocalic [ʔ] as an optional indicator of extra emphasis on an initial vowel, thus [ˈʔɔːfl] *awful*, [aɪ ˈʔæm] *I AM*. This prevocalic [ʔ] cannot be assigned to /t/, since it contrasts with [tʰ], as [ʔɪn] *IN* vs. [tʰɪn] *tin*. Common sense suggests it be assigned to no segmental phoneme, but be treated instead as part of the phonetic correlate of extra emphasis: from a segmental point of view it is an allophone of zero. Hence in one environment [ʔ] is assigned to /t/, in another to zero. This instance of **overlapping allophones** violates biuniqueness.

When in Cockney we find *cotton* usually pronounced [ˈkɒʔn], but sometimes [ˈkɒtən], while *reckon* is usually [ˈreʔn] but sometimes [ˈrekən], one sees an attractive case for allowing [ʔ] to count also as an allophone of /k/. Adherence to the principles of taxonomic phonemics, however, forces one to phonemicize [ˈreʔn] as /retṇ/ (or even as /ˈretən/, as actually done by Sivertsen 1960). The [ʔ] of [aɪˈʔæm] is an instance where we want to be allowed to regard a phonetic segment as having no corresponding underlying phonological unit – to be able to **insert** a speech sound in a particular specifiable phonetic environment as we convert the underlying string of phonemes into the surface string of speech sounds which realize it. Another clear example of insertion is the 'intrusive *r*' which most English people use in phrases such as *Kenya*[r] *and Uganda, the magnolia*[r] *in the garden*.

Sometimes we want to be able to do the opposite, namely to **delete** an item. This means having an underlying phonological unit which receives no overt phonetic realization at all. A variety of optional elisions can be readily handled in this way, as when in slow speech one says *support* as two syllables (RP [sə'pɔːt]), but in faster or more casual speech as one syllable (RP [spɔːt]). If we allow the principle of deletion in the rules relating phonemes and allophones, we can regard the phonemic representation as an unchanging /sə'pɔːt/.

Another extremely desirable relaxation of strict biuniqueness concerns the possibility of a single phonetic segment being the realization of a string of two or more phonological segments. An example is the syllabic [n̩] which most accents have in words like *hidden* [-dn̩]. There are compelling reasons for regarding this [n̩] as the realization of underlying /ən/. These include the morphological fact that the *-en* suffix is pronounced [ən] in other environments (*swollen*); possible free variation between [n̩] and [ən] in some other environments (*station*); the possibility in some accents of getting [n̩] as the realization of a /ə/ and a /n/ which belong to different words in the sentence ([hædn̩aɪs 'deɪ] *had a nice day*); and the extreme difficulty experienced by many native speakers of English, including some of those undergoing training in phonetics, in perceiving the difference between [n̩] and [ən]. But this analysis is not available under any phonological theory which regards phonemicization as the assignment of speech sounds to phonemes, the phonemes being classes ('families') of speech sounds fulfilling certain requirements.

Difficulties also arise with the notion of contrastiveness ('distinctiveness', 'opposition'), when this is seen as a necessary condition for phonemic difference. Contrastiveness sometimes works in one direction only. For example, RP and similar accents have a type of assimilation which causes a phrase such as *good girl*, /'gʊd 'gɜːl/, to be optionally pronounced ['gʊg̚ 'gɜːl], where [g̚] denotes a velar plosive without audible release (since phonetically there is a single velar with a long hold phase extending right across the word boundary). In the phrase *big girl* ['bɪg˺ 'gɜːl] we have no hesitation about assigning [g˺] to /g/. To maintain the biuniqueness principle of taxonomic phonemics we should have to regard the assimilated pronunciation of *good girl* as involving the phoneme /g/ at the end of *good*, since we cannot assign [g˺] sometimes to /g/ and sometimes to /d/. This is indeed the analysis adopted by writers within the taxonomic-phonemic framework, e.g. Gimson (1980). But it is not without its absurdities. In *big girl* the first /g/ can optionally be realized as an audibly released [g], so that here /g#g/ varies (freely or stylistically) between [g˺ g] and [gə g]. In the assimilated pronunciation of *good girl*, however, this option is not available: the putative /g#g/ can only be [g˺ g], never [gə g]. Coherent allophonic rules to account for this difference cannot be formulated. And the contrastiveness is one-way in that there is no contrast between [d] and [g˺] in the environment exemplified by *good girl*, since [d] can be replaced by [g˺] without any change of meaning or oddness; yet there is a phonemic contrast between [g˺] and [d] in the same environment as exemplified in *big girl*, where to replace [g˺] by [d] would yield the nonsensical **bid girl*.

There are other alternations which are asymmetrical in their operation, too. In RP any word that can be pronounced with the sequence [uːə] can alternatively be pronounced with [ʊə], thus *brewer* ['bruːə ∼ brʊə], and similarly with *steward, fewer, fluent* etc. One is tempted to say that [uːə] and [ʊə] are in free variation. However, it is not the case in this accent that any word with [ʊə] can alternatively be pronounced with [uːə]: words such as *poor, sure, cure, during* can be pronounced with [ʊə], thus [pʊə] etc., but never (in RP) with [uːə]. The alternation is not symmetrical.

Interestingly enough, RP [ʊə] is involved in another asymmetrical alternation. It is on the whole true that words such as *poor, sure, cure, during* – those [ʊə] words which do not have [uːə] as an alternative possible pronunciation – can alternatively be pronounced with [ɔː], thus [pɔː], [ʃɔː] etc. Yet the great majority of words which can be pronounced with [ɔː] have no alternative with [ʊə]: *paw, shore, boring, thought* etc.

The conclusion to be drawn is that phonology needs to consist mainly of rules relating underlying, relatively abstract phonological representations (phonemic representations) to surface, concrete phonetic representations, rather than with principles for assigning phonetic segments to phonemes or other more general units. Thus taxonomic phonemics has come to be displaced in linguistic theory by various versions of so-called **generative phonology**. With a generative approach we can, for instance, include in the phonological description of RP the rules (12) and (13)

(12)   /ʊə/ → [ɔː]
(13)   /uːə/ → [ʊə]

as optional or style-dependent stages in the path from underlying phonemic representation to surface phonetic representation. If *poor* has the underlying representation /pʊə/, and *fluent* the underlying representation /fluːənt/, then rule (12) allows *poor* the variant [pɔː], while rule (13) allows *fluent* the variant [flʊənt]. This is more satisfactory than insisting that every phonetic [ɔː] be assigned to the phoneme /ɔː/ and every phonetic [ʊə] to the phoneme /ʊə/.

In the accent of Cardiff, south Wales, what appears to be an identical [ɾ] is used both in words such as *three* [θɾiː], *through*, *thriving* and in words such as *bottom* ['bɒɾəm], *letter*, *beautiful*. Taxonomic phonemics, strictly applied, would require us to assign all cases of [ɾ] to the same phoneme, which is absurd. Generative phonology allows us to derive one set of cases from an underlying /r/ and the other set from underlying /t/.

1.2.9 Phonological rules

Whereas the goal of taxonomic phonemics is to classify the observed phonetic phenomena (above all as allophones of phonemes), the goal of generative phonology is rather to specify the pronunciation of sentences. Within the overall framework of a transformational generative grammar, the phonological component consists of **rules** which map an underlying, abstract representation (the 'systematic-phonemic' representation) onto a more concrete phonetic representation (the 'systematic-phonetic' representation). It is hypothesized that words are stored in the speaker's mental lexicon in a form analogous to the systematic-phonemic representation. When any word is actually uttered, its shape is successively modified as it undergoes the phonological rules which apply to it. The input to the body of rules is the stored form; the output is the form uttered in a given context.

For example, the word *bad* has (in the standard accents) the underlying representation /bæd/. The (optional) RP rule of Dealveolar Assimilation is potentially triggered whenever a word ending in an alveolar stop occurs before a word beginning with a bilabial or velar stop. Hence in the phrase *bad girl* we can derive the surface form [bæg], as discussed in 1.2.8.

Rules may be **context-free** or **context-sensitive**. A context-free rule applies under all circumstances, in all phonetic environments. But all, or almost all, phonological and phonetic rules are context-sensitive: they apply only in certain environments. In most accents, for example, the aspiration of /p, t, k/ applies only before stressed vowels:

(14)   Voiceless plosive → Aspirated / __ Stressed vowel

where the symbol → means 'goes to, becomes, is rewritten as', / means 'in the environment', and __ in the structural formula means the place in which the rule applies. Rule (14) therefore supplies aspiration to the voiceless plosives in the words *pin, toss, carry, appoint, return, account,* but not to those in *rip, lost, back, supper, letter, lacquer, persuade, tomorrow, connection.* In fact rule (14) is not quite exact as it stands: the specification of the environment must be revised so as to exclude cases where /s/ precedes within the syllable, e.g. *spin, staff, skull, aspire, restore, askance*; and in many accents provision must be made for possible aspiration in final position.

A rule-based phonology is extremely powerful. Rules can be used not only to alter segments or to specify them in detail; with them we can also delete segments or insert them, or even change their order (metathesis); we can coalesce two adjacent segments into one, or 'disalesce' one segment into two. Using the symbol Ø ('zero'), we can formulate the insertion of [r] in *Kenya and Uganda* or *the magnolia in the garden* as (15):

(15)   Ø → r / ə __ # # Vowel

The deletion of [ə] in *support* and similar words takes the form (16):

$$(16) \quad \partial \rightarrow \emptyset \left/ \begin{bmatrix} \text{Voiceless} \\ \text{consonant} \end{bmatrix} - \begin{bmatrix} \text{Voiceless} \\ \text{consonant} \end{bmatrix} \begin{bmatrix} \text{Stressed} \\ \text{vowel} \end{bmatrix} \right.$$

One way of formulating the rule coalescing /ən/ to [n̩] in *hidden* etc. would be (17):

(17)   ən → n̩ / $\begin{bmatrix} \text{Stressed} \\ \text{vowel} \end{bmatrix}$ [Plosive] —

(This is a first approximation to Syllabic Consonant Formation.)

The classical treatment of English in terms of generative phonology is Chomsky & Halle's *The sound pattern of English* (1968, hereafter referred to as *SPE*). Their treatment goes well beyond rules of the relatively superficial kind we have been discussing so far. They also attempt to cater for all the alternations observable in the shape of English morphemes, i.e. to include in the phonology all of what has traditionally been called morphology. Thus on the basis of alternations such as *electric–electricity*, *critic–criticize*, *medical–medicine*, they recognize a rule of Velar Softening which changes underlying /k/ to [s] in certain environments. (The rule has to be restricted to the Greek and Latin part of English vocabulary, since the /k/ in *king, kitty, kite, mannikin* remains [k] in spite of a following /ɪ ~ aɪ/.) Their rules also predict stress patterns for words and phrases.

In this work we exclude 'morphological' rules of this kind from consideration. Partly this is because they are in many cases not productive, which is to say they are not applied to new material to produce new phonetic forms; partly it is because in everything except final details they are applicable equally to all accents of English. But mainly it is because I consider them much too powerful: they make possible such a large number of rival alleged underlying patterns that we disappear into a haze of indeterminacy.

1.2.10 Natural classes

Phonological rules do sometimes operate on individual phonemes or sound-types (e.g. [p] or [i]). More usually, though, they are less limited: they operate rather on **natural classes** of sounds (e.g. voiceless plosives, or front vowels). Natural classes are classes of sounds which share common **features**, and can be defined by fewer features than are needed to define any single member of the class. To define the natural class of voiceless plosives we need to mention voicelessness and plosion; but to define the particular voiceless plosive [p] we need to add reference to labiality. In this sense the natural class consisting of English /p, t, k/ is simpler or more general than the single-member class consisting of /p/. It is a general linguistic principle that one strives to make the descriptive rules as simple, i.e. as general, as possible.

The nature of the universal phonetic feature system which each language draws its stock of distinctive features is still the subject of some controversy. Rather than enter into these questions in the present work, I have preferred to name natural classes involved in rules by using traditional phonetic terminology. So rule (14) above appeared as

(14)   Voiceless plosive → Aspirated / __ Stressed vowel

rather than as (14′) or (14″):

$$(14')\quad \begin{bmatrix} -\text{voi} \\ -\text{cont} \end{bmatrix} \rightarrow [+\text{asp}] / \underline{} \begin{bmatrix} +\text{stress} \\ +\text{syll} \end{bmatrix}$$

$$(14'')\quad \begin{bmatrix} -\text{voice} \\ \text{stop} \end{bmatrix} \rightarrow [\text{aspirated}] / \underline{} \begin{bmatrix} +\text{stress} \\ \text{V} \end{bmatrix}$$

I shall also make use of the abbreviations C and V (Consonant and Vowel respectively), so that (14) can also be written as (14‴):

(14‴)   Voiceless plosive → Aspirated / __ ′V

Adherents of particular feature systems will readily be able to convert these formulations into the sort they favour.

In rule formulations the convention applies that any feature characterizing the input which is not altered by the rule continues to characterize the output. Thus the output of rule (14‴) will be a segment which remains voiceless and plosive. In the case of [p], which enters as bilabial (as well as being voiceless and a plosive), the output is bilabial, voiceless, plosive – and aspirated, i.e. [pʰ].

1.2.11 A case in point: the velar nasal

One of the principal concerns in phonology in the period since the publication of *SPE* has been to find well-motivated grounds for constraining phonological rules and restricting the set of possible underlying representations. In this work I shall assume underlying representations which are very similar to the surface forms: I shall not assume anything very much deeper than the taxonomic phoneme. Using a generative rather than a taxonomic model enables us to escape the absurdities and difficulties of 1.2.7–8 above; positing rather concrete underlying representations facilitates our concentration of attention on the subject-matter under discussion, which is variation in pronunciation (and not, for instance, in morphology) among the various forms of English.

An example of a border-line case is the velar nasal. English clearly possesses a voiced velar nasal sound type, [ŋ] as in *sing, think, angle* (in the standard accents [sɪŋ], [θɪŋk], [æŋgl]). More precisely, there are a number of slightly different sound types groupable under the general name of velar nasal, since in this case as in all others there is typically a degree of co-articulation with preceding and/or following segments. But does English have a velar nasal **phoneme**? Is the underlying representation of *sing* /sɪŋ/ or something else? In view of the existence of minimal pairs of the type *sing* [sɪŋ] vs. *sin* [sɪn], *bang* vs. *ban*, *rung* vs. *run* vs. *rum*, the taxonomic-phonemic answer is that there clearly is a phoneme /ŋ/, since there is no other phoneme to which the sound type [ŋ] can plausibly be assigned. The generativist, however, usually argues that there is no underlying phoneme /ŋ/ and that all surface occurrences of [ŋ] are derived by rule from underlying /n/ or /ng/. Two rules are needed for this: a rule of Nasal Assimilation, (18), and a rule of Final [g] Deletion, (19).

(18) $\begin{bmatrix} \text{Alveolar} \\ \text{nasal} \end{bmatrix} \rightarrow [\alpha \text{ Place}] / \underline{\quad} \begin{bmatrix} \alpha \text{ Place} \\ \text{Stop} \end{bmatrix}$

Here α is a 'Greek letter variable' which can assume any value appropriate for the feature in question. Whatever value for the Place of Articulation feature is specified for the Stop in the right-hand environment, rule (18) supplies the same Place value to the nasal.

(19) $g \rightarrow \emptyset$ / Nasal $\underline{\quad}$ #

The incorporation of rules (18) and (19) into the grammar leads one to posit underlying forms and derivations for *sing, think,* and *angle* as in (20) (where we ignore for the moment the question of the syllabicity of the final lateral).

(20)

	sing	*think*	*angle*	
Underlying phonological representation	# sɪng #	# θɪnk #	# æŋgl #	input
by (18)	# sɪŋg #	# θɪŋk #	# æŋgl #	
by (19)	# sɪŋ #	n.a.	n.a.	
Delete boundary symbols	sɪŋ	θɪŋk	æŋgl	output

The /g/ in *angle* is not deleted by (19) because it is not followed by
#. To make this analysis work correctly, it is obvious that words
such as *longing, banger* must include an occurrence of # between
stem and suffix, / # lɒng # ɪng # /, / # bæng # ə(r) # /; and this corresponds to their morphology. We have derivations as in (21).
(Accents vary as to whether there is a final /r/. Vowels also vary in
some of these examples.)

(21)

	longing	*banger*
Underlying phonological representation	# lɒng # ɪng #	# bæng # ə(r) #
by (18)	# lɒŋg # ɪŋg #	# bæŋg # ə(r) #
by (19)	# lɒŋ # ɪŋ #	# bæŋ # ə(r) #
Delete boundary symbols	lɒŋɪŋ	bæŋə(r)

Certain problems do, however, arise with this approach. In the
standard accents the words *stronger, strongest, younger, youngest,
longer* and *longest* retain [g] after the [ŋ], although the morphological
boundary present would lead us to expect them to lose the [g] by
rule (19). The adjective *wrong* is normally not gradable, but if
one forces a comparative *wronger* and superlative *wrongest* most
speakers seem to produce forms without [g]. So it seems best to
regard *stronger*, etc., as exceptions. The words *strong, young,* and
long must include in their phonological specification in the lexicon
an indication that for them – exceptionally – rule (19) does not apply
when the suffixes *-er* (comparative) and *-est* (superlative) are
attached.

This illustrates the general point that certain words may be
phonologically irregular. Just as certain verbs are irregular in the
morphology of their past tense, so certain adjectives are irregular in
the phonology of their comparative and superlative.

There are a few words which are irregular in the other direction: a
post-nasal [g] undergoes deletion from them even though they do
not meet the structural description of rule (19). Examples include
gingham ['gɪŋəm], *Langham* ['læŋəm], and (for some speakers only)
dinghy ['dɪŋɪ]. They cannot plausibly be regarded as including a

boundary # after the nasal: even though the *-ham* of *gingham* and *Langham* may once have been a living suffix, it cannot now be synchronically so considered.

Once we admit rule (19) to our phonological description, we can account more simply for the difference between the standard accents and the midlands/north-of-England accents mentioned in 1.2.4 above. Instead of positing a difference in the inventory of consonant phonemes, all we need say is that the accents which say [θɪŋg] etc. lack rule (19). If they have no rule (19), they delete no post-nasal [g]s.

In some lower-class west-of-Scotland and Northern Ireland speech, however, pronunciation such as ['fɪŋər] *finger* are found. We can account for this by saying that for them rule (19) takes the slightly different form (19'):

(19')   g → Ø / Nasal __

In this formulation the rule serves to delete every post-nasal [g], whether followed by a boundary or not. (Actually, it will probably be necessary to restrict the rule so that it does **not** apply before a stressed vowel, in words such as *engage*.)

A committed generativist does not have to stop here. What about the standard pronunciation of words such as *thumb, climb, lamb*? The spelling suggests the possibility of recognizing final underlying /b/ in such words and widening rule (19) so as to delete not only final [g] but also final [b] when a nasal precedes. As velars and labials belong to the natural class of 'non-coronal' consonants (as opposed to the 'coronal' dentals, alveolars, retroflexes and palato-alveolars), we reformulate (19) as (19'').

(19'') $\begin{bmatrix} \text{Non-coronal} \\ \text{consonant} \end{bmatrix}$ → Ø / Nasal __ #

This allows derivations such as (22).

		thumb	*timber*	*land*	*sing*
(22)	Underlying phonological representation	# θʌnb #	# tɪnbə(r) #	# lænd #	# sɪng #
	by (18)	# θʌmb #	# tɪmbə(r) #	# lænd #	# sɪŋg #
	by (19'')	# θʌm #	n.a.	n.a.	# sɪŋ #
	Delete boundary symbols	θʌm	tɪmbə(r)	lænd	sɪŋ

Yet these derivations for *thumb* and *timber* are questionable. Since [m], unlike [ŋ], does occur initially, and clearly contrasts medially with [mb] in words where no # can be posited (*camel* vs. *gambol*, *summer* vs. *number*), we must admit /m/ to the inventory of possible underlying consonant phonemes. Thus we are faced with an indeterminacy as far as the underlying shape of *thumb* is concerned: it could just as well be /#θʌm#/, /#θʌmb#/, or /#θʌnb#/, and there is no way of telling which. Allowing even the very moderate degree of abstractness implied by rules (18) and (19″) inevitably leads to uncertainty in phonemic shape. And of course in an account of present-day pronunciation we should not be justified in appealing either to the history of English or to the spelling to enable us to choose between the rival possible underlying representations.

If we stick to the traditional taxonomic-phonemic view that /ŋ/ is a phoneme, we avoid both this indeterminacy and the necessity of treating *gingham* etc. as exceptions.

1.2.12 Optional rules, variable rules

Rules may be either **obligatory** or **optional**. An obligatory rule is applied whenever its structural description is met. Rule (14) above, however formulated, specifies aspiration for every voiceless plosive occurring in the environment of a following stressed vowel. Optional rules, on the other hand, describe a situation of free variation; it is a matter of random choice whether an optional rule is applied on a given occasion or not. Thus an accent where absolute-final /t/ varies freely between aspirated [tʰ] and unaspirated [t⁼] (and /p/ and /k/ vary likewise) has the optional rule (23):

$$(23) \quad Opt \begin{bmatrix} \text{Voiceless} \\ \text{plosive} \end{bmatrix} \rightarrow \text{aspirated} \; / \underline{\quad} \|$$

where the symbol ‖ means 'end of utterance, major clause boundary'. When randomly triggered, rule (23) will supply aspiration to the final consonant of *Wait!*, thus [weɪtʰ]; when randomly not triggered, it will not, so that the output will be [weɪt⁼].

Rules may be either **categorial** or **variable**. A categorial rule applies independently of stylistic or social considerations. Its operation does not depend on such factors as the degree of formality of the occasion or the social class, age, sex, or carefulness of the speaker. A variable rule does depend on non-linguistic considerations of this kind. For example, we find that in many parts of Britain final /t/ can be pronounced in any of three ways: with weak aspiration, [tʰ]; with simultaneous alveolar and glottal closures, [tʔ]; or with a glottal closure only, [ʔ]. This situation can be shown formulaically as (24) (after Trudgill 1974a: 156).

(24) /t/ → x < [tʰ] ∼ [tʔ] ∼ [ʔ] > / __ #
      x = f(style, class)

This form of notation, and the concept of variable rules, were first introduced by Labov (1969); they are still a matter of some controversy.

Given that we admit the notion of variable rules, it may still be difficult to determine whether a given rule (which we observe to apply sometimes, and sometimes not to apply) is optional or vairable. Our answer may vary according to whether we are attempting to describe an idiolect (an individual speaker's competence, his internalized knowledge of his language) or the speech of a whole community. Variability observable within a community does not necessarily imply variability within the individual idiolects that constitute the speech community.

A further complication is that rules sometimes apply only to certain parts of the vocabulary, or more readily to some parts than to others. For example, a rule may apply to familiar words more readily than to learned words; or not apply to proper names; or apply to native words but not to borrowed words. It appears that sound changes often spread gradually through the vocabulary, usually spreading from the more everyday words to the less familiar ones (**lexical diffusion**).

The RP alternation between [ʊə] and [ɔː] is perhaps a case in point. It can be viewed as optional, inasmuch as I find I sometimes say [ˈʃʊəlɪ] and sometimes [ˈʃɔːlɪ] for the word spelt *surely*. As far as I can tell, this alternation is random. It appears to be true, though, that people who share a similar background to me but are older are more likely to say [ˈʃʊəlɪ], while those ditto who are younger than me are more likely to say [ˈʃɔːlɪ]. This implies that the rule is to be seen as a variable one, with x a function of the speaker's age. Then there are other words subject to this alternation in the community which

I say pretty consistently with [ʊə], e.g. *moor*; and there are people who consistently use [ɔː] in certain words where I fluctuate, such as *poor*. Even to describe the RP-speaking speech community's usage adequately would require a combination of optionality, variability, and lexical specification in this rule.

1.2.13 Rule ordering

In their path from the underlying, memory-stored phonological representation to the actual surface (detailed phonetic) representation words, and the sentences made up out of them, typically undergo several rule-determined modifications. Sometimes the order in which the rules apply in such a 'derivation' is critical.

In RP, as we have see, *fluent* can be ['fluːənt] or [flʊənt]; in general, any word which can have [uːə] can alternatively have [ʊə]. We posit a rule of Smoothing (3.2.9 below) to account for the alternation. A word such as *poor* can be either [pʊə] or [pɔː]; there are many other words which fluctuate similarly between [ʊə] and [ɔː], and we posit a rule of CURE Lowering (3.2.7) to account for this. It is clear, though, that the output of Smoothing (uːə → ʊə) must not be permitted as the input to CURE Lowering (ʊə → ɔː), since this would give rise to unattested variants such as *[flɔːnt] for *fluent*, in accordance with derivation (25):

(25) Input   fluːənt
      by Smoothing   flʊənt
      by CURE Lowering flɔːnt   = incorrect output

We can avoid this error by ordering Smoothing after CURE Lowering. A form resulting from the operation of Smoothing can then never be an input to CURE Lowering. As it is often expressed, the relationship between Smoothing and Lowering is not a **feeding** one. Correct derivations of *fluent* and *poor* are shown in (26), where the incorrect rule order of (25) has been reversed to prevent one rule feeding the other.

(26) Input   fluːənt   pʊə (= output if optional
                                   rules not selected)

      by CURE Lowering –   pɔː
      by Smoothing   flʊənt –
                     flʊənt pɔː = correct output if
                                   optional rules selected

Another subcase of the general RP Smoothing rule converts [aʊ] to [ɑː] before a following vowel, as *tower* [taʊə ~ tɑːə], *bowing* [baʊɪŋ ~ bɑːɪŋ]. There is also a rule of R Insertion in RP and similar accents (3.2.3 below), which inserts [r] between a non-close vowel and a following vowel, as *far off* [ˈfɑː ˈɒf] → [ˈfɑːr ˈɒf]. It is clear that we must not allow Smoothing to feed R Insertion, since if we did we should derive incorrect forms such as *[tɑːrə], *[bɑːrɪŋ]. Therefore R Insertion precedes Smoothing.

Yet another rule, Unstressed H Dropping, permits the deletion of [h] in certain unstressed syllables, so that *with his friends* may have either [hɪz] or [ɪz]. Is there an ordering relationship between Unstressed H Dropping and R Insertion? We can investigate the question by trying out both possible orders, as in (27) and (28), where they are applied to the phrase *for his friends*. (The input for *for* is taken as [fə], which presuppose that the rule of Weakening has already applied to change the underlying [ɔː] of [fɔː] to [ə].)

(27)	Input	fə hɪz ˈfrɛndz	
	by Unstressed H Dropping	fə ɪz ˈfrɛndz	
	by R Insertion	fər ɪz ˈfrɛndz	= correct output

(28)	Input	fə hɪz ˈfrɛndz	
	by R Insertion	–	(structural description not met, so rule cannot apply)
	by Unstressed H Dropping	fə ɪz ˈfrɛndz	= incorrect or questionable output

We certainly want to be able to derive [fər ɪz ˈfrɛndz], the output of (27), and must therefore allow Unstressed H Dropping to feed R Insertion. The correct order for the two rules seems accordingly to be as in (27). The output of (28) is questionable: some speakers of the accent in question may have [fə ɪz ˈfrɛndz] as a possibility, though most probably do not. If we want to allow it as a possible output, it can be accounted for by keeping the order as in (27), but making R Insertion optional in this environment (as it certainly is in many others).

We have shown that the three rules of Unstressed H Dropping, R Insertion, and Smoothing must apply in that order. The ordering of CURE Lowering with respect to Unstressed H Dropping and R Insertion is immaterial, but it must precede Smoothing.

A phonological theory which allows ordered rules offers a more satisfactory account than taxonomic-phonemic phonology when dealing with certain problematic bodies of data. A well-known instance is illustrated by the words *writer* and *rider* in certain American and Canadian accents of English. In a typical Canadian accent, for example, these words are pronounced ['rəidə] and ['raɪdə] respectively. Prima facie, this seems to constitute a minimal pair establishing a phonemic opposition between a putative /əi/ and /aɪ/, since they contrast in an identical environment. Inspection shows, however, that in all other environments [əi] and [aɪ] are in complementary distribution, [əi] occurring before a voiceless consonant and [aɪ] elsewhere. Furthermore, voiceless [t] does not occur contrastively in the environment 'V __ V. All of these facts fall into place if we recognize two ordered rules in the phonology of this accent: one of PRICE Raising (vol. 3, 6.2.4) and one of T Voicing (3.3.4 below), statable as (29):

(29)   PRICE Raising $aɪ → əi / — \begin{bmatrix} C \\ -\text{voiced} \end{bmatrix}$

           T Voicing $t → d / \; 'V — V$

Assuming, in line with the morphology, that the underlying phonological representation of *writer* is /raɪt # ər/ and that of *rider* /raɪd # ər/, we have the following derivations (30):

(30)	writer	rider	
Input	raɪt # ər	raɪd # ər	
by PRICE Raising	rəit # ər	–	
by T Voicing	rəid # ər	–	
Delete boundaries etc.	rəidə	raɪdə	= output

If the rules were allowed to apply in the reverse order, we should have derivations (31), with an output incorrect for the accent we are considering.

(31)	writer	rider
Input	raɪt # ər	raɪd # ər
by T Voicing	raɪd#ər	–
by PRICE Raising	–	–
Delete boundaries etc.	raɪdə	raɪdə

1.2.14 Polylectal and panlectal phonology

To what extent is the English language a single entity, to be described in all its diversity by means of a single body of rules? To restrict an account of English phonetics to the pronunciation of a single speaker – to a single idiolect – is obviously unsatisfactory, in view of the fact that language is above all a social phenomenon, used principally for communication and social interaction, not for solipsistic communing with oneself. But if we attempt to describe the output of the whole speech community, the entire collective of English speakers, we may well find it impossible to reconcile their variability with the qualities we expect to find in a linguistic description or grammar: the qualities of being coherent, structured, discrete, and self-consistent. In particular, we may not be able to reconcile such a whole-language description with the aim of modelling in our grammar the competence of the ideal speaker–hearer, the knowledge he has of his language.

Dialectologists and historical linguists have demonstrated the feasibility of accounting for differences between dialects or accents in terms of their different historical development from a common ancestor (cf. chapter 3 below). Generative phonology has shown how this can be extended to synchronic description, in that variations between speakers, or more generally between language varieties, can largely be accounted for by positing differences in relatively superficial rules or their ordering, the underlying representations being common to all varieties of the language. In the strongest version of this thesis, the grammar of a language should aim to cover all the dialects or accents of the language under description. Such a **panlectal** grammar is justified, it is claimed by its adherents, not merely as a descriptive device enabling us to summarize variety differences in convenient form, but more significantly as furnishing a model of the adult speaker's ability to understand, interpret and even predict the speech of those who speak a different accent from his own.

An early theoretical attempt to cope with accent variability was the **diaphone** put forward by Jones (1962: ch. 27) as 'a family of sounds consisting of an "average" sound used by many speakers in a given word together with deviations from this used as equivalents by other speakers' (1963: xxxv). In this sense the different qualities found in DRESS in different accents constitute a single diaphone. 'Each variety of sound contained in a diaphone may be termed a "diaphonic variant" or a "free variant".' In a rival terminological tradition, the variants themselves are termed diaphones, and are grouped by the descriptivist into a **diaphoneme** (thus, for instance, *PEAS*).

The diaphone/diaphoneme approach runs into difficulties as soon as we have to deal with systemic differences between accents (1.3.4 below) rather than mere differences in phonetic realization (1.3.2 below). Do we set up different diaphonemes for the vowel of NORTH and that of FORCE? Some speakers maintain an opposition in such words (*warn* pronounced differently from *worn*), but many others do not. For those who do not, must we assign their undifferentiated vowel to two diaphonemes simultaneously? Alternatively, if we set up just one diaphoneme, how do we treat the opposition undoubtedly preserved in the speech of those who do distinguish these pairs? Again, for many speakers the vowel of FORCE is to be equated phonemically with that of GOAT (e.g. /fors, got/). For others it is not (e.g. /fɔːs, goʊt/). How then is one to diaphonemicize the vowels of FORCE?

Only by making the diaphonemic representation a rather remote, underlying form, linked to actual surface representations in given accents by a long chain of rules – only in this way could we resolve the obvious difficulties of the taxonomic diaphoneme. For example, we can assume that words such as *eight, straight* have a velar fricative in their underlying phonemic representation, thus perhaps /eːxt, streːxt/ (or, with vowels represented in pre-Vowel Shift form, /æːxt, stræːxt/). Given that words such as *late, mate*, have no such underlying /x/, we can readily write rules which give an [ɛɪ]-type output for *eight* and *straight*, but an [eː]-type output for *late* and *mate*, in those north-of-England accents which make this distinction. The majority of accents, which make no such distinction, would merely include a rule deleting /x/ at an appropriate moment. There are other accents, however, which have minimal pairs such as *mane* [meːn] vs. *main* [mɛɪn], with *late* not rhyming with *wait*. In these accents *wait* is usually (though not necessarily) homophonous with *weight* and a rhyme for *eight, straight*. To accommodate them in a panlectal grammar of English, we must recognize an underlying phonemic contrast which will surface as [e:] in the one case, and as [ɛɪ] in the other. To accommodate all the accents discussed in this paragraph, we need both the presence vs. absence of underlying /x/ and the underlying monophthong vs. diphthong opposition. Otherwise we shall not be able to distinguish appropriately between the three lexical sets represented by *straight, late*, and *wait* respectively. Yet it would be absurd to attribute the knowledge of the distinction between these three lexical sets to the large majority of speakers of English for whom all three words rhyme perfectly. A panlectal grammar is thus a linguist's construct which cannot correspond to the goal of making the grammar a model of the native speaker–hearer's competence (knowledge of his language).

The same difficulty arises in connection with the intrusive [r] of RP and similar accents. The only plausible explanation of its origin is through rule inversion (as discussed in 3.2.3 below). This implies that RP *star, Shah* are underlyingly /stɑ:, ʃɑ:/, with the linking/ intrusive [r] of the sandhi forms [stɑ:r, ʃɑ:r] inserted by rule. In rhotic accents such as GenAm, however, there is no doubt that *star* contains an underlying /r/ as well as its surface realization. Thus the underlying representations are different in the two accents: but this conclusion is incompatible with the panlectal hypothesis of a shared underlying form for all accents.

A useful discussion of this issue is offered by Luelsdorff (1975), in connection with the description of American Black English. He proposes the term the **Dependence Principle** for the typical generativist/polylectalist approach requiring that the description of a given dialect may be converted into an adequate description of a related dialect by the addition, deletion, and reordering of a relatively small number of rules. He argues that it 'has the undesirable result of making the adequate description of a dialect impossible without recourse to the data of some other variety of the language. Since generative grammars are representations of the linguistic competence of individual speaker–hearers, this principle must be rejected.' Instead, Luelsdorff offers the **Independence Principle**: 'that each dialect may be adequately described in its own terms, i.e. without reference to the data of related dialects.... These independently motivated individual descriptions may then be compared with an eye to pointing out their similarities and differences, leaving the extent and nature of dialect differences an essentially empirical question.' In this work I have adopted this latter approach: entities such as my standard lexical sets are to be seen only as a linguist's constructs, not as a part of any speaker's competence.

It does not follow that a degree of polylectalism is to be rejected. Every speaker who has grown up in a speech community where there is sharp social stratification in speech is familiar with the facts of sociolinguistic variation in that locality – though not necessarily at a conscious level. It is normal for such a speaker to be able to vary his accent 'upwards' or 'downwards', not only stylistically, in different social contexts, but also to imitate the speech of those higher up or lower down the social scale than himself. If he can do this accurately – as many speakers seem able to – then, it would seem, we must allow that his internalized knowledge of his language, i.e. his grammar, is to that extent polylectal not only receptively but also productively. It is to recognize this fact that we admit variable rules to the grammar.

1.3 How accents differ

1.3.1 Introduction

There are two possible ways to set about describing differences between accents. We can compare their different historical developments, or we can compare their different synchronic states.

Historically, we can describe the various changes which have occurred since, say, Middle English, or in general since the period when the ancestors of the accents in question first diverged. We can list for each accent the rules which have been added to (or lost from) the grammar, together with possible changes in rule order, rule inversions, and so on. We can tabulate the splits and mergers that have taken place, and analyse the restructurings which followed as rules ceased to be productive. Chapter 3 below makes some attempt in this direction.

In the alternative, synchronic, approach, we attempt to describe the existing accents as they are. We investigate the differences in phonetic detail. We examine possible differences in phonological structure (phonotactic distribution). We ask whether the phonemic systems of the various accents are isomorphic (i.e. whether there is a one-to-one relationship between the phonemes of accent A and those of accent B). We look for differences in the use of particular phonemes in particular words or morphemes.

Section 1.3 is devoted to this second approach to the problem of comparing accents. In essence, this approach was first suggested by Trubetzkoy, who wrote (1931):

Les différences phoniques existant entre deux dialectes peuvent être de trois sortes: elles peuvent concerner le système phonologique, ou bien la réalisation phonétique des divers phonèmes, ou encore la repartition étymologique des phonèmes dans les mots. D'après cela nous parlerons de différences dialectales phonologiques, phonétiques et étymologiques.
[Phonic differences between two dialects may be of three kinds: they may concern the phonological system, or the phonetic realization of the various phonemes, or the etymological distribution of the phonemes in words. Accordingly we shall speak of phonological, phonetic, and etymological differences between dialects.]

Trubetzkoy's 'phonological' differences are my **systemic** differences, discussed in 1.3.4; his phonetic differences are my **realizational** differences, discussed in 1.3.2; and his etymological differences are my **lexical-incidential** differences, discussed in 1.3.5. Trubetzkoy did not take account of **phonotactic** (structural) differences, discussed in 1.3.3.

1.3.2 Phonetic realization

The simplest kind of difference between accents is a difference in phonetic detail – in the phonetic realization of a given phoneme.

For example, the vowel in words such as *coat, nose, snow* (referred to in this work as GOAT words) shows considerable variation. As discussed in 2.2.14 below, it is monophthongal in some accents, but diphthongal in others; as a diphthong it may be narrow or wide, with a starting-point which is front, central, or back. Thus in RP it is generally [əʊ], but may also be more lip-rounded, [ɵʊ], or less so, [əω]; there are also old-fashioned back variants, [oʊ] etc., and variants with a front starting-point, [ëʊ]; some variants have very little diphthongal movement. In the south-east of England wider diphthongs are common, thus [ʌʊ] etc. In Scotland and various other places a monophthongal realization is usual, [oː] or a shorter [o].

Similarly, the vowel in words such as *out, loud, now* (the MOUTH words) shows a wide range of variation (2.2.18 below). Although usually diphthongal, it can also be monophthongal, as in the Cockney variants [æː] and [aː]. As a diphthong, it can have a starting-point ranging from back [ɒʊ] (South African) to front [ɛʊ] (provincial south of England), as well as the more widespread intermediate types [aʊ], [a+ʊ]. There are also variants with less than open central starting-points, [əʊ]. and so on.

Differences such as these can be regarded as resulting simply from differences of detail in the phonetic realization rules applying to the particular phonemes in question.

Although the most obvious realizational differences relate to vowels, there are also cases involving consonants. For example, there are accents in the north of England and in Scotland where /p, t, k/ are never aspirated, so that *pin, tin, kin* have [p⁼, t⁼, k⁼], as against the [pʰ, tʰ, kʰ] of other accents. Indeed, accents that do have aspiration of voiceless plosives may differ in just how many milliseconds of aspiration (on average) they have in a given phonetic context.

This brings us to the observation that phonetic details may vary in a context-sensitive manner; that is, one of the points of difference between two accents may be a matter of a particular positional allophone. The Canadian [əɪ] allophone of /aɪ/ discussed in 1.2.13 above is a case in point. This allophone, the consequence of the rule of PRICE Raising, occurs only in the environment of a following phonologically voiceless consonant, as in *nice, write, lifelike*. In all other environments, as *ride, tie, line, fire*, the realization of /aɪ/ in this accent is much the same as in most other North American accents.

In Irish English the consonant /l/ is generally clear in all environments. In RP, GenAm, and many other accents two perceptibly different allophones may be distinguished, clear and dark. The details of the environment in which the dark allophone is used vary, however: thus intervocalically, as in *silly*, RP uses clear /l/, thus ['sɪlɪ], while GenAm uses dark, thus ['sɪɫi]. In this word, as in others where /l/ is intervocalic (*valley, yellow, column*), RP thus sides with Irish English against GenAm; compare words such as *belt, milk, halt*, where RP and GenAm agree in having dark /l/, but Irish English uses a clear variety.

Most accents use a post-alveolar or retroflex approximant for intervocalic /r/ in words such as *very, sorry, arrow*. A certain kind of RP has free variation here between the approximant and an alveolar tap, [ɾ]; for some speakers the variation may be stylistic. In the working-class accent of Liverpool, a tap in this phonetic environment is the norm, with [ɾ] thus being a positional allophone of the phoneme otherwise realized in the accent as an approximant.

Accents clearly vary in the details of **segment duration**. Although vowel duration has been well studied, at least where it is contrastive, we know relatively little about differences in consonant duration. The duration of aspiration is not the only case where differences obviously exist: in the intervocalic /d/ of *ready*, for example, we face a range of durational possibilities extending from the very short tap of a typical American accent to the rather long plosive of a typical Welsh accent, with other accents occupying intermediate positions.

Realizational differences of this kind have no strictly linguistic function. But they play an important part in making a given regional or social accent recognizable as such.

1.3.3 Phonotactic distribution

Accents may differ in the environments in which particular phonemes do or do not occur. This may be looked at from either of two angles: as differences in the constraints on **phonotactic distribution** of given phonemes, or as differences in the phonological **structures** (syllable types, etc.) which are permitted.

The phonotactic distribution of a given phoneme is the set of phonetic contexts in which it may occur. At one level this can be trivial. It is not important, for instance, if one accent is adjudged to permit word-initial /vr/ (as in *vroom!*, *vraic*, *vrille*, where these items happen to be known and used), where another bars this initial cluster possibility.

At another level it can be of great importance. One fundamental division in English accent types depends upon a difference in phonotactic distribution of the consonant /r/. In the **rhotic** accents (3.2.2 below) /r/ can occur, with an overt phonetic realization, in a wide variety of phonetic contexts, including preconsonantal and absolute-final environments, thus *farm* [fɑrm], *far* ‖ [fɑr]. In the **non-rhotic** accents /r/ is excluded from preconsonantal and absolute-final environments, thus *farm* [fɑ:m], *far* ‖ [fɑ:]. The rhotic accents include those typical of Scotland, Ireland, Canada, Barbados, certain western parts of England, and most of the United States, including GenAm. The non-rhotic accents include those typical of Australia, New Zealand, South Africa, Trinidad, certain eastern and southern parts of the United States, and most of England and Wales, including RP.

One difficulty with this dichotomy is that it is possible to argue, for certain accents at least, that an occurrence of the phoneme /r/ is present underlyingly in the critical environments, but that it is obligatorily vocalized or deleted by rule so that it is not present phonetically. It is perhaps natural for those whose own speech is rhotic to look at non-rhotic accents as if this were the correct analysis; in this case, the definition of rhotic and non-rhotic would have to refer to the absence vs. the presence of such a rule in the accent under description. For reasons explained in 1.2.14 above I consider this view misguided, at least as far as it applies to accents such as my own.

There are also accents that can be classified as semi-rhotic, having lost preconsonantal /r/ but retaining it in certain word-final environments: thus Jamaican, with *farm* [fa:m] but *far* ‖ [fa:r]. And one could call some southern speech (both British and American) hyper-rhotic, since it not only retains all historical /r/s but also has /r/ at the end of words such as *comma, China*. (This phenomenon is distinct from the use of intrusive /r/ at the end of such words by those whose speech is non-rhotic.)

Although rhoticity is by far the most important case of a difference in phonotactic distribution, it is not the only one. From a strict phonemic point of view, it can be argued that the quality of the vowel at the end of words such as *happy* is a difference in phonotactic distribution, since it is a question of the range of environments in which the phonemes /i:/ (FLEECE) and /ɪ/ (KIT) respectively occur (or indeed whatever other vowel phoneme the final segment in *happy* is analysed as belonging to.)

1.3.4 Phonemic systems

Accents may differ in their phonemic systems, i.e. in the number or identity of the phonemes they use.

For instance, most accents of English have two distinct vowel phonemes in the close back area, a short /ʊ/ as in *foot* and a long /uː/ (which it may be convenient on other grounds to write in some cases without length marks, thus /u/) as in *boot*. This also means that *good* /gʊd/ is not a rhyme for *mood* /muːd/. But in Scottish English there is only a single phoneme, /u/, which corresponds to these two phonemes of other accents. Thus in a Scottish accent *foot* /fut/ is a perfect rhyme for *boot* /but/, and *good* /gud/ for *mood* /mud/. Scottish English therefore has one fewer phoneme at this point in its vowel system than other accents: it differs from them **systemically**. English people and Americans may discuss whether they prefer to use the pronunciation /rʊm/ or /ruːm/ for *room*; but the question is meaningless to a Scot, who has no such choice.

All accents of England make a difference between pairs such as *stock* and *stalk*, RP /stɒk/ vs. /stɔːk/. So do many accents elsewhere, including traditional GenAm. In some Scottish and Irish speech, though, as well as in Canada and in certain parts of the United States, *stock* and *stalk*, like *don* and *dawn* or *cot* and *caught*, are homophonous because the vowel system of these accents contains only a single phoneme in the open back area, as against the two of accents which distinguish *stock* from *stalk*.

An example of a possible systemic difference among the consonants arises in Scottish, Welsh and Irish English, with the possibility of there being a voiceless velar/uvular fricative /x/ in the consonant system of these accents – a phoneme missing from the consonant systems of RP and of most other accents. The opposition is illustrated by the minimal pair *loch* vs. *lock*.

In 2.3 below we show that it is convenient for some purposes to divide the vowel system up into part-systems. One part-system, part-system A (the 'short' vowels) has six members in some accents of English, as illustrated in the non-rhyming items *pit, pet, pat, pot, cut,* and *put*. But a broad local accent of the north of England has only five members of the part-system, since *cut* and *put* have the same vowel and thus rhyme. Similarly, the words *rush* and *push* rhyme in north-of-England five-short-vowel accents, but not where there are six contrasting short vowels.

In part-system B (long front-tending vowels or diphthongs) GenAm and RP have only one mid-height phoneme, that of *face* and similar words. But in some local accents of England and Wales there are two contrasting phonemes corresponding to the one of the standard accents: these accents distinguish a long monophthong /eː/ from a diphthong /ɛɪ/ so as to keep *Dane* distinct from *deign* and to cause *late* not to rhyme with *eight*. This means that they have one more contrasting item in part-system B than the standard accents.

It often happens that a given phonemic opposition is neutralized in certain phonetic environments. For example, the opposition of /p/ vs. /b/ is neutralized in the environment #s— (1.2.7 above). The set of contrastive units operating in a position of neutralization may be referred to as a **subsystem**. For example, in Belfast speech the opposition between short /ɔ/ and long /ɔː/ may be illustrated by heterophonous pairs such as *cot* vs. *caught*, *stock* vs. *stalk*. But before voiced consonants the opposition is neutralized, so that for example *don* = *dawn* [dɔːn], while *cod* and *fraud* rhyme. This accent thus differs subsystemically from RP, where the corresponding opposition (/ɒ/ vs. /ɔː/) operates before voiced consonants just as much as before unvoiced.

The American southern neutralization of /ɪ/ vs. /ɛ/ before nasals (*pin* = *pen*, although *bit* ≠ *bet*) is a subsystemic difference vis-à-vis accents that have no such neutralization.

The classification of accents presented in 2.3 below is based upon systemic differences, being a typology of vowel systems.

1.3.5 Lexical distribution

Accents (and indeed individual speakers) often vary in the phonemes they select for the lexical representation of particular words or morphemes: that is, they differ in the incidence of phonemes in a given lexical item or items. Thus every speaker has at his disposal both an /iː/ (as in *beet*) and an /aɪ/ (as in *bite*). In the word *either* some speakers use their /iː/, so that it rhymes with *breather*, but others use their /aɪ/, so that it rhymes with *lither*. (Others again may use some other vowel, so that *either* rhymes neither with *breather* nor with *lither*. And speakers may fluctuate between the two pronunciations in a stylistically-determined way, or at random.)

As far as *either* is concerned, the question is trivial; at most it will apply equally to the item *neither*. But by observing a given speaker's vowel in these two words we can make no predictions about his pronunciation of any other words, say *price* or *fleece* or *hippopotamus*. It is an atomistic question about a particular lexical item or pair of items. Similarly with *tomato* (stressed vowel like that of *father* or *fat* or *fate*).

Facts of this kind about accents have also been termed 'selectional' (O'Connor 1973: 182). They have also, vaguely, been termed 'distributional'; but this term, if unqualified, is open to confusion with differences in phonotactic distribution such as were discussed in 1.3.3 above. I have called them 'incidental' (Wells 1970), but will now prefer the names **lexical-incidental** or **lexical-distributional**.

Lexical-distributional differences are important where a substantial body of words behave in a parallel fashion. One such body comprises the items listed in 2.2.7 below as the standard lexical set BATH. Most accents have contrasting vowel phonemes of the /æ/ and /ɑː/ type, as in *trap* and *palm* (or *father*) respectively. Given these two vowels, though, some accents use /æ/ in *bath, staff, grass, basket,* while others use /ɑː/. The choice between these two vowels in this lexical set is of indexical importance in distinguishing high vs. popular accents in the north of England, in distinguishing northern from southern accents in England as a whole, and in distinguishing between the two standard accents RP and GenAm.

The issue of lexical distribution of particular phonemes in particular words is distinct from the realizational issue concerning, for example, the phonetic quality associated with /æ/. Thus a front open [aˑ] quality in BATH words might arise either because the TRAP vowel in the accent in question is rather open in realization, or because the PALM vowel is rather front. In the first case BATH words would belong with TRAP (a 'flat-BATH' accent, 2.2.7 below), in the second with PALM ('broad-BATH').

A typical north-of-England accent and RP both contain the contrasting phonemes /ʊ/ and /uː/, as in *put* and *boot* respectively. The lexical distribution of these phonemes in the two accents corresponds on the whole. But there are a few words in which the northern accent has /uː/ in spite of RP /ʊ/, thus *hook, cook, look*. The same lexical-distributional characteristic applies also to typical Irish accents (though not in the north of Ireland, where there is no such phonemic opposition).

Most popular controversies about 'right' and 'wrong' pronunciation concern issues of lexical distribution. They take realization, phonotactics, and phoneme system for granted. Should *accomplish* have the vowel of STRUT or the vowel of LOT? Does *Nazi* rhyme with *Benghazi*, or should it have /-ts-/? Should *controversy* be stressed on the first syllable or on the second? But not 'how much nasalization should there be in the stressed vowel of *accomplish*?' or 'does an intramorphemic /ts/ cluster in *Nazi* (or *pizza*, or *curtsey*) violate English phonotactic principles?' or 'is the first syllable of *contemplate* identical with, or distinct from, the name *Kahn*?'. It is clear that issues of lexical distribution are psychologically very much more real than other kinds of difference between accents.

1.3.6 Further considerations

Differences in lexical incidence correspond to differences in the phonological shape of the representations stored in the speaker's mental lexicon. Differences in phonotactic distribution and phonemic system in principle reflect varying conditions imposed on the phonological representations as a whole in the mental lexicon. Differences in phonetic realization reflect differences in the rules which operate on stored forms to produce a phonetic output.

This four-way classification of accent differences is one springing naturally out of a taxonomic-phonemic approach to phonology, and is subject to the possible shortcomings of this approach. Wherever phonemicization is in doubt (i.e. wherever there is some argument about the nature of the stored forms), this classification is correspondingly uncertain.

Consider, for example, an accent such as Cockney where – to simplify somewhat – a vocoid [ʊ] is used in all environments where RP has a lateral non-vocoid [ɫ], thus *milk* [mɪʊk] (RP [mɪɫk]), *shelf* [ʃɛʊf] (RP [ʃɛɫf]), *middle* ['mɪdʊ] (RP ['mɪdɫ]). Is this essentially a difference just in the realization of /l/ in non-prevocalic position (so that [mɪʊk] is still phonemicized as /mɪlk/, etc.)? Or are we to say that Cockney has a special restriction on the phonotactic distribution of /l/ (excluding it from non-prevocalic position), together with a wider phonotactic distribution of /w/ (if we take Cockney *milk* as /mɪwk/)? Or does the Cockney vowel system contain a whole set of additional diphthongs not included in the RP system – /ɪʊ, ɛʊ/ etc.? Our answer must depend on the phonological analysis we make of the Cockney [ʊ] which results from L Vocalization.

Some Americans pronounce *can't* as [kæ̃t] (compare *cat* [kæt]). If we treat this minimal pair as evidence for the presence of a phoneme /æ̃/ in the vowel system, contrasting with non-nasalized /æ/, (as advocated for example by Pilch 1976: 132), then we shall have to say that this accent differs systemically from accents which preserve the historical /n/ in *can't* as [n]. If on the other hand we reject this analysis, preferring to regard [æ̃] as the realization of an underlying phoneme sequence /æn/, then the difference is merely one of realization.

Those who believe that RP *start* [stɑːt] and *north* [nɔːθ] contain underlying /r/, and consider that their underlying representations are of the type /stɑrt, nɔrθ/, would see the RP–GenAm difference at this point as being simply one of realization (compare GenAm [stɑrt, nɔrθ]). Those who agree with me in rejecting this analysis, and posit instead RP underlying /stɑːt, nɔːθ/, will see the difference as one of phonotactic distribution (and therefore as a difference in underlying representation, since the phonotactic constraints are constraints upon lexical representation).

1.3.7 Consequences: rhymes, puns, and intelligibility

Differences between accents, other than those differences which are merely realizational, typically result in words which rhyme in one accent not rhyming in another; in puns which work in one accent not working in another; and in utterances spoken with one accent being potentially misunderstood by a hearer who uses another.

Words of one syllable are said to rhyme when they are phonologically identical from the vowel onwards, as *face–place, rope–soap, saw–flaw*. In polysyllabic words, or sequences of words, there must be phonological identity from the vowel of the stressed syllable up to the end, as *happy–snappy, better–letter, edited–credited, stop it–drop it*. As with the majority of rhymes, these work equally in all accents. The English cultural tradition, unlike the French, requires also that the consonants preceding the stressed vowel differ, so that we hesitate to accept as rhymes pairs such as *apply–reply*, or homophones such as *sight–site*.

The phonological identity on which rhyme depends does not necessarily imply phonetic identity. The pair *lose–fuse* is a good rhyme even in the kind of RP which has a clear allophonic difference between the [uː] of *lose* and the advanced [ʉː] of *fuse* (where this allophone is conditioned by the preceding /j/): phonologically, as /luːz/ and /fjuːz/, they rhyme.

As a literary device, rhyme follows certain special conventions. Our traditions allow a moderate use of **eye-rhymes** (such as *word–sword*, *love–move–grove*, which 'rhyme' only from an orthographic point of view), while conceding only grudging acceptance of certain phonetically perfect **ear-rhymes** (such as those involving words of differing morphological constitution, e.g. *packed–fact*, *stand it–bandit*). And of course diachronic changes may mean that words which were perfect ear-rhymes for the poet who used them now rhyme no longer:

> Blow, blow, thou winter wind,
> Thou art not so unkind ...   (Shakespeare, *As You Like It*)

> I am monarch of all I survey ...
> From the centre right round to the sea ...
> (Cowper, *Verses Supposed to be Written
> by Alexander Selkirk*)

Since Shakespeare wrote, *wind* has lost its variant with the PRICE vowel and become established as /wɪnd/ only; in the two hundred years since Cowper, *sea* has settled down (in most accents) with the vowel of FLEECE, not that of FACE.

The conservatism of literary traditions tends to restrict ear-rhymes in serious verse to those which work in all accents. Hence the reluctance in England to exploit what are in RP perfect ear-rhymes, such as *corn–dawn, finer–China, scarf–laugh*. Comic verse, on the other hand, readily accepts such rhymes, but has to sacrifice the effect of perfect rhyme for part of its potential audience.

> Sure, deck your lower limbs in pants:
> Yours are the legs, my sweeting.
> You look divine as you advance;
> Have you seen yourself retreating?

– writes Ogden Nash, but the effect is spoilt if one pronounces /ədˈvɑːns/ in RP instead of the usual American /ədˈvænts/.

> Why is the milk from a red cow white
> If it always eats green grass?
> It seems so odd, it can't be right,
> It really seems a farce ...

– sings a comedian in a London pantomime, but the rhyme only works for those who say /grɑːs/ (not /græs/) and /fɑːs/ (not /fɑrs/). The *Wizard of Oz* song that rhymes *dinosaurus* with *forest* and then *la-di-das* with *Oz* is satisfactory in GenAm (/-sɔrəs, fɔrəs(t)/; /-dɑz, ɑz/), but falls very flat if one attempts to sing it with a British accent (/-sɔːrəs, fɒrɪs(t)/; /-dɑːz, ɒz/).

There are plenty of puns which work satisfactorily in all accents: 'I asked him if he'd trussed the turkey; he said, "Yes, with my life."' But there are many others which do not. 'Why is a cosh-boy like a journalist?' 'Because they're both ['ɛdɪtəz] (head-hitters/ editors)' – this sort of pun will delight London schoolchildren, with their H-dropping accent, but will be incomprehensible to those of Glasgow, Dublin, or Ottawa. Nor does the name *Nicholas* offer the same punning potential (*knickerless*) in a rhotic accent as it does in a non-rhotic. A London comedian can speak of Reg Varney and his brother Manto (sc. Mantovani), but not a Belfast comedian. An RP wit, but not an Irish one, can allude to chefs who, like journalists, refuse to reveal their /sɔːsɪz/.

When American feminists objected not only to the giving of women's names to tropical storms but also to their being called hurricanes /ˈhɜrəkeɪnz/, the second point was lost on the British, for whom *hurricane* /ˈhʌrɪkən/ does not contain the same vowel as *her* /hɜː/. And even Dorothy Parker's famous sentence illustrating the use of the word *horticulture* ('You can lead a horticulture, but you cannot make her think') fails for those who use /ɪ/ in the second syllable of *horticulture* but /ə/ in the preconsonantal weak form of *to*.

There are several other potential puns which risk foundering on /ɪ/ vs. /ə/ as weak vowels. They include the honeymoon salad made of *lettuce alone*. Although the cinema (the *pictures*) becomes the *fleas and itches* in Australian rhyming slang, it could not do so in London, where /ˈpɪtʃəz/ and /ˈɪtʃɪz/ do not rhyme.

The richest source of misunderstandings between speakers with different accents is probably **realizational overlap**, the situation where the realization of phoneme /A/ in one accent is phonetically identical (or at least perceptually identical) with the realization of phoneme /B/ in another accent. There was the genuine case (known to me) of the Canadian who explained that his child was *autistic*, expecting commiseration, but instead receiving congratulations –

on its being *artistic*. Although these two words are clearly distinguished within either accent, it so happens that the Canadian
realization of the first overlaps with the RP (etc.) realization of the
second, as [ɑ'tɪstɪk]. Another misunderstanding of which I have
personal knowledge happened to an American southerner who
asked for an *egg* in a British Railways buffet car. He received a
whisky (a Haig, an 'Aig, [ən 'ɛɪg]). But I fear that the Londoner
is apocryphal who, invited back for coffee by a visiting American,
upset him by accepting the invitation ['ʌp jɔːr 'æəs], sc. *up (at) your
house*.

A combination of realizational overlap and lexical-distributional
difference is responsible for the well-known RP (etc.) vs. American
difficulty over *impassable* and *impossible*, [ɪm'pɑːsəbl̩]. (This may
even cause confusion between Maine and Illinois.) It is perceived
realizational overlap alone which is responsible for the joke which is
heard in assorted versions in assorted places:

> Q. Define the meaning of the word *sex*.
> A. It's what ɑ people have coal delivered in.

In the north of England, the variable ɑ takes the value 'posh' (RP
/sæks/ perceived as identical with northern local /sɛks/); in the
south of England and among RP speakers it takes the value 'Australian' or 'South African'.

Some confusions are due not so much to realizational overlap as
to inaccurate perceptions of contrasts made in both relevant
accents. Thus an Ulsterman who accuses Londoners of not distinguishing between *life-belts* and *life-boats* is just wrong, even though
the phonetic distance between London [bɛʊʔs] and [bʌʊʔs] is not as
great as between Ulster [bɛlts] and [bots].

It often happens that accent A keeps messages *x* and *y* phonetically distinct, while accent B does not. In such cases speakers of
accent A might reasonably accuse speakers of accent B of failing to
speak clearly; but to speakers of accent B the accusation seems
unjustified. *He's a little* [hɔːs], says the Englishman, and the Scotsman rightly charges him with failing to make clear whether he's a
little *horse* or a little *hoarse*. To the Englishman this is just a good
pun which just cannot be disambiguated without lexical changes.
Both Scots and Englishmen find it ridiculous for a midwestern
American to be unable to make clear in pronunciation the difference

between *fairies* and *ferries*; the Scot and the American, but not the average Englishman, can distinguish phonetically between *to carve* and *to calve*; while only the Scot could fail to signal phonetically the distinction between *pooling* and *pulling*. Nor is this sort of observation restricted to words in isolation: the Englishman will not make clear, in ordinary conversational style, whether *the moat had been sprayed with oil* or *the motor'd been sprayed with oil* (I quote an instance of confusion which I once witnessed – phonetically both can be [ðə 'məʊtəd ...]), while for the Scot or the midwesterner it would be quite exceptional **not** to make the difference very clear.

To a large extent one can predict homophones, and the potential confusions they may cause, by considering the phonemic contrasts and phonotactic constraints which apply in a given variety of English. Take the pair *splendid–splendoured/splendored* (as in *Love is a many-splendor'd thing*). Who would be likely to make the spelling mistake 'Love is a many-*splendid* thing'? Not the speaker of a rhotic accent, who pronounces /r/ in *splendo(u)red* but not in *splendid*. Not the speaker of an accent which has resisted the Weak Vowel Merger (2.2.25 below), who has /ɪ/ in *splendid* as against /ə/ (with or without following /r/) in *splendo(u)red*. Only the speaker of an accent such as Australian, which is non-rhotic and has undergone the Weak Vowel Merger, so that both words are pronounced identically as ['splendəd]. The contrast in pronunciation will be greatest in an accent which is rhotic and has unmerged weak vowels, e.g. Barbadian, with ['splɛndɪd] vs. ['splɛndɚd]. Compare Irish (rhotic, merged weak vowels) ['splɛndəd] vs. ['splɛndɚd]; and RP (non-rhotic, unmerged weak vowels) ['splendɪd] vs. ['splendəd].

Similar considerations apply to pairs such as *chatted–chattered*, *tended–tendered*, *offices–officers*, *arches–archers*, except that there are increasingly many people in England, for instance, who have these pairs as homophones not because they lack the weak /ɪ/ vs. /ə/ opposition but because for them the lexical-distributional shape of the suffixes *-ed* and *-es* (in their allomorphs containing a vowel) is /əd, əz/ rather than the traditional and RP /ɪd, ɪz/. These speakers, like Australians, will also be liable to make spelling mistakes of the type 'Justice was *metered* out', 'The church is *foundered* upon a rock' – authentic examples which must arise from the metanalysis of ['miːtəd] and ['faʊndəd] as /miːtə # d/, /faʊndə # d/, instead of /miːt # əd/, /faʊnd # əd/.

1.3.8 Rhythmical characteristics

This account of differences between accents has so far ignored the 'prosodic' or 'suprasegmental' features of speech – matters such as rhythm, stressing, intonation, and voice quality. Regrettably, we are far from being able to give a coherent account of how these vary from accent to accent, even though it is clear that they too have an important indexical rôle helping the hearer to recognize particular accents and, indeed, individual speakers.

It is not clear whether the **syllable**, as a phonological entity, is equally important in all varieties of English. In most accents – though not all – one observes a difference in syllabication between *selfish* and *shellfish* or *waifish* ('She looked kind of lost, she had a waifish appearance') and *crayfish*. This difference can be attributed to the differing place of the syllable boundary. This boundary, which we may symbolize $, tends to correspond with any major morpheme boundary (#) there may be, so that we have on the one hand *self # ish* ['sɛlf$ɪʃ], *waif # ish* ['weɪf$ɪʃ], and on the other hand *shell # fish* ['ʃɛl$fɪʃ], *cray # fish* ['kreɪ$fɪʃ]. Typical realizational consequences relate to (i) the duration of the sonorant segments of the first syllable, with [ɛl] and [eɪ] shorter in *selfish*, *waifish* than in *shellfish*, *crayfish*, and/or to (ii) the quality of the [f], which is stronger when syllable-initial, in [-$fɪʃ], than when syllable-final, in [-f$ɪʃ]. The same kind of considerations apply to *peace-talks* vs. *pea-stalks*, etc., discussed above (1.2.6). In morphologically simple words the general rule in English seems to be that any doubtful consonants belong with a stressed rather than an unstressed syllable: thus *dolphin* and *hyphen* are *dolph$in*, *hyph$en*, like *selfish* and *waifish* and unlike *shellfish* and *crayfish*. *Bicker* is, except for the initial /p/ vs. /b/, identical in pronunciation with *picker*, even though *bicker* is morphologically indivisible while *picker* (one who picks) is *pick # er*; so we may assume that both are phonetically syllabicated [-ɪk$-]. (A speaker does also have the option of indicating the # explicitly by slowing down at the boundary, lengthening the [k] and altering the rhythm; but this is done only for special extra clarity in *picker*.)

Yet there are in the north of England certain accents in which the *selfish–shellfish*, *waifish–crayfish* differences either do not exist phonetically at all, or are at least very much smaller than in other accents. These are the accents which seem to be characterized by a typical 𝆏 𝆏 rhythm in disyllables such as *hoping, party, icing, selfish* – words which in other accents have 𝆏˙ 𝆏˙ or 𝆏 𝆏, the 𝆏 𝆏 type being reserved for compounds (*shellfish*) or word sequences. In an interesting and original article, Abercrombie (1964) has drawn attention to rhythmic differences of this kind. He suggests that in words of the *hoping* class lowland Scottish applies the 𝆏 𝆏 rhythm, various other accents (including RP) 𝆏 𝆏, and a Yorkshire accent 𝆏 𝆏. This analysis agrees well with the facts; but it is suggestive rather than exhaustive as a treatment of the complications of English speech rhythm.

Accents also vary in **pace**: that is, in the general rate of speech, measurable as the mean number of syllables uttered per second. There exists a general tendency for urban speech to be faster than rural speech, as can be seen by comparing the accent of London with that of Wiltshire, that of New York City with that of Texas, or that of Melbourne with that of rural Australia. It must be confessed, however, that to state the existence of this tendency is to make an impressionistic claim rather than to report a substantiated fact. In any case, it is only a general tendency. Particular urban or rural areas do not necessarily conform to it. Particular speakers from a given geographical background to not necessarily conform, except in a general statistical way, to the norm for their locality. And any individual varies his pace of utterance in accordance with situational factors or personal whim (Ramsaran 1978).

Rhythmic qualities in speech derive from the interaction of many factors. In addition to characteristics of pace, segment duration, and syllabication, a further factor, perhaps the most important of all, is **stressing**. Stress can be seen phonetically as the consequence of additional respiratory and articulatory muscular effort on certain syllables, with an auditory correlate of increased loudness. In practice, though, it is through the effects of stress on intonation that a syllable is usually most readily recognized as being stressed. Thus for instance in comparing front-stressed *insight* with end-stressed *incite* we detect the stressedness of the stressed syllable not so much by loudness as by the location of the pitch change as we say (in RP or GenAm) –

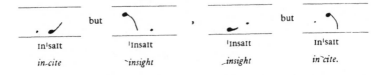

While the details vary, the principle involved appears to apply to all native accents of English (though for speakers of English as a second or foreign language, and in particular Africans and South Asians, stress and intonation constitute an area where native-speaker-like patterns are only rarely achieved).

Stress can also be seen as a lexical category, in that almost every word in the mental lexicon has one or more of its syllables marked as [+ stress]. (The exceptions are **clitics**: the common minor-category words such as articles, pronouns, conjunctions, which are basically unstressed, although they may receive stress for emphasis in a sentence or when cited.)

One of the controversial claims made by Chomsky & Halle (1968) is that lexical stress in English is predictable by rule. The rules are, however, exceedingly complex, and there are many exceptions that can be catered for only in an ad-hoc way by juggling various types of alleged boundary.

A lexical stress will surface as a phonetic stress unless some rule intervenes to suppress or shift it. But it will receive additional audibility through pitch prominence (as discussed above) only if the intonation pattern of the utterance allows it.

There are obviously many instances of particular words or categories of words having different lexical stress patterns in different accents. Even within the same geographical and social framework, this is the sort of question that laymen argue about: do we say *'exquisite* or *ex'quisite*, *'controversy* or *con'troversy* (UK), *'inquiry* or *in'quiry* (US)? These are differences of lexical distribution, like those concerning the pattern of phonemes in lexical representations (1.3.5 above). As is well known, the location of stress has implications for vowel quality: *controversy* with stress on the first syllable is (in RP) ['kɒntrəvəsɪ] or (with strong third syllable) ['kɒntrəvɜːsɪ], but with stress on the second syllable it is [kən'trɒvəsɪ].

1.3.9 Intonation

All native forms of English make the distinction between **accented** syllables and others: accented syllables are not only stressed but also pitch-prominent. (In the metalanguage of those for whom stress is a multi-valued feature, this distinction is described as a difference of stress level.) Words in an utterance which are in some pragmatic sense important (new, not repetitious) are highlighted by having an accent placed upon them, while those that are pragmatically unimportant (given, repetitious) receive nothing more than stress. Within an intonation group, the last such accented syllable carries particular pitch prominence; it is termed the nucleus (synonyms: 'tonic', 'intonation center'). It is on the vowel of the nuclear syllable that the characteristic tone movement of the intonation group begins (rise, fall, fall-rise etc.).

Although there may occasionally be difficulties in finding clear criteria for identifying the location of nuclei in practice, it appears that the concept of intonation nucleus is valid for all varieties of native English (though certainly not for all languages). It is the location of the nucleus that gives the well-known distinctions of the type illustrated in (32).

(32a)   It was an ex'tremely 'good 'plan
(32b)   It was an ex'tremely 'good ˌplan
(32c)   It was an ex'tremely ˌgood ˌplan

Version (32a) has the last accent on *plan*, which is of course also stressed; -*treme-* and *good* will normally be stressed and may also be accented. In (32b) the last accent is on *good*; *plan* will normally be stressed but not intonationally prominent. In (32c) the last, and only, accent is on -*treme-*; *plan* will, and *good* may, be stressed but not accented.

The semantic focus signalled by (32a) is unmarked. Version (32b) would usually occur in response to a question such as 'What sort of a plan did they put forward?', so that *plan* is repetitious. Version (32c) would occur in response to a question such as 'Was their plan a good one, do you think?', making both *plan* and *good* repetitious.

Although these general principles may apply to all kinds of English, there are extensive differences of detail, largely still uninvestigated. West Indians, for instance, sometimes use nucleus placements such as (33a), where other speakers would use (33b).

(33a)   She 'thinks I will 'marry her, | but I 'don't 'want to 'marry her.
(33b)   She 'thinks I will 'marry her, | but I 'don't 'want to ,marry her.

The repertoire of possible nuclear tones, and the phonetic shape they take, clearly varies very greatly from one accent to another; again, this is something still largely unexplored by dialectologists and phoneticians. (The former have largely ignored the question; the latter have mostly restricted their descriptions to the standard accents as taught to foreign learners.) The question is both a phonological and a phonetic one. On the one hand, we need to know what is the number of terms in the system (how many distinct nuclear tones are there?). On the other hand, we must ask what are the realizational details (allotones) of each distinctive tone in all its various possible phonetic environments. There is also the very important problem of the meaning of particular tones: does the fall-rise of accent A mean the same thing as the fall-rise of accent B? It is this problem that the outside investigator finds most difficult to approach satisfactorily.

Suppose that an American and an Ulsterman are in conversation together. The American might ask, ,What's a ,ruff? The Ulsterman might answer, A, sort of ,bird. Both might use a low-level prenuclear pattern, with a rise on the nucleus: ⸱ ⸱ ✓ . This pattern seems to be typical of tentative questions in American English, but of statements in Ulster English. Hence to the American the Ulsterman sounds as if he is not so much answering as asking a further question, A sort of bird?. But that would be to perceive the intonation patterns of one accent through the filter of the intonation patterns of another accent.

Even if both accents make a phonological distinction between rise and fall tones (as they do), there are two possible lines of explanation here. One is that this is a case of realizational overlap. The Ulster fall (exemplified here), we could say, has a perceptually very prominent onglide, with little if any actual falling pitch in this particular phonetic context (nucleus on final syllable of group). Hence there is a realizational overlap between an American rise and an Ulster fall. The other is that the meaning of rise and fall tones differs in the two accents (just as *cot* means one kind of bed in the

90

United States, another kind of bed in the United Kingdom). Under this assumption the Ulster response statement is indeed systemically a rise. But we should say that one of the meanings of a rise in Ulster English is 'neutral statement', a meaning which is conveyed by a fall in American English. In their interesting study of Belfast intonation, Jarman & Cruttenden (1976) opt essentially for this second line of explanation.

Certain British urban accents seem to have a similar (but different) tendency to use rising tones in circumstances where most other kinds of English have falling tones: among them are those of Birmingham, Liverpool, Newcastle-upon-Tyne, and Glasgow, each with its own differences of detail. In his analysis of Liverpool intonation, Knowles (1978) partly follows the first of our two lines of explanation, arguing that the RP low rise and the Liverpool skipping high-low tone can both be derived from an underlying fall-rise (in many accents of England actually surfacing as a phonetic fall-rise): all are used in the same type of yes–no question.

But our ignorance in this area is still very great. In this work, regrettably, I can do no more than make odd remarks about such intonation pattern characteristics of particular accents as have come to my notice.

1.3.10 Voice quality

Voice quality, in the widest sense of the term, is a further area, indexically important, where our ignorance of the facts is considerable. Yet it seems that very many regional and social accents have an associated typical voice quality. One can reasonably describe a speaker as having a typical 'Norwich voice' (or 'Glasgow voice', or 'RP voice', or 'Canadian voice'). Speakers whose actual phonetic segments are virtually identical can nevertheless sound quite different. Even where there are slight segmental differences, they can often be attributed to some overall difference in articulation. In each case it is a question of **setting** (Honikman 1964).

In Laver's model of voice quality (Laver 1968, building on Abercrombie 1967: ch. 6; see now also Laver 1980), the two main components are setting and 'the anatomical and physiological foundation of a speaker's vocal equipment'. The latter is genetically and individually determined, and can therefore be excluded from consideration when we are discussing regional and social accents (except insofar as their speakers may constitute a genetically distinct population; and anatomy and physiology are of course the basis of our ability to identify individual speakers as being young or old, male or female). Settings, for Laver, are 'long-term muscular adjustments . . . of the speaker's larynx and supralaryngeal vocal tract'. They may have been acquired by social imitation, or idiosyncratically by individuals; but they quickly become unconscious and quasi-permanent. They fall into two types: those relating to the larynx, and those relating to the supralaryngeal vocal tract.

Larynx settings can be divided into three groups: phonation types, pitch ranges, and loudness ranges. Among phonation types (Catford 1964), as well as the obvious 'voiced' and 'voiceless' states of the glottis, important possibilities include 'creak' (which can be combined with voice as 'creaky voice') and 'murmur' (also termed 'breathy voice'). Obviously no variety of English uses either creaky voice or murmur to the exclusion of ordinary voice; but some accents do seem to tend to use particular special phonation types as frequent options, or in particular phonetic contexts (including their use as part of particular intonation patterns). Thus Norwich working-class speech has been described by Trudgill (1974a: 186) as having a tendency to use creaky voice, while Norwich middle-class speech shows no corresponding tendency; on the other hand it has often been pointed out that RP-speaking men tend to go into creak towards the end of an utterance spoken with a low fall nuclear tone.

Characteristic settings for pitch and loudness include the high and wide pitch range associated with American Black speech, the low pitch range of a Texan drawl, and the soft loudness range of a Scottish Highlands accent.

Settings of the supralaryngeal vocal tract can be divided into four groups: longitudinal, latitudinal, those relating to tension, and those relating to nasalization. Longitudinal modifications involve the raising or lowering of the larynx from a neutral position. Latitudinal modifications involve a constriction or expansion of the vocal tract at some particular point, and include various types of pharyngalization and labialization, as well as settings corresponding to segmental secondary articulations (velarization, palatalization, alveolarization). Tension modifications involve the degree of overall muscular tension and its effect on the acoustic characteristics of the vocal tract: little is known about them. Nasalization and denasalization involve the operation of the soft palate (the velopharyngeal sphincter) and the consequent prevalence or scarcity of nasal resonance.

Within this framework one might, for instance, describe a typical Texan or Canadian male voice quality as 'lowered larynx voice', and that of working-class Norwich as 'raised larynx voice'. The characteristic voice quality of working-class Liverpool speech (Scouse) is velarized, involving a shift of the tongue's centre of gravity backwards and upwards (Knowles 1974, 1978). Similar qualities are found in the English West Midlands and sometimes in New York. In north Wales a pharyngalized voice quality is frequently encountered. The accent of lowland Scottish speakers typically involves tense voice, whereas that of American southerners involves just the opposite. Many accents are regarded as characterized by nasalization, including many of those of the United States, Australia, and England.

The last-mentioned term, nasalization, is one which is often used in a rather vague and inaccurate manner. Partly this is because it is popularly applied as a term of disparagement even to voice qualities that do not in fact involve nasalization. Partly it is because the auditory effect of nasalization can result from modifications which do not involve the soft palate (e.g. the electronic removal of voiceless fricatives from a recording of normal speech: Abberton 1973).

As Laver points out, voice quality can also act as an index to membership of occupational groups. Actors, clergymen, drill sergeants, are all popularly believed (rightly or wrongly) to have particular characteristic voice qualities.

1.4 Why accents differ

1.4.1 Why innovations arise

The fundamental reason why accents differ is that languages change. English pronunciation changes as time passes; and the developments which have arisen and become established in different places and among different social groups have not been identical. Present-day pronunciation patterns reflect the changes which have taken place, modifying earlier pronunciation patterns. In order to attempt an explanation of why different accents and different we must therefore explore why innovations in pronunciation tend to arise and what makes them spread.

Why do innovations arise? One popular view is that all change is decay and corruption, and that new pronunciation patterns are a result of human laziness and slovenliness. Although this view is absurd as a full explanation of sound change, it does include an element of truth. The **principle of least effort** leads us to tend to pronounce words and sentences in a way which involves the minimum of articulatory effort consistent with the need to maintain intelligibility. If a simple articulatory gesture works just as well as a complex one, there is a natural tendency to prefer it, thus rendering the articulatory movements in speech simpler. For example, a voiceless [t] between vowels, as in *better* or *atom*, involves not only a tongue-tip movement up to the alveolar ridge and away again, but also a switching off and on again of the vibration of the vocal cords. It is simpler, and requires fewer motor commands to the organs of speech, if the vibration of the vocal cords is continued throughout the alveolar articulation. The outcome is a 'voiced *t*', as in the typical American pronunciation of these words (3.3.4 below). Another way of simplifying [t] is to abandon the alveolar component, concentrating all the articulatory modifications (switch-off of voicing, plosive occlusion) at the glottis. The outcome in this case is a glottal plosive, [ʔ], as in the typical Cockney (and wider British) pronunciation ['beʔə, 'æʔəm]. Or the alveolar articulation may not be abandoned, but merely carried out in a half-hearted way, so that no complete occlusion is effected: the outcome here is the alveolar slit fricative of Irish English (vol. 2, 5.3.8). The principle of least effort provides a post hoc explanation of each of these rival developments, but offers no guide as to why one rather than another should develop. Nor does it explain why intervocalic /t/ should undergo these developments while intervocalic /p/ or /k/ or /f/ or /ʃ/ do not.

Maximal simplification of an articulatory gesture is achieved if we abolish it entirely; the maximal simplification of a segment is its deletion. Hence we can reasonably attribute the loss of historical /r/ in specified environments in the non-rhotic accents to the principle

of least effort: to pronounce *start* as ['stɑt] is simpler than to pronounce it as ['stɑrt]. (But it would be easier still to pronounce it as
['stɑ] or as ['sɑ].)

Some segment types are more **natural** than others: they are
learnt earlier by children, they are found more widely in the languages of the world, and pronunciation changes tend to work
towards them. Naturalness is not quite the same thing as articulatory simplicity. For example, it is evident that the natural lip position for vowels is unrounded for open and front vowels (as [a, e, i])
but rounded for non-open back vowels (as [o, u]). Other vowel
types occur (e.g. [ø, y, ɤ, ɯ]), but less commonly. Now when
English velarized [ɫ] is simplified by the loss of its alveolar lateral
component (L Vocalization, 3.4.4 below), the articulatory residue is
a back close vocoid resulting from the raising of the back of the
tongue which was responsible for the 'darkness' of dark /l/. This is a
vowel or semi-vowel of the [ɤ] type: closish, back, but unrounded.
In many areas where L Vocalization has occurred, e.g. in popular
London speech, the resultant vocoid is in fact usually rounded, and
thus similar to [o] or [ʊ], thus *middle* ['mɪdo] etc. Although this
roundedness necessitates an additional articulatory movement,
namely lip rounding, it does result in a segment type which is more
natural than it would have been otherwise.

Many of the articulatory movements in speech involve great
precision of timing. In a word such as *mince* ['mɪns], for example,
three adjustments of the organs of speech are required in order to
effect the transition from [n] to [s]: the tongue tip has to come away
from the alveolar ridge, converting the complete occlusion into a
fricative-type narrowing, the soft palate has to rise, converting the
nasal into an oral articulation, and the vocal cords have to stop
vibrating. Unless all three changes happen simultaneously, a tran-
sitional segment will result. For example, if the soft palate completes
its rising movement before the tongue tip comes away from the
alveolar ridge, an epenthetic plosive will come about, thus ['mɪnts].
Not surprisingly, this is a common pronunciation variant in this
kind of word.

Not only certain segment types, but also certain sequential possibilities are more natural than others. For instance, it appears that –
other things being equal – a regular alternation of consonants (C)
and vowels (V) is more natural than clusterings of one type or the

other. Thus the treatment of /r/ in non-rhotic accents results in more natural sequences than were present historically or persist in rhotic accents, since ['bɔː juː, bɔːrɪŋ, bɔːd] for *bore you, boring, bored/board* are CVCV, CVCVC, CVC, while rhotic ['bɔːr juː, bɔːrɪŋ, bɔːrd] (etc.) involve two clusters of [r] plus another C.

Nevertheless, English is a language which allows a good deal of consonant clustering within syllables as well as sequences across syllable boundaries. A way of reducing the articulatory complexity of strings of consonants is through **assimilation**, the process whereby a sound is made phonetically more similar to the sounds constituting its phonetic environment. We know, for instance, that the word which is nowadays *ant* /ænt/ had an Old English form *ǣmete*; regular vowel developments would give a present-day form *amt* /æmt/ (compare traditional-dialect *emmet*). The change from [m] to [n] before a following [t] is an assimilation which results in an obvious articulatory simplification, namely the elimination of a labial movement. As its spelling implies, *nature* was once pronounced with intervocalic [tj]. The current form with [tʃ] represents the outcome of a coalescent assimilation, whereby an alveolar plosive followed by a palatal semivowel combined into a palato-alveolar affricate. Various types of assimilation operate as optional rules in current English, though as a mechanism of sound change assimilation seems to be of minor importance.

As children learn to speak, it can be observed that they tend to replace complex or less natural segments and sequences with simpler or more natural ones. As their pronunciation habits mature, they normally move on to master the adult-type sounds which they hear around them. But this does not always happen: sometimes, instead, they retain an infantile makeshift into adult life. Where this happens among a whole community rather than just with individual speakers, we have a mechanism whereby sound change may come about. For example, the dental fricatives [θ] and [ð] are relatively unnatural segment types, rare among the languages of the world and learnt late by children. Compared with them, the labiodental fricatives, [f] and [v], are more natural; and children, as is well known, readily substitute them for the difficult dentals, thus *thing* [fɪŋ], *mouth* [maʊf], *mother* ['mʌvə], etc. The prevalence of these pronunciations among adult working-class Londoners or American blacks can thus be regarded as a persistent infantilism.

But perhaps the same is true of most sound changes. The alternative development, found in Ireland, the West Indies, New York and elsewhere, replaces the dental fricatives with dental or alveolar plosives, [t, d] etc. These, too, can be seen as more natural than [θ, ð].

1.4.2 System preservation

Ease of articulation, if allowed free rein, would lead to nothing but a uniform grunt, perhaps [ɑː], for every word in the vocabulary. It is held in check principally by the countervailing pressure of the **necessity to preserve intelligibility** and thus facilitate communication. Several of the innovations mentioned so far tend to lead to the loss of certain contrasts and thus to the creation of new homophones and new opportunities for misunderstanding. Allowing [t] to become voiced risks making *latter* and *ladder* identical in sound, causing uncertainty between *waiting* in the river and *wading* in it, or between a lamb which is *bleating* and one which is *bleeding*. Allowing an epenthetic [t] in *mince* risks making it homophonous with *mints*, so that 'Go and buy some [mɪnts]' is ambiguous (at least where *mince* is the everyday name for minced beef or hamburger, as in England). Dropping the /r/ from *bored/board* may make this word homophonous with *bawd*, or lead to confusion between a *flaw* and a *floor*. Using [f] for standard /θ/ will bring about confusion between *I thought* and *I fought*, or between *three tickets* and *free tickets*. Although there are accents which have to tolerate these potentialities for confusion, it is not surprising that there are other accents which have failed to adopt the various sound changes which lead to them.

The obvious usefulness of preserving distinctions reinforces the natural human tendency towards conservatism in social institutions, language among them. Superficial appearances to the contrary notwithstanding, children to tend to model themselves upon their parents and upon societal norms. In pronunciation this implies the accurate imitation of existing pronunciation patterns, and hence resistance (on the whole) to the principle of least effort.

Indeed, some sound changes can be accounted for by saying that they tend not just to preserve but even to increase the auditory distinctiveness of particular phonemic contrasts. The development

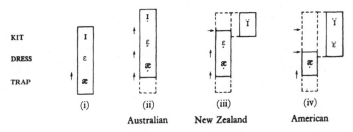

Fig. 4 Diagrammatic representation of push-chains, (i)–(iv), resulting from the raising of [æ] in (i). (Relationships shown are schematic only. No phonetic identity is claimed, for instance, between the 'American' and 'New Zealand' qualities for the KIT vowel.)

of a diphthong [oʊ] for the earlier monophthong [oː] in words such as *coat* (3.1.12 below) has increased the perceptibility of the distinction between *coat* and *caught* [kɔːt], since it reinforces a difference on the vowel height dimension with a difference of diphthong vs. monophthong. The subsequent centring or fronting of the first element of the diphthong (thus [kəʊt, keʊt]) makes the distinction even more unmistakable.

Where sounds are rather close to one another in auditory space, a change in the realization of one phoneme may lead to a change in another, adjacent, phoneme, so as to reduce possible confusion between them. Given that a change takes place in /æ/ whereby it becomes closer, approaching [ɛ], there is going to be a risk of confusion between *bad* and *bed*, *gnat* and *net*, etc., unless this other vowel changes in its turn, by becoming closer (as has happened in southern-hemisphere English), or else by becoming somewhat centralized (as in the United States). There may then be a knock-on effect on /ɪ/, making it too become closer (as in Australian) or central (as in New Zealand). Such a chain of events is known as a **push-chain** (fig. 4).

A sound which undergoes a change may also leave behind it a vacuum, as it were, in the auditory space it formerly occupied. An adjacent sound may then move in such a way as to fill this vacuum, or at least so as to restore the same auditory distance as previously obtained. This process, too, many affect several members of a vowel or consonant system; it is known as a **drag-chain** (fig. 5). The fronting of the [ɑː] of *father* towards [aː], something which has

Fig. 5 Diagrammatic representation of drag-chain resulting from the raising of [æ]

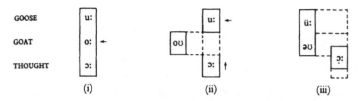

Fig. 6 Successive stages of a chain (?) consequent upon the diphthonging of [oː]

happened in certain kinds of American English as well as in Australian and New Zealand, is perhaps to be explained as a drag-chain effect consequent on the raising of [æ].

Where several members of a system have all undergone related changes, it may be difficult to decide whether a push-chain is involved, or a drag-chain. After the [oː] of *goat* had become diphthongal, the [ɔː] of *thought* in much of England (and in the southern hemisphere) moved closer, till it now overlaps on what was once the auditory territory of GOAT – a drag-chain effect. But at about the same time the [uː] of *goose* has tended to become a central rather than a back vowel. Is this a push-chain effect following the raising of the THOUGHT vowel? Or is it in fact the primary change, with the raising of the THOUGHT vowel depending on it in a drag-chain relationship? It is difficult to say.

1.4.3 Splits and mergers

Some sound changes lead to alterations in the system of oppositions. In some cases a phoneme undergoes a **split**, so that what was previously a single phoneme now becomes two, as its erstwhile allophones achieve independent phonemic status. In other cases phonemes undergo a **merger**, so that what were previously contrasting phonemes now cease to contrast, becoming merged into a single phoneme.

The process of phoneme splitting can be slow. Typically, what happens is that a positional allophone develops into an independent phoneme because of changes in the environments in which it occurs. In the history of RP, long /iː/ acquired an allophone [iə] in the environment of a following /r/ (3.2.1 below). As long as the following /r/ was preserved, the centring diphthong remained a co-allophone of the [iː] used in other environments. But then the new possibility arose of giving zero realization to the /r/ if it was pre-consonantal or final. At first, no doubt, this was an optional omission: at this moment we might speak of the /iː/ phoneme **cracking**, since the burden of distinguishing between *bead* [biːd] and *beard* [biə(r)d] now began to fall on the vowel quality (monophthong vs. diphthong) rather than on the presence vs. absence of the [r]. As soon as the loss of the [r] became categorial, we can regard the phoneme split as accomplished: this variety of English had acquired the phoneme /iə/ (/ɪə/). The new phoneme was in opposition to the /iː/ which remained in other environments: this is demonstrated by minimal pairs such as *bead* [biːd] vs. *beard* [biəd], which show the monophthong and diphthong (previously allophones of the same phoneme) contrasting in the same environment. From now on, new generations of children learning the language presumably stored [iə] in a way distinct from [iː], whereas previously [iər] had been stored as /iː/ plus /r/: the lexical representation of *beard* had undergone **restructuring**. (The point at which this happens remains a controversial one for phonologists. It is possible to argue that alternations such as *fear* [fiə] – *fearing* [fiərɪŋ] provide grounds for children to continue to analyse [iə] as realizing underlying /iːr/, even in cases like *beard* where there is no alternation; and this may be favoured by their exposure to other accents of English in which /r/ retains its overt phonetic realization.)

Sound changes do not always apply to all lexical items which apparently meet their structural description. For example, the change from short [a] to long [aː] (later [æ], [ɑː]) in the history of RP applied, among other environments, before /nt # /, as in *slant, grant, plant, shan't, can't*, etc. For reasons that are not clear, it never extended to the words *pant, cant*, and *rant*. The item *ant* seems to have vacillated, but has now firmly ended up with the short vowel. The sound change was evidently subject to gradual **lexical diffusion** through the vocabulary items which met the structural description of the sound change in question; but this lexical diffusion was then arrested before all the relevant items had undergone the change. This meant the elevation to phonological status of what would otherwise have been an allophonic change: earlier /a/ split into contrastive modern /æ/ and /ɑː/. (We discount at the moment the fact that modern RP /ɑː/ actually has several other sources as well.)

Decay of an allophone-conditioning environment and interrupted or incomplete lexical diffusion are major factors in the causation of phonemic splits.

If a sound change affects phoneme /x/ in such a way that it comes to have the set of realizations $[a_1, a_2, \ldots]$ which are identical in each relevant environment with the realizations of phoneme /y/, then the two phonemes become indistinguishable phonetically: they merge. Within the last century, RP /ɔə/ and /ɔː/ have merged in just such a way. Previously, *wore* /wɔə/ was distinct in pronunciation from *war* /wɔː/. When /ɔə/ became subject to the sound change I have called Monophthonging (3.2.1 below), and thereby acquired the realization [ɔː], it became impossible to distinguish /ɔə/ from /ɔː/, since they were realized identically. New generations grew up unaware that the words had ever been distinguished from one another in pronunciation, generations for whom *wore* and *war* are perfect homophones. The phoneme /ɔə/ has been eliminated from the system. (In London, both words are often pronounced [wɔə], rather than [wɔː]. This does not affect the point at issue, namely that the phoneme merger renders them identical in pronunciation, whatever the phonetic realization of the merged phoneme.)

Both splits and mergers inevitably involve an alteration in the phonemic system: splits increase the number of terms in a system, mergers reduce it.

1.4.4 Regularization

Some sound changes can be explained on the grounds that they lead to greater simplicity in the grammar (in the widest sense of this term, i.e. including phonology). This involves simplifying not the physical movements of the articulators but the abstract mental plan of the language which underlies our ability to speak it.

There is always a pressure to remove irregularities by bringing

irregular forms under the general rule. In verb morphology, for
example, the irregular *strive–strove–striven* is under pressure to
become *strive–strived–strived* (compare *arrive–arrived–arrived*).
The less well-known and frequently used a word is, the more it is
susceptible to this kind of pressure.

Some rule changes represent regularizing simplifications. An
allophonic rule which makes /t/ take the phonetic shape [ʔ] in all
syllable-final environments is simpler (more general) than one
which makes it do so only before certain consonants. The current
British trend towards general syllable-final glottalling thus constitutes a rule simplification.

Any phoneme merger reduces the number of contrasting items in
the system and therefore constitutes a simplification. Where a
particular opposition is not much exploited for distinguishing
words (has a low functional load), it may well be eliminated. In this
sense the Scottish loss of the FOOT–GOOSE opposition (so that *good*
and *mood* come to rhyme) is a simplification, since it removes the
necessity to distinguish between /ʊ/ and /uː/ in the lexicon.

Certain phoneme splits may also be seen as leading to greater
regularity. A system may contain 'empty spaces', i.e. unexploited
intersections of feature values which are exploited otherwise. For
example, a plosive system comprising just /p, t, k, b, d/ would have a
gap at the point where a */g/ might be expected. There seems to
exist a general systemic pressure in languages to fill gaps of this sort,
perhaps at first allophonically, and then by phonemicizing what
was previously allophonic. This is perhaps the fundamental mechanism whereby English first developed voiced fricatives /v, ð, z, ʒ/
(although dialect mixture and French superstrate influence may
also have played a part).

When foreign words are borrowed into English they are usually
made to conform to English patterns. Full integration implies
a phonological reinterpretation in terms of English phonemes
arranged in patterns which follow English phonotactic constraints.
Thus for instance French *façade* [faˈsad] is anglicized as RP
/fəˈsɑːd/, rhyming with *card*, and as General American /fəˈsad/,
rhyming with *rod*, while *revue*, French [ʀəˈvy], becomes /rɪˈvjuː,
rəˈvju/, acquiring the typical English cluster /vj/ while losing the
un-English vowel [y]. Not all foreign words undergo complete
integration: in particular, learned terms taken from languages

widely studied tend to retain unintegrated elements. The word *genre*, from French [ʒɑ̃:ʀ], is notorious in this respect, being very difficult to recast in English phonetic form.

It is not only foreign borrowings that may be regularized in this way. **Folk etymology** is the reinterpretation of a learned word in terms of familiar morphemic components, as when *asphalt* (RP /'æsfælt/) takes the popular form *ash-felt* /'æʃfelt/. A recent example is *polyurethane* (paint) pronounced as if written *polyurethene*, with the familiar -*thene* of *polythene*. Similarly the name of the flower *phlox* may be treated as a plural, acquiring a new singular form /flɒk/.

A similar kind of reinterpretation makes learned words conform to familiar phonotactic patterns. Here is the explanation of the common pronunciation of *et cetera* with /-ks-/: English has a large number of words beginning with an unstressed vowel plus /ks/, as *exceed*, *exciting*, *accept*, but no other words in /Vts-/.

Spelling pronunciation and other effects of orthography are considered in 1.4.6 below. Another mechanism potentially responsible for sound change, hypercorrection, is treated in 1.4.7. One must admit, though, that there remain certain sound changes for which none of the explanations we have put forward can reasonably be held responsible. One such is the current change in England from /gz/ to /kz/ in words such as *exist*, *exhaust*, *example*. We can label it **dissimilation** (making contiguous segments less similar to one another), but this explains nothing.

1.4.5 Why innovations spread

Let us suppose that some phonetic innovation arises through one of the mechanisms just discussed. Two fates are possible: either it will catch on, or it will die stillborn. If it catches on in the immediate social and geographical area where it first arose, then again either fate may await it: it may spread to a wider area, and indeed may eventually come to operate in all the various accents of English. Alternatively it may remain restricted to a small group of speakers, and later in due course die out again.

It will spread only if it is imitated. It will be imitated only if it is felt to be in some sense admirable and worthy of imitation. This will happen only if the speakers who use it are perceived as setting the fashion.

Fashions are set by various groups at various times. On the whole, though, trend-setters are urban rather than rural and metropolitan rather than provincial. So the commonest pattern is for an innovation to arise in a large city, particularly the political capital, and to spread out from there to other cities, thence to towns, and thence to villages, in rather the same way that fashions in clothes or hair-styles do. This is why country speech is conservative or old-fashioned, while city speech is innovative and up-to-date.

In respect of social class, it is obvious that many sound changes have spread from higher social strata to lower. The upper or upper middle class on the whole define the standards of speech as of most other matters, and other classes gradually pick up their ways of doing things. This is why working-class speech is often relatively old-fashioned, and why for instance it is only the working class in the north of England who still use traditional-dialect. A good example of phonetic conservatism in England is rhoticity: we find it only in certain geographical areas (overwhelmingly rural) and in certain social classes (lower middle and below), since it is here that the RP custom of R Dropping has been slowest to catch on.

RP in England, and this or other accents elsewhere, enjoy **overt prestige**. People agree that this is the correct way of speaking, that speakers with this accent 'have no accent'. Such an accent is a de facto **standard**. It is considered appropriate for public use – a suitable accent for a newsreader, an ambassador, a classical actress, a barrister, a general, a society hostess. A standard accent exerts constant pressure upon any non-standard accent. For example, a television reporter coming to work in London may be made to feel provincial and ridiculous if he or she retains a working-class northern accent. The same applies to someone with an American southern accent going to work in Chicago. The speaker with the non-standard accent tends, consciously or unconsciously, to modify his accent in the direction of the standard. And so those innovations which happen to have taken place in the standard accent tend to spread out to other accents.

But this is not the only possible direction in which innovations may spread socially. It has been shown that some changes have spread from lower social strata to higher. An excellent example in England is H Dropping (3.4.1 below). This characteristic, although overtly strongly stigmatized, has nevertheless spread out from its presumed origin in London Cockney to its present predominance throughout all urban England except the Tyneside area. But it has never been a characteristic of middle-class or upper-class speech: on the contrary, it is perhaps the strongest social shibboleth to exist in the accents of England. Its spread cannot be explained except through the concept of **covert** prestige. This is the unacknowledged prestige which attaches to working-class speech (particularly that of certain large cities), leading to the adoption of its characteristics in steadily widening circles. It appears that it is the speech of middle-working-class males which exerts this covert prestige (rather than the speech of the upper or lower working class, or that of working-class women).

We have seen above (1.1.6) that women's speech tends to differ from men's, other things being equal, by being like that of a higher social class. Given that there are two prestige sources from which new sound changes are imitated and spread, an overt upper-middle-class one and a covert middle-working-class one, we should expect that the first sort of change would be spearheaded by women, and the second sort by men. The two foci from which change radiates would thus be upper-middle-class women and middle-working-class men. For one recent change, at least, it has been demonstrated that just this was the case: Trudgill (1972) shows that in Norwich the change from [ɑ] to [ɒ] in LOT words actually spread out from both foci simultaneously. The influence of RP was felt first in women's speech, and the influence of Cockney first in men's speech; it is a coincidence that in this instance both led in the same direction, namely towards the replacement of the [ɑ] of the older Norwich local accent by the RP/Cockney [ɒ].

Groups which are imitated lose their exclusiveness by this fact. A trend-setting group sets a new fashion; others join the trend and adopt the fashion; and the trend-setting group is no longer in the forefront of fashion. So it has to adopt another new fashion, set another trend, in order to maintain its distinctive position. We may suppose that in the early twentieth century smart RP speakers initiated the switch from [oʊ] to [əʊ] in GOAT words. When all sorts of middle-class and other speakers followed suit, the trend-setters (speakers of what Gimson calls 'advanced RP', 1980: 6.32) launched a new fashion, for [eʊ]. It was unfortunate for them that social changes in Britain in the 1960s and 1970s then robbed them of their position as the most admired and imitated group. Over the last quarter-century all the signs are that the covert prestige of working-class speech is acting as a more potent source of innovation than the overt prestige of advanced RP. Mainstream RP is now the subject of imminent invasion by trends spreading from working-class urban speech, particularly that of London – Glottalling, L Vocalization, *happy* Tensing, and so on. The use of [eʊ] in GOAT is almost the hallmark of an ageing trendy.

1.4.6 The influence of literacy

Most native speakers of English can read and write. From the point of view of the linguistic history of mankind, this is an exceptional situation. But it is a fact of great importance for the development of English pronunciation, since widespread literacy tends to affect the pronunciation people use.

People are consciously aware of the spelling of a word in a way in which they are not consciously aware of the pronunciation. In English-speaking culture there is much greater awareness of letters and spelling than there is of sounds and pronunciation. Terms such as 'vowel' and 'consonant' are applied by the layman to letters, not to sounds. Ordinary people know how many letters there are in the alphabet, but have no idea how many phonemes there are in the phonemic inventory of their accent. The fact that comparatively few people can consistently avoid spelling mistakes, that there is widespread uncertainty about the written form of many common words, does not invalidate this point. The spelling tends to be taken as the fundamental, real shape of a word, and the pronunciation as secondary and derivative. That this is absurd does not prevent its happening. For example, native speakers of English will often have the intuition that *snow* ends in /w/, while *toe* does not. A phonologist can make out a case that both these words end in /w/, or that neither does; but for most accents of English there are no grounds whatever, other than spelling, for saying that one does and the other does not.

English spelling notoriously fails to correspond consistently to pronunciation. This is the root cause of the various effects we consider in this section.

The foremost effect is **spelling pronunciation**. One can set up reading rules for English which allow one, with probability though in no way with certainty, to infer the pronunciation on the basis of the spelling. For example, the spelling *oi* almost always corresponds to the pronunciation /ɔɪ/ (i.e. the vowel of CHOICE). Therefore in a word such as *tortoise*, traditionally pronounced with a second syllable /təs/, a new pronunciation with /tɔɪs/ (or /tɔɪz/) tends to arise through the influence of the spelling. I hear this new pronunciation around from time to time; it is possible that bit by bit it will catch on and eventually supplant the /təs/ form.

There are many words in which this process has already operated so as to replace a traditional form with a new one based on the spelling. The /w/ in *quote, swore, swollen, backwards, Edward, inward, Ipswich* dates only from the nineteenth century; *sword* and (in Britain, at least) *Norwich* have remained unaffected, while the /w/-less form of *inwards* has given rise to a doublet form *innards* 'internal parts'. In the case of *towards* we can observe a spelling-based form with /-ʹw-/ gradually displacing the older /tɔːdz, tɔrdz/.

It is to spelling pronunciation that we must attribute the occasional use of a strong vowel (that of DRESS) in plural -*es* or verbal -*ed* in place of the usual reduction vowel. The same applies to the newsreaders' pronunciation of *guerrilla*, encouraged recently by the BBC to make this word different in sound from *gorilla*.

There are many vocabulary items which we first come across in writing. Rather than hearing from a parent or teacher, or from a member of our peer group, we encounter them in a newspaper or book. In these circumstances we have no alternative but to infer a pronunciation on the basis of the reading rules we have internalized. The spread of secondary and higher education means that this process is by now a very potent source of spelling pronunciations, so much so that a considerable proportion of the learned vocabulary is without generally agreed single uniform pronunciations. I think I represent the majority of educated people when I pronounce *micro-organism* with /ʹmaɪkrəʊ-/; but I am aware that there is a substantial minority who say /ʹmɪkrəʊ-/. On the other hand I well remember my feeling of shame as an adolescent schoolboy when I gave the Classical Sixth a talk about the Minoan Linear B tablets and stated that they contained *inventories*, pronouncing this as /ɪnˈventərɪz/: in discussion the teacher pointedly referred to /ˈɪnvəntrɪz/. I have used the latter pronunciation ever since.

It is to spelling pronunciation that we owe such forms as *proven* with the GOAT vowel (but *prove* still always with the GOOSE vowel), *linguistic* as /lɪŋɡjʊˈɪstɪk/ rather than /lɪŋˈɡwɪstɪk/, or *vehicle* with /-h-/. In each of these cases the newer spelling pronunciation is currently in competition with a traditional form. In the case of *covert*, the new form RP /ˈkəʊ'vɜːt/, GenAm /ˈkoˈvɜrt/ represents a triumph of spelling pronunciation over both tradition and the link with *cover* reflected in the older /ˈkʌvət/, /ˈkʌvərt/.

A special category of spelling pronunciation is what we might call **continental vowelism**. This chiefly involves giving to the spelling letters *a*, *e*, and *i* the values of PALM, FACE, and FLEECE, rather than those of FACE, FLECE, and PRICE respectively. It is known, for instance, that *armada* used to be RP /ɑːˈmeɪdə/; this pronunciation has been entirely displaced by /ɑːˈmɑːdə/, which certainly corresponds to Spanish [arˈmaða] more closely than the earlier form. *Gala*, too, now usually has /ɑː/, though the older /eɪ/ form is still sometimes heard. *Apparatus* and *data* are following the same path. Phoneticians cannot make up their minds between /eɪ/ and /iː/ in *lenis*. A similar reason lies behind *trauma* /ˈtraʊmə/ alongside /ˈtrɔːmə/.

Educated people are thus aware that words in or from foreign languages are subject to somewhat different reading rules from those applying to English. But they are often vague about them, and about the different rules applicable to different foreign languages. Many resulting pronunciations are absurd in that they reflect neither the reading rules of English nor those of the language from which the word in question comes. For example, there is an awareness based on French that /dʒ/ is an English-type consonant, for which /ʒ/ is the 'foreign' equivalent. But when this leads to *raj*, *Taj Mahal*, *mah-jongg*, or *adagio* with /ʒ/ instead of /dʒ/ (although the languages of origin have affricates in these words), we have what might well be called a **hyperforeignism**. Another consonant well-known for being foreign is a voiceless velar fricative, which for some educated speakers could reasonably be counted as a marginal loan-phoneme in their English, /x/. But when it is used in *machismo*, *Boccherini*, *Sarajevo*, or *tovarisch* (in the original languages [tʃ, kk, j, ʃʃ] respectively), it is a hyperforeignism deriving from inadequate reading rules. (And even more so in *Munich* /'mjuːnɪx/ instead of /'mjuːnɪk/, German *München* ['mʏnçən].)

The converse of spelling pronunciation is **pronunciation spelling**, the creation of a new spelling form on the basis of the pronunciation. Hence we have *fridge* and *telly*, informal abbreviations of *refrigerator* and *television* (where possible spellings *frig(e)* and *tele* would be misleading). Hence also common-sense though counter-etymological spellings such as *gormless* or *to scarper*. And this is of course the basis for the vast body of spelling mistakes which speakers of English continue to commit. I find *ambivolent*, *alsation*, *villify*, *derrogate*, and *a smuggler-come-gangster* in my daily newspaper within a single week, together with a further crop (*hyperthetical*, *pronounciation*, *cheek by jowel*) which tell us interesting facts about the pronunciation used by the writer. My students in London often write *uvular* when they mean the *uvula* – a mistake which Scots or Canadians would presumably have no difficulty in avoiding. And the rear cover blurb of the British edition of Chomsky 1975 includes the spelling *analagy* for *analogy*, in spite of the claim that (if Chomsky is to be believed) [ə'næylədʒɪ] has an underlying phonemic form of the type /ænælɔg + j/ (compare ['ænə'lɒdʒɪkl]), which ought to prevent people making that particular spelling mistake.

Other pronunciation phenomena which depend on literacy include **acronyms** (*derv*, *SALT*, *NATO*) and **initialese** (*US*, *BBC*, *EEC*).

An interesting type of spelling pronunciation has entered into the creation of abbreviatory forms such as *prop-shaft*, *con-rod*, and *rad* (= radiator). Neither *propel* nor *propellor* nor any other derivative has initial /prɒp-, prɑp-/; so in *prop-shaft* this vowel must be attributable to the spelling. The same applies to *connect(ing)* and the *con-* of *con-rod*. *Radiator* and all derivationally related forms have /reɪd-/, making /ræd/ *rad* explicable only in terms of orthographic influence.

Place-names and personal names are notoriously subject to spelling pronunciation: who could infer that *Costessey* near Norwich rhymes with *bossy*, or that *Goondiwindi* in Queensland is [gʌndə-'wɪndi]? Sometimes they are affected by pronunciation spelling, too, as when *Kirkby* near Liverpool, locally /'kɜːbi/, gets pronounced /'kɜːkbi/ or spelt *Kirby* by outsiders.

1.4.7 External influences

Where an individual or a community ceases to use one language exclusively and adopts another one, whether partially or wholly, then the old language will tend to exert a certain influence on the new one. This is known as the **substratum** effect.

For our present purposes we are interested in cases where a community speaking some language other than English has now adopted English. Certain of the phonetic characteristics of their accent of English may be explained as due to the substratum of the former language. In the British Isles it seems likely that this applies to elements of the Welsh and Irish accents of English, and to the post-Gaelic accents of Scotland (though not to most Scottish speech). It is perhaps the explanation of the clear [l] even in non-prevocalic environments in south Walian, Irish, and Highland Scottish accents, e.g. *milk* [mɪlk] (elsewhere usually [mɪɬk]).

Where the other language is retained as a first language, English being acquired in addition, the relationship is properly one of **interference** rather than of substratum. The situation then is comparable to a French or German accent of English in the mouths of those for whom French or German respectively is the mother tongue. Patterns of interference may themselves become institutionalized, as has happened in the case of Indian English (vol. 3, 9.1).

No sharp line can be drawn between interference effects and substratum effects, since the deciding factor is the maintenance of the other language as the first language. As Welsh has gradually yielded ground to English in Wales, one can say that what began as interference effects when English was an imperfectly acquired second language have now very generally become substratum effects as English assumes the rôle of majority first language.

Similar effects sometimes apply even when there is no general trend towards the abandonment of one language in favour of another, but two languages are used side by side in a largely bilingual community. Thus some of the characteristics of South African English may be attributable to Afrikaans, many of the white population of South Africa having good command of both these languages. The other language in such a situation is known as the **adstrate** language.

The first languages of immigrants in Britain, North America and Australia seem in general not to leave any effects on pronunciation beyond the first or second generation. For the first generation, of course, there is typically very considerable interference from the first language: Spanish-accented English in New York or San Antonio, Punjabi-accented English in Bradford. If, as seems possible, a stable bilingualism becomes established among some local-born communities of recent immigrant origin, we should expect more permanent effects on the local accent.

1.4.8 Altering one's accent

It often happens that an adolescent or adult, that is someone past the critical age of first-language learning, wishes to alter his accent. This may be for a temporary purpose such as acting a part in a play or doing impressions, or it may be in response to a longer-term alteration in the speaker's life-style, as when people move into a new social or geographical environment and alter their speech to fit.

Insofar as it does not merely exploit what are already the latent capacities of our built-in variability, acquiring a new accent can be seen as consisting mainly in adding new, late rules to our existing phonological competence. In some cases it also requires new phonological specifications for particular individual items in the vocabulary.

How easy is it to alter one's accent, and how consistently can one do it? For someone who is highly motivated, changing some aspects at least is quite straightforward; but to change other aspects may inevitably be very difficult. Only a small minority can succeed in acquiring truly native-speaker-like command of an accent first attempted in adult life. A point-by-point comparison of the original accent and the target accent can reveal the reasons for difficulty.

Where the point of difference between the two accents is just a question of realization (1.3.2 above), the speaker's problem is merely one of learning to articulate the target realization and to substitute it for the original realization. For example, a Cockney speaker can acquire an RP realization of the GOAT vowel simply by changing every one of his [ʌʊ]s to [əʊ]. Formulaically, his **adaptation rule** can be stated as (34).

(34) ʌʊ → əʊ

To imitate a non-aspirating northern or Scottish accent an actor would have to de-aspirate every /p, t, k/. We could represent this as (35) or, probably more realistically, as (36).

(35) $\begin{bmatrix} \text{Voiceless} \\ \text{Plosive} \end{bmatrix} \rightarrow [-\text{aspirated}]$

(36) $[+\text{aspirated}] \rightarrow [-\text{aspirated}]$

The reason for preferring formulation (36) is that it would constitute a simple addition to pre-existing rules, whereas (35) would have to replace one, namely the context-sensitive rule supplying aspiration to syllable-initial /p, t, k/.

Where the realization difference between the two accents applies only in certain phonetic contexts, the change is easy if it involves **generalization**, i.e. relaxing the environment condition on a rule. A Canadian actor, in whose native accent /aɪ/ has the positional allophone [əi], would, in order to talk with an RP or GenAm accent, have to eliminate the occurrences of [əi], extending the principal allophone [aɪ] to all environments. This can be formulated as (37):

(37) əi → aɪ

Adding (37) to Canadian phonology gives the desired output [naɪs] for *nice*, etc., without disturbing the already satisfactory realization of the vowel in *ride*, etc. Similarly a speaker of RP or GenAm wishing to talk with an Irish accent has to make all instances of /l/ clear, i.e. change every [ɫ] to [l]:

(38) ɫ → l

— which yields the desired Irish-style output [bɛlt], [mɪlk] etc.

But the change is more difficult if it goes in the other direction, i.e. if a new realization is to be applied in certain phonetic environments only. A speaker wishing to acquire the Canadian distribution of the /aɪ/ allophones has to learn to apply rule (39), which is context-sensitive.

(39) aɪ → əi / — $\begin{bmatrix} \text{-voiced} \\ \text{C} \end{bmatrix}$

Providing he correctly identifies the restricted environment for the application of this rule ('before a voiceless consonant only'), all will be well. He will get [əi] in *nice, fight, like*, etc., while keeping [aɪ] in *ride, my, arrive*, etc., just as in authentic Canadian. There is no need to learn off by heart lists of words for which the change is or is not appropriate: the phonetic environment suffices. Applying the adaptation rule without the needed restriction on its environment would produce the inappropriate forms [rɔid], [mɔi], [ə'rɔiv], etc. Such overgeneralization leads to **hyperadapted** pronunciations, or **hypercorrections**.

Similarly, an Irishman wanting to sound like an RP speaker must apply the context-rule l → ł / except before a vowel or /j/. Without the restriction on the environment, the rule would yield hyperadapted pronunciations such as [łɛs] or ['sɪłi].

Where the difference between the original accent and the target accent is a systemic one, the adaptation is easy if the original accent **overdifferentiates** with respect to the target accent, but fraught with difficulty if it **underdifferentiates**. Scottish English has only one phoneme, /u/, where GenAm, like other accents, has two, /ʊ/ and /u/. GenAm thus overdifferentiates with respect to Scottish, and an American who wants to put on a Scottish accent need have little difficulty in this area: he merely replaces both his /ʊ/ and his /u/ by a uniform [u]. That is, he adds to his phonology the adaptation rule ʊ → u, which turns [gʊd] into [gud], leaving [mud] as [mud]. (An adaptational realizational adjustment will also be required.) But a Scotsman wishing to talk with an American accent faces a much more difficult problem. His task is to split his /u/ in two. In some words it must be altered to [ʊ], thus *good, put, bull*, etc.; but in others it must undergo only slight realizational modification to sound like GenAm /u/, thus *mood, boot, pool*. Formulaically, he must apply a rule of the type (40).

(40)   u → ʊ in certain words only

The Scotsman's problem is thus one of deciding which words are appropriately said with [ʊ] and which with [u]. He cannot use the phonetic environment to decide; the spelling offers little in the way of reliable help. Not surprisingly, hypercorrections (resulting from wrong decisions on this question) are very common when Scotsmen attempt to assume another accent.

An upwardly-mobile English northerner has a similar problem with the short vowels (Part-system A). He has to split his /ʊ/. To achieve an accent nearer to RP, he must keep [u] in some words, e.g.

put, full, good, push, cushion. But in others – *cut, dull, blood, rush, percussion,* the majority in fact of his original /ʊ/ words – he must change [ʊ] to an opener vowel of the [ʌ] type. His adaptation rule (41) succeeds in many cases, but not in all.

(41) ʊ → ʌ in certain words only

Rule (41) correctly changes *cut,* for example, from [kʊt] to [kʌt]; but it yields hypercorrect forms like [pʌt], ['kʌʃn̩] when applied to a word for which it is inappropriate. And again there is no way for the northerner to know whether it is appropriate or not, short of learning lists of words off by heart. His is the typical problem of under-differentiation.

Where accents differ in the phonotactic distribution of phonemes, the accent-changer again may or may not have a problem. Restricting the distribution of a phoneme is relatively simple; extending it is likely to lead to hypercorrections. For the speaker of a rhotic accent to assume non-rhoticity is quite a straightforward matter. He needs merely to apply the /r/-deletion rule (42).

(42) r → Ø except before a vowel

This yields a non-rhotic distribution of /r/, correctly deleting it in *far, farm,* etc., but retaining it in *red, berry, far away.* Inspection of the phonetic environment is all that is needed in order to decide whether or not it is appropriate to apply the rule.

But the speaker of a non-rhotic accent wishing to adopt a rhotic accent has more of a problem. He needs an /r/-insertion rule (43) to turn [fɑm] into [fɑrm] etc. (We ignore the question of the length of the vowel.)

(43) Ø → r after certain vowels in certain words only

The 'certain vowels' for the environment of (43) are those after which he is in most cases already accustomed to using linking /r/, namely /ɑ:, ɔ:, ɜ:, ə, ɪə, ɛə, ʊə/ (in RP), but not /i, eɪ, əʊ, æ/ etc. Yet the /r/-insertion rule will still yield hypercorrections if applied indiscriminately after the correct vowels. It will change not only *farm, banner, corn, beer,* but also *calm, Anna, dawn,* and *idea,* to the inappropriate [kɑrm, 'ænər], etc. Once again, application of the rule has to be restricted to certain words only. In fact, knowledge of spelling helps: anyone who can spell correctly will be able to identify the words where change is appropriate by the *r* in the orthographic representation. Experience shows, however, that it is very difficult for a Londoner, for example, to avoid using absurd pronunciations like [dɔrn], [aɪˈdɪər] when imitating an American or Scottish accent. When personally attempting this feat, I find that constant conscious vigilance is called for (and I am fortunate enough to be a good speller).

Problems also arise where the target accent has phonotactic distribution constraints which are less obvious. Thus a Scotsman, for instance, trying to acquire RP, may well not be aware that in RP /əʊ/ cannot occur before /r/ within the same morpheme. The adaptation rule [o] → [əʊ] works satisfactorily in *goat, nose, snow,* etc.; but it falls down on words such as *four, boring, course.* These in a Scottish accent are /for/, /ˈborɪŋ/, /kors/. The rule just mentioned will change them to [fəʊr], [ˈbəʊrɪŋ], [kəʊrs]; other adaptation rules then apply to give the Scottish pseudo-RP pronunciations [fəʊə], [ˈbəʊrɪŋ], [kəʊs]. To achieve the proper RP output [fɔː], [ˈbɔːrɪŋ], [kɔːs], we need rule (44), which reflects the restricted phonotactic distribution of /r/ in RP.

(44) [o] → $\left\{ \begin{array}{l} \text{[ɔː] / \_\_ r} \\ \text{[əʊ] elsewhere} \end{array} \right\}$

(Actually, to convert all the various Scottish vowels before /r/ into RP, we need something more elaborate, namely the successive rules of Pre-R Breaking, Laxing, and R Dropping discussed in 3.2.1–2 below.)

Changes in the lexical distribution (incidence) of phonemes are not difficult if they concern just one or two individual words: it is then just a matter of learning a new pronunciation for each word involved. But where large numbers of words are involved there can be difficulties and striking instances of hypercorrection. This happens, for example, with the BATH words. A speaker of a flat-BATH accent, a Yorkshireman for instance, who wants to acquire the prestigious RP broad-BATH lexical distribution, ought to apply a rule a → ɑː in certain words only, learning by heart which individual words are involved. But the danger is that he may instead apply a context-sensitive rule such as (45), changing from [a] to [ɑː] whenever the phonological environment of (45) is satisfied.

(45)
$$a \rightarrow \text{ɑ:} \; / \; \left\{ \begin{array}{l} \_\_ \; \begin{bmatrix} -\text{voiced} \\ \text{fricative} \end{bmatrix} \\ \_\_ \; \text{ns, nt, mpl} \end{array} \right\}$$

While appropriately changing *pass*, *castle*, *disaster*, *sample*, etc., to [pɑːs, 'kɑːsl] etc., this rule also yields hypercorrections such as *gas* [gɑːs], *tassel* ['tɑːsl], *aster* ['ɑːstə], *ample* ['ɑːmpl] (compare RP [gæs], ['tæsl], etc.). Again it is a question of learning which words it is appropriate to modify and which words not.

It is particularly awkward, in the case of adaptation rules which require to be lexically specified, when two potential candidates for the rule occur in close proximity. The item *gas-mask* is notorious: northern /gasmask/ plus rule (45) yields ['gɑːsmɑːsk] (RP ['gæsmɑːsk]). A similar example with the /ʊ–ʌ/ opposition is *good luck*, where northern /'gʊd 'lʊk/ can readily be hypercorrected to ['gʌd 'lʌk].

Hypercorrections are unlikely if the speaker wishing to adopt a new accent is able to identify the cases where change is appropriate by reference to the phonetic environment. Where they cannot be so identified, and must therefore be lexically determined, hypercorrections are to be expected.

2

Sets and systems

2.1 The reference accents

2.1.1 Introduction

The accent which enjoys the highest overt prestige in England is known to phoneticians as **Received Pronunciation** (for short, **RP**). This name is less then happy, relying as it does on an outmoded meaning of *received* ('generally accepted'). But it is so well established that I have decided to retain it here. The accent in question is sometimes popularly referred to as 'BBC English' or even 'Standard English'. It is what English people mean when they say that someone 'hasn't got an accent' (though to Americans it is a typical British accent). I myself have elsewhere called it **Southern British Standard** (Wells & Colson 1971), inasmuch as it is generally taken as a standard throughout southern Britain (i.e. in England and perhaps Wales, but not in Scotland).

Geographically, RP is associated with England, though not with any particular locality within England. It is the most general type of educated British pronunciation (although there are many highly educated English people who do not use it). Socially, it is characteristic of the upper and upper middle class, insofar as members of the latter class, sociologically defined, speak with an accent not localizable within England. Occupations perhaps most typically associated with RP are barrister, stockbroker, and diplomat. Most of those who speak it have spoken it since childhood; they have not needed to go to speech classes in order to acquire it. Typically they belong to families whose menfolk were or are pupils at one of the 'public schools' (exclusive private schools standing outside the state education system). Until the early 1970s, this was the accent demanded in its announcers by the BBC.

Depending on the criteria used, RP may be circumscribed more or less narrowly (a matter to which we return in vol. 2, 4.1). Even with the more generous definitions, though, not more than about 10 percent of the population of England could be considered as RP speakers.

With the loosening of social stratification and the recent trend for people of working-class or lower-middle-class origins to set the fashion in many areas of life, it may be that RP is on the way out. By the end of the century everyone growing up in Britain may have some degree of local accent. Or, instead, some new non-localizable but more democratic standard may have arisen from the ashes of RP: if so, it seems likely to be based on popular London English.

In the United States there is no accent whose status and rôle correspond to that of RP in England. Except to some extent in the east, it is grammar (morphology and syntax) rather than pronunciation that people make stereotypic judgments about (foreign accents and Black English are exceptions to this generalization). A recognizably local accent in the United States can only come from the east or the south. In particular, the accents of eastern New England, metropolitan New York, and the coastal and inland south are readily localizable as such.

'**General American**' is a term that has been applied to the two-thirds of the American population who do not have a recognizably local accent in the sense just mentioned. This is the type of American English pronunciation taught to learners of English as a foreign language – 'the type of American English which may be heard, with slight variations, from Ohio through the Middle West and on to the Pacific Coast' (Prator & Robinett 1972). Nevertheless, 'General American' is by no means a uniform accent; and this is one of the reasons why the name 'General American' is nowadays looked at somewhat askance, and why it is here written with defensive quotation marks (which are dropped from here on). We shall discuss the kind of variability found in General American (hereafter GenAm, for short) in vol. 3, 6.1. Meanwhile, it is convenient to use it as a basis for comparison. (We assume a relatively conservative variety, in which for example *don* is pronounced differently from *dawn* and *hoarse* differently from *horse*.)

2.1.2 The vowel system of RP

RP has a vowel system which may be set out as (46).

(46)

ɪ	ʊ	iː			uː	ɪə		ʊə
e		eɪ	ɔɪ	əʊ		ɛə	3ː	ɔː
	ʌ							
æ	ɒ		aɪ	aʊ			ɑː	

checked	*free*

Not counting /ə/, which is restricted to weak (unstressed) syllables, there are nineteen vowels in the system. Of these the six traditionally 'short' vowels /ɪ, e, æ, ʌ, ɒ, ʊ/ are indeed of relatively short duration when compared with their 'long' counterparts in identical surroundings; nevertheless their duration does vary considerably according to phonetic environment, and they have certain quite long allophones. Distributionally, they stand apart in that – unlike the long vowels and diphthongs – they are subject to the phonotactic constraint that they do not occur in a stressed monosyllable with no final consonant. Hence they are labelled **checked**; the final consonant in *fit* /fɪt/, *rent* /rent/, *cat* /kæt/, *cup* /kʌp/, *shock* /ʃɒk/, *put* /pʊt/ can be interpreted as checking the pulse of air for the syllable and its vowel. But in *key* /kiː/, *play* /pleɪ/, *fear* /fɪə/, *snow* /snəʊ/, *two* /tuː/ etc. the vowel occurs free of any checking consonant; hence such vowels (or diphthongs) are labelled **free**. 'Free' vowels may also occur before a checking consonant (e.g. *keep* /kiːp/). This means that in the environment of a following final consonant the whole vowel system has the potentiality of occurrence, but in the environment ＿# only the free vowels are available.

The terms 'checked' and 'free' must be interpreted as applying to stressed syllables only: in RP both /ɪ/ and /ʊ/ can occur with no following consonant in an unstressed syllable. For /ɪ/ this is the case in a large number of words such as *happy* /ˈhæpɪ/, *city* /ˈsɪtɪ/, *coffee* /ˈkɒfɪ/; for /ʊ/ there are only a few optional words such as *value* /ˈvæljʊ ~ ˈvæljuː/ plus weak forms such as /tʊ/ for *to* (otherwise /tuː, tə/). In both cases the opposition between the short and the phonetically corresponding long vowel (ɪ – iː, ʊ – uː/) carries virtually no functional load in this environment.

The use of one vowel or another in particular words (lexical items) can be illustrated by tabulating their occurrence in the set of keywords (47), each of which – as established later in this chapter –

stands for a large number of words which behave the same way in respect of the incidence of vowels in different accents.

(47)	KIT	ɪ	FLEECE	iː	NEAR	ɪə
	DRESS	e	FACE	eɪ	SQUARE	ɛə
	TRAP	æ	PALM	ɑː	START	ɑː
	LOT	ɒ	THOUGHT	ɔː	NORTH	ɔː
	STRUT	ʌ	GOAT	əʊ	FORCE	ɔː
	FOOT	ʊ	GOOSE	uː	CURE	ʊə
	BATH	ɑː	PRICE	aɪ	*happ*Y	ɪ
	CLOTH	ɒ	CHOICE	ɔɪ	*lett*ER	ə
	NURSE	ɜː	MOUTH	aʊ	*comm*A	ə

Words such as *diary, sapphire* are often pronounced in RP with [aə] or [aː], thus ['daːrɪ, 'sæfaː], and it might be thought that this diphthong or monophthong ought to be included as a phoneme in the vowel system. It can, however, be treated as a realization of the phonemic sequence /aɪə/ rather than as a separate phoneme. See below, 3.2.9.

2.1.3 The vowel system of GenAm

GenAm has a vowel system which may be set out as (48).

(48)							
ɪ	ʊ	i			u		
ɛ	ʌ	eɪ	ɔɪ		o	3	ɔ
æ			aɪ	aʊ		ɑ	

    checked   *free*

There are also [ə] and [ɚ], which are restricted to weak (unstressed) syllables. Otherwise, the system comprises the fifteen vowels set out above. Vowel length (duration) is not as important in GenAm as in some other accents; all vowels vary somewhat in duration depending on their phonetic environment. We can still, however, distinguish two classes of vowel on the basis of phonotactic distribution. The five checked vowels, /ɪ, ɛ, æ, ʌ, ʊ/ are precluded from occurring in a stressed monosyllable with no final consonant, while the remaining vowels ('free') are not subject to this constraint.

The mid and close free vowels may be either monophthongal [i, e, u, o], or diphthongal [ɪi, eɪ, ʊu, oʊ], and either possibility could be chosen as the basis for the phonemic symbol. Checked vowels, too, are often diphthongal, particularly in the environment of a following liquid, e.g. /hɪl/ [hɪəɫ] *hill*, /hɪr/ [hɪəɹ], /wɛl/ [wɛəɫ] *well*. It is simpler to write FLEECE, GOOSE and GOAT with single-letter symbols; but I have written FACE as /eɪ/ rather than /e/ to avoid confusion vis-à-vis RP DRESS.

There is also a problem of phonemicization in the vowel symbolized above as /ɜ/. It occurs in words such as *nurse* /nɜrs/, *sermon* /'sɜrmən/, and is always followed by /r/. Many pronouncing dictionaries and introductory phonetics courses for American students use a single symbol for /ɜr/, namely /ɝ/, thus /nɝs, 'sɝmən/. In favour of this analysis is the phonetic fact that in the usual GenAm pronunciation the r-colouring is spread throughout the whole vowel ([ɝ] = [ɜ] plus r-colouring). I have preferred the analysis and notation /ɜr/ because of its parallelism with /ɑr/ and /ɔr/. These, too, as in *farm* /fɑrm/ and *form* /fɔrm/, often involve an r-coloured vowel as the realization of /Vr/; and writing /ɜr/ allows us to regard the relationship between RP /fɜːm/ *firm* and GenAm /fɜrm/ as parallel to that between RP /fɑːm/ and GenAm /fɑrm/, RP /fɔːm/ and GenAm /fɔrm/.

If we treat [ɝ] as underlyingly /ɜr/, it is logical to treat [ɚ] as underlyingly /ər/, thus *further* /'fɜrðər/ ['fɝðɚ].

The opposition between [ɜr] and [ər] is tenuous and may be absent (a possible minimal pair is *foreword* /'fɔrwɜrd/ vs. *forward* /'fɔrwərd/). This raises the further possibility of treating '/ɜ/' and /ə/ as phonologically identical, so that [ɝ, ɚ] would be taken as underlyingly /ər/ (*further* /'fərðər/). And since there may be no real opposition between /ʌ/ (*love* /lʌv/) and /ə/, there is also the possibility of analysing [ɝ, ɚ] as /ʌr/.

Leaving aside this and other problems in the phonological analysis of GenAm, we turn to the question of the use of one vowel or another in particular words (lexical incidence). This can be shown, as in 2.1.2 above, by using the standard set of keywords, (49).

(49)

KIT	ɪ	FLEECE	i	NEAR	ɪr
DRESS	ɛ	FACE	eɪ	SQUARE	ɛr
TRAP	æ	PALM	ɑ	START	ɑr
LOT	ɒ	THOUGHT	ɔ	NORTH	ɔr
STRUT	ʌ	GOAT	o	FORCE	or
FOOT	ʊ	GOOSE	u	CURE	ʊr

BATH	æ	PRICE	aɪ	*happ*Y	ɪ
CLOTH	ɔ	CHOICE	ɔɪ	*lett*ER	ɚ
NURSE	ɜ˞	MOUTH	aʊ	*comm*A	ə

In GenAm *diary* seems to be pretty consistently trisyllabic, /ˈdaɪərɪ/, while *sapphire* is disyllabic, /ˈsæfaɪr/. Such words do not pose the problem of analysis they do in RP.

2.1.4 The two vowel systems compared

When we compare the pronunciation of particular words in the two accents, we find that in many respects there is a good match: for example, almost all words that have /iː/ in RP have the corresponding /i/ in GenAm, and vice versa: thus *creep, sleeve, key, people* and hundreds of other words. Likewise /aɪ/, transcribed identically for the two accents, and used in both cases for *ripe, arrive, high, try* and many other words.

In other cases, though, the match is not one-to-one but two-to-one or one-to-two. In *stop, dodge, romp*, etc., RP /ɒ/ corresponds to GenAm /ɑ/; but in *cough, gone, Boston*, etc., it corresponds to GenAm /ɔ/. Conversely, in *stop, dodge, romp*, etc., GenAm /ɑ/ corresponds to RP /ɒ/; but in *father, psalm, bra*, etc., it corresponds to RP /ɑː/. The matter of presence or absence of /r/ means that we also get a correspondence between the RP diphthong /ɪə/ (which we interpret as monophonemic) and the GenAm sequence /ɪr/ (which we interpret as biphonemic): thus *beer, fear, period*, etc.

Investigation shows that in spite of these complications we can successfully match the vowels in RP and GenAm forms of particular words for the vast bulk of the vocabulary. There is a residue of oddities like *tomato*, where RP /ɑː/ corresponds to GenAm /eɪ/, a correspondence reflected in very few other items. (Note also the different treatment of foreign words and names exemplified by *Rachmaninov*, RP /rækˈmænɪnɒf/, GenAm /rɑkˈmɑnɪnɔf/.)

This matching furnishes us with the framework of **standard lexical sets** which we use not only for comparing RP and GenAm but also for describing the lexical incidence of vowels in all the many accents we consider in this work. It turns out that for vowels in strong (stressed or stressable) syllables there are twenty-four matching pairs of RP and GenAm vowels. We identify each pair, and each standard lexical set of words whose stressed syllable exhibits the correspondence in question, by a keyword, which we shall always write in SMALL CAPITALS. Thus the correspondence between RP /iː/ and GenAm /i/ is the basis for the standard lexical set FLEECE. The keywords have been chosen in such a way that clarity is maximized: whatever accent of English they are spoken in, they can hardly be mistaken for other words. Although *fleece* is not the commonest of words, it cannot be mistaken for a word with some other vowel; whereas *beat*, say, if we had chosen it instead, would have been subject to the drawback that one man's pronunciation of *beat* may sound like another's pronunciation of *bait* or *bit*. As far as possible the keywords have been chosen so as to end in a voiceless alveolar or dental consonant: a voiceless consonant minimizes the likelihood of diphthongal glides obscuring a basic vowel quality, while coronality (alveolar or dental place) minimizes the possible allophonic effect of the place of a following consonant. An exception here is TRAP for the /æ/ correspondence, where no items in /-t, -s, -θ/ are altogether suitable; another one is PALM.

The list of the twenty-four correspondences and keywords follows, (50). In 2.2 below we analyse the content of the standard lexical set defined by each of them.

(50) The standard lexical sets

	RP	GenAm	keyword			RP	GenAm	keyword
1.	ɪ	ɪ	KIT		13.	ɔː	ɔ	THOUGHT
2.	e	ɛ	DRESS		14.	əʊ	o	GOAT
3.	æ	æ	TRAP		15.	uː	u	GOOSE
4.	ɒ	ɑ	LOT		16.	aɪ	aɪ	PRICE
5.	ʌ	ʌ	STRUT		17.	ɔɪ	ɔɪ	CHOICE
6.	ʊ	ʊ	FOOT		18.	aʊ	aʊ	MOUTH
7.	ɑː	æ	BATH		19.	ɪə[1]	ɪr	NEAR
8.	ɒ	ɔ	CLOTH		20.	ɛə[1]	ɛr	SQUARE
9.	ɜː[1]	ɜr	NURSE		21.	ɑː[1]	ɑr	START
10.	iː	i	FLEECE		22.	ɔː[1]	ɔr	NORTH
11.	eɪ	eɪ	FACE		23.	ɔː[1]	or	FORCE
12.	ɑː	ɑ	PALM		24.	ʊə[1]	ʊr	CURE

[1] with /r/ following before a vowel only.

In the rest of this work standard lexical set keywords will also be used to refer to (i) any or all of the words belonging to the standard lexical set in question; and (ii) the vowel sound used for the standard lexical set in question in the accent under discussion. Rather than using expressions such as 'short *i*' for example, we shall speak of the KIT vowel or simply of KIT.

It can be seen by comparing the vowel systems qua systems that the differences between the two accents in this respect are (i) that RP has a systemic contrast between /ɒ/ and /ɑː/ which is lacking in GenAm; and (ii) that RP has separate 'centring diphthong' phonemes /ɪə, ɛə, ʊə/, which are lacking in GenAm (although phonetic [ɪə, ɛə, ʊə] are found as allophones of /ɪ, ɛ, ʊ/). The first of these systemic differences is catered for by the standard lexical sets LOT, PALM, and CLOTH, the second by the sets NEAR, SQUARE, CURE and KIT, DRESS, FOOT. A diagram, (51), may make the relationship clearer. (For the latter group we include examples with /r/ after the vowel.)

		RP	GenAm	
(51a)	*father, bra*	ɑː	ɑ	= PALM
	stop, rod	ɒ	ɑ	= LOT
	cross, cough	ɒ	ɔ	= CLOTH
(51b)	*mirror, spirit*	ɪr	ɪr	= KIT
	nearer, weary	ɪər	ɪr	= NEAR
	fears, beard	ɪə	ɪr	
	merry, herald	er	ɛr	= DRESS
	Mary, area	ɛər	ɛr	= SQUARE
	pairs, scared	ɛə	ɛr	

2.1.5 RP and GenAm: further comparison

In 2.1.4 we considered the vowel systems of the two reference accents and the lexical correspondences between them. We go further into this question as we consider each standard lexical set in turn in 2.2 below. Meanwhile, it may be helpful to look briefly at the other respects in which the two accents differ from one another. In particular, we must consider their consonant systems, and examine the phonetic realization and phonotactic distribution of both vowels and consonants.

The consonant systems are easily disposed of: they are identical, and can be set out as follows (52).

(52)	Plosives, affricates	p		t		tʃ	k
		b		d		dʒ	g
	Fricatives	f	θ	s		ʃ	
		v	ð	z		ʒ	
	Nasals	m		n			ŋ
	Approximants, liquids	w		l	r	j	h

The obstruents (plosives, affricates, fricatives) come in pairs distinguished by the phonological feature [± voice]; the sonorants are not so distinguished. (On the phonemic status of /tʃ/ and /dʒ/, see 1.2.5 above; on that of /ŋ/, see 1.2.11 above.)

In phonetic realization there are a number of differences between RP and GenAm, of which the most important are those relating to THOUGHT (RP /ɔː/, GenAm /ɔ/) and GOAT (RP /əʊ/, GenAm /o/). These are discussed in 2.2 below. In some instances a difference in symbolization might seem to imply a greater phonetic difference than in fact exists, as when we write DRESS /e/ in RP but /ɛ/ in GenAm. Among the consonants, there is a notable difference between the two accents in the realization of the liquid /l/, which is in general 'darker' (more velarized) in GenAm than in RP, particularly in intervocalic position in words such as *jelly, pillow* (GenAm ['dʒɛɬɪ, 'pɪɬou]; RP ['dʒɛlɪ, 'pɪləʊ]). There is also a difference in the realization of /t/ in intervocalic position, where GenAm usually has a voiced tap [ɾ], a pronunciation which is rare in RP (RP /t/ remaining voiceless in all environments): thus *letter, putting* (GenAm ['lɛɾɚ, 'pʊɾɪŋ], RP ['lɛtə, 'pʊtɪŋ] (3.3.4 below).

Turning to differences in phonotactic distribution, by far the most important are those relating to /r/. In RP the liquid /r/ is subject to the severe phonotactic constraint that it can occur only before a vowel: the sequences /rC/ and /r‖/ are excluded. GenAm is not subject to any such constraint. Thus where GenAm has /r/ followed by a consonant, RP lacks it; examples (with first the GenAm form, then the RP) are *sharp* /ʃarp/, /ʃɑːp/, *form* /fɔrm/,

/fɔːm/, *beard* /bɪrd/, /bɪəd/, *cures* /kjʊrz/, /kjʊəz/. Where GenAm has word-final /r/, RP lacks it unless the next word follows closely and begins with a vowel; examples are *car* /kɑr/, /kɑː(r)/, *war* /wɔr/, /wɔː(r)/ *fear* /fɪr/, /fɪə(r)/, *pure* /pjʊr/, /pjʊə(r)/. Where GenAm has /r/ followed by a vowel, so does RP; examples are *very* /ˈvɛrɪ/, /ˈverɪ/, *narrow* /ˈnɛro/, /ˈnærəʊ/, *serious* /ˈsɪrɪəs/, /ˈsɪərɪəs/, *arrive* /əˈraɪv/. (Syllabic [l̩], for this purpose, counts as a vowel: *coral* /ˈkɔrl̩/, /ˈkɒrl̩/.) As some of these examples show, there are also differing constraints in the two accents on the vowels which may occur before /r/.

The cluster /hw/ remains a possibility for many Americans, as in *white* /hwaɪt/, *which* /hwɪtʃ/. In RP this survives only as artificial pronunciations; the usual forms have plain /w/, thus /waɪt/, /wɪtʃ/. Many Americans also lack the clusters /tj, dj, nj/, as in *mature, during, nuclear* /məˈtʊr, ˈdʊrɪŋ, ˈnuklɪər/ (compare RP /məˈtjʊə, ˈdjʊərɪŋ, ˈnjuːklɪə/).

These and other differences between the two reference accents are discussed from a historical perspective in 3.2 and 3.3 below.

There are hundreds of words exhibiting differences of lexical incidence between RP and GenAm, thus *tomato* RP /təˈmɑːtəʊ/, GenAm /təˈmeɪto/. Others differ in stress, as *address* RP /əˈdres/, GenAm usually /ˈædrɛs/. As this example shows, there are many instances where the British incidence also has some currency in the United States (in this case, the less frequent GenAm /əˈdrɛs/); or vice versa, as in the case of the GenAm form of *primarily*, /praɪˈmɛrəli/, which has made considerable headway in England at the expense of the traditional form, RP /ˈpraɪmərɪlɪ/. A *cuckoo* is usually /ˈkʊku(ː)/ on both sides of the Atlantic; yet in America, but not in England, there is a variant /ˈkuku/.

A list of some other words with incidence differences follows. *Advertisement* RP /ədˈvɜːtɪsmənt/, GenAm often /ˈædvərtaɪzmənt/; *anti-* RP /ˈæntɪ/, GenAm usually /ˈæntaɪ/; *ate* RP usually /et/, GenAm /eɪt/ (i.e. the DRESS vowel in RP, the FACE vowel in GenAm; though FACE is also found in RP); *ballet* RP /ˈbæleɪ/, GenAm often /bæˈleɪ/; *Bernard* RP /ˈbɜːnəd/, GenAm usually /bərˈnɑrd/; *beta* RP /ˈbiːtə/, GenAm /ˈbeɪtə/; *borough* RP /ˈbʌrə/, GenAm /ˈbɜro/; *clerk* RP /klɑːk/, GenAm /klɜrk/; *depot* RP /ˈdepəʊ/, GenAm /ˈdipo/; *detail* RP /ˈdiːteɪl/, GenAm usually /dɪˈteɪl/; *docile* RP /ˈdəʊsaɪl/, GenAm /ˈdɑsl̩/; *erase* RP /ɪˈreɪz/, GenAm /ɪˈreɪs/; *figure* RP /ˈfɪgə/,

GenAm /ˈfɪgjər/; *herb* RP /hɜːb/, GenAm usually /ɜrb/; *inquiry* RP /ɪŋˈkwaɪərɪ/, GenAm often /ˈɪŋkwəri/; *iodine* RP /ˈaɪədiːn/, GenAm usually /ˈaɪədaɪn/; *laboratory* RP /ləˈbɒrətrɪ/, GenAm /ˈlæbrətɔri/; *leisure* RP /ˈleʒə/, GenAm /ˈliːʒər/; *lever* RP /ˈliːvə/, GenAm usually /ˈlevər/; *lieutenant* RP /lefˈtenənt/, GenAm /luˈtɛnənt/; *massage* RP /ˈmæsɑːʒ/, GenAm /məˈsɑʒ/; *neither* RP mainly /ˈnaɪðə/, GenAm mainly /ˈniðər/ (but both pronunciations are found in both countries; similarly *either*); *nonsense* RP /ˈnɒnsəns/, GenAm /ˈnɑnsɛns/; *omega* RP /ˈəʊmɪgə/, GenAm /oˈmigə, oˈmeɪgə, oˈmɛgə/; *process* (n.) RP /ˈprəʊses/, GenAm /ˈprɑsɛs/ (the plural in GenAm is often /ˈprɑsəsiz/); *progress* RP /ˈprəʊgres/, GenAm /ˈprɑgrɛs/; *quinine* RP /kwɪˈniːn/, GenAm /ˈkwaɪnaɪn/; *record* (n.) RP usually /ˈrekɔːd/, GenAm /ˈrɛkərd/; *schedule* RP /ˈʃedjuːl/, GenAm /ˈskɛdʒul/; *shone* RP /ʃɒn/, GenAm /ʃon/; *suggest* RP /səˈdʒest/, GenAm /səgˈdʒɛst/; *thorough* RP /ˈθʌrə/, GenAm /ˈθɜro/; *vase* RP /vɑːz/, GenAm usually /veɪs/ ('if it costs more than $9.95 it's a /vɑz/'); *vermouth* RP /ˈvɜːməθ/, GenAm /vərˈmuθ/; *wrath* RP /rɒθ, rɔːθ, rɑːθ/, GenAm /ræθ/; *Z* RP /zed/, GenAm /zi/. Note also the strong forms of *of*, *from*, and *was*, which all have /ɒ/ in RP but often /ʌ/ in GenAm.

2.2 Standard lexical sets

2.2.1 KIT

The standard lexical set KIT is defined as comprising those words whose citation form in the two standard accents, RP and GenAm, has the stressed vowel/ɪ/. The two accents agree substantially in the lexical incidence of this vowel in stressed syllables; some GenAm words with /ɪ/, however, belong with NEAR (2.2.19). Phonetically it is a relatively short, lax, fairly front and fairly close unrounded vocoid [ɪ], centralized from, and somewhat closer than, cardinal 2. Some of the words belonging to this lexical set are listed in (53).

The KIT vowel has the traditional name 'short I'. It derives in most cases from the short /i/ of Middle English, and is most commonly spelt *i* or, less commonly, *y*. Where /ɪ/ occurs in unstressed syllables it is spelt in a wide variety of ways.

Most accents have a vowel in KIT words generally similar to the above. Among the more noticeable variants, however, are the following. In the West Midlands of England it may be rather more [i]-like, i.e. closer and fronter. In accents of the southern hemisphere (vol. 3, chapter 8) it is, under certain circumstances, articulated as a central rather than as a front vowel, i.e. as [ɪ]. One form of this development is discussed in vol. 3, 8.3.8, the KIT Split. Here, and in American southern speech, KIT is particularly subject to **shading** (the development of different allophones conditioned by the place of articulation of the following consonant). Very open, [ʌ]-like qualities are found in some kinds of Scottish speech.

(53) KIT *ship, bit, sick, stitch, stiff, pith, this, wish,*
            rib, kid, dig, bridge, give, his,
            dim, skin, sing, fill,
            milk, limp, hint, drink, lift, list, plinth, mix,
            slither, vision, spirit, dinner, silly, winter, sister, . . . ;
            myth, symbol, rhythm, Syria, . . . ;
            pretty, England, English,
            build, guilt,
            women, sieve,
            busy, business.

2.2.2 DRESS

The standard lexical set DRESS is defined as comprising those words whose citation form in RP has the stressed vowel /e/ and in GenAm /ɛ/. The two accents agree substantially in the lexical incidence of this vowel; some GenAm words with /ɛ/, however, belong with SQUARE (2.2.20). Phonetically it is a relatively short, lax, front mid unrounded vocoid: [e] in RP, but somewhat opener, [ɛ̞], in GenAm. Some of the words belonging to this lexical set are listed in (54).

The DRESS vowel has the traditional name 'short E'. It derives in most cases from the short /e/ of Middle English, and is most commonly spelt *e*. Another origin, applying in several very common words, is Middle English long /ɛː/ via a shortening process; this is reflected in the spelling *ea*.

Most accents have a vowel in DRESS words generally similar to the above. Among the more noticeable variants, however, are the following. In the southern hemisphere it is typically closer, [e] or even more so. Old-fashioned types of both Cockney and RP tend to closer varieties than are now general. In much of the north of

England the vowel is opener, [ɛ] or even more. Of diphthongal variants, a closing offglide before certain voiced consonants, [eᶦ ~ ɛᶦ] is found in Cockney and, to a more noticeable degree, in popular American speech in the south and elsewhere; a centring offglide, [ɛə] is common in the American midwest.

In American southern the opposition of DRESS vs. KIT is neutralized before a nasal (*pin = pen*). In Scottish English DRESS is often split into /ɛ/ and /ë/.

(54) DRESS *step, bet, neck, fetch, Jeff, mess, mesh,*
ebb, bed, egg, edge, rev, fez,
hem, pen, bell,
shelf, hemp, tent, theft, best, sex, next,
effort, method, terror, tenor, jelly, centre/center, pester, . . . ;
threat, sweat, deaf, death,
bread, dead, head, health, realm, meant, breast,
ready, jealous, pleasant, weather, treacherous, . . . ;
any, many, Thames,
friend, says, said, Leicester, bury.

2.2.3 TRAP

The standard lexical set TRAP is defined as comprising those words whose citation form in RP and GenAm has the stressed vowel /æ/. This comprises all cases of RP /æ/, but not all cases of GenAm /æ/, others of which belong with BATH. Phonetically, /æ/ is a front nearly open unrounded vocoid, [æ], approximately halfway between cardinals 3 and 4. It occurs in checked syllables only. Some of the words belonging to this lexical set are listed in (55).

The TRAP vowel has the traditional name 'short A'. It derives in almost all cases from Middle English short /a/, and is nearly always spelt *a*.

It is a striking fact that the current trend in pronunciation of this vowel is towards a closer, longer, perhaps tenser or diphthongal quality in the United States, but towards an opener, [a]-like, monophthongal quality in England. The latter is possibly to be seen as a reaction against the closer, [ɛ ~ ɛᶦ] type of realization associated with Cockney. But closer variants of /æ/ are also typical of southern-hemisphere English. Fully open qualities, [a] or [a-], are typical of the north of England, most of Wales, and Ireland; in Northern Ireland and in Scotland the possibility of a TRAP–PALM

Merger may lead to central and indeed back qualities in TRAP words. Open [a] is also usual in the West Indies, where in popular speech TRAP may be merged with LOT.

Lengthening of this vowel is common in the south of England and in North America. This may well apply selectively to the lexicon, so that some words have a lengthened vowel and others do not in a way which is not phonetically predictable (vol. 3, 6.1.4). In the United States the long variant is often diphthonged, giving typical pronunciations such as *bad* [bɛːəd ∼ beːəd] alongside [bæːd]. These variants contrast strikingly with the [bad] of regional British speech and even more with the [bɑd] etc. of popular Belfast.

(55) TRAP *tap, cat, back, batch, gaff, math(s), mass, dash,*
cab, mad, rag, badge, have, jazz,
ham, man, hang, shall,
scalp, lamp, ant, hand, thank, lapse, tax,
arrow,[1] *carriage,*[1] *banner, abbey, tassel, cancel, panda,* . . . ;
plaid.

[1] GenAm also with /ɛ/.

2.2.4 LOT

The standard lexical set LOT is defined as comprising those words whose citation form has the stressed vowels /ɒ/ in RP and /ɑ/ in GenAm. This comprises a large majority of cases of RP /ɒ/, the remainder being allocated to CLOTH. It comprises a smaller proportion of cases of GenAm /ɑ/, others of which belong under PALM and START.

Phonetically, RP /ɒ/ is typically a back, nearly open, weakly rounded vocoid, [ɒ̞], somewhat less open than secondary cardinal 5; GenAm /ɑ/, on the other hand, is a central fully open unrounded vocoid, ranging from (retracted) [a] to (advanced) [ɑ]. The RP vowel is relatively short, and restricted to checked syllables; the GenAm one is typically longer, and occurs (because of the PALM–LOT Merger, 2.3.4 below) in free syllables too. Some of the words belonging to this lexical set are listed in (56).

The LOT vowel has the traditional name 'short O'. It derives in most cases from Middle English /ɔ/. Other, less common, sources include Middle English /a/ in the environment of a preceding /w/, as *quality*. The vowel is usually spelt *o*, and less commonly *a*.

In Britain the predominant type of vowel in LOT words is back and rounded, [ɒ ~ ɔ], though with the recessive unrounded variant [ɑ] in parts of the south of England remote from London. Southern Ireland, like Canada and most of the United States, typically has an unrounded vowel as in GenAm. In North America, rounded RP-type realizations are restricted to eastern New England, parts of the coastal south, and west Pennsylvania: in the latter of these, but not all others, the LOT vowel has merged with the THOUGHT vowel. There is considerable sociolinguistic variability with the LOT vowel in the West Indies, popular speech often reflecting a merger of LOT with TRAP, while higher-prestige speakers carefully maintain the distinction. In the southern hemisphere, RP-type [ɒ] is general.

In non-rhotic accents where LOT is (surface-) phonemically distinct from both START (= PALM) and THOUGHT, it may lie phonetically between them so that the appropriate symbolization is /ɑ(:)/ for START, /ɒ/ for LOT, and /ɔ(:)/ for THOUGHT. This is the case in RP and many British accents, as well as in southern Ireland, the southern-hemisphere accents, and eastern New England. In other non-rhotic accents, though, LOT is phonetically unrounded and fronter than START, thus lying phonetically between START and TRAP. This is the case in metropolitan New York and in much of the American south. If we continue to use the symbol /ɑ/ for LOT in these accents, then we need some other symbol for START: normally /ɑ:/ or /ɑə/ will suffice, although *PEAS* uses Kurath's '/ɑ/'.

(56) LOT *stop, pot, sock, notch, Goth,*
           rob, odd, cog, dodge,
           Tom, con, doll,
           solve, romp, font, copse, box,
           profit, possible, proverb, bother, rosin,
           honest, ponder, . . . ;
           swan, quality, yacht, wasp, watch, squabble,
           waffle, . . . ;
           knowledge, acknowledge.

2.2.5 STRUT

The standard lexical set STRUT is defined as comprising those words whose citation form in RP and GenAm has the stressed vowel /ʌ/. The two accents agree very substantially in the lexical incidence of this vowel. Phonetically, /ʌ/ is a relatively short, half-open or slightly opener, centralized-back or central, unrounded vocoid. Distributionally, it is restricted to checked syllables. Some of the words belonging to this set are listed in (57).

The STRUT vowel has the traditional name 'short U'. It derives mostly from Middle English short /u/, though also sometimes from a shortened /oː/, and is one of the two possible outcomes of the FOOT–STRUT Split (3.1.7 below). The vowel is usually spelt *u* or *o*, less commonly *ou* or *oo*.

There is considerable phonetic variation in this vowel among local accents, though everywhere where it contrasts with the vowel of FOOT we find that /ʌ/ is mid or opener than mid, ranging from [ɣ+] in certain accents of the north of England through the [ɔ] of Irish or West Indian accents to the strikingly front quality, almost [a], of Cockney. Of the standard accents, GenAm characteristically has a somewhat backer quality of /ʌ/ than present-day RP, [ʌ+] as against [ɐ]; Scottish and Canadian speech are usually like GenAm in this respect, but southern-hemisphere accents like RP.

In Wales, and in some (higher-prestige) midlands and north-of-England accents, STRUT words have stressed [ə], in consequence of the STRUT–Schwa Merger (vol. 2, 5.1.3, 4.4.2). A central [ɜ] is found in some American southern accents. Even in GenAm it may well be considered that stressed [ʌ] and unstressed [ə] are co-allophones of one phoneme.

In areas where the FOOT–STRUT Split has not applied in popular speech, or is still in the process of gradual diffusion, relatively open, STRUT-like qualities may be encountered as hypercorrections in FOOT words, as ['ʃʌɡə] *sugar*.

(57)　STRUT　*cup, cut, suck, much, snuff, fuss, rush,*
　　　　　　　rub, bud, jug, budge, buzz,
　　　　　　　hum, run, lung, dull,
　　　　　　　pulse, bulge, punch, lump, hunt, trunk,
　　　　　　　butter, study, punish, number, mustn't, Guthrie, . . . ;
　　　　　　　done, come, love, mother, stomach,
　　　　　　　monk, tongue, onion, money, front, . . . ;
　　　　　　　touch, enough, young, double, southern, country, . . . ;
　　　　　　　blood, flood.

2.2.6 FOOT

The standard lexical set FOOT is defined as comprising those words whose citation form in RP and GenAm has the stressed vowel /ʊ/.

The two accents agree substantially in the lexical incidence of this vowel; some GenAm words with /ʊ/, however, belong with CURE (2.2.24) Phonetically, /ʊ/ is a relatively short, lax, fairly back and fairly close vocoid [ʊ], usually weakly rounded. Distributionally it is restricted, as a stressed vowel, to checked syllables. Some of the words belonging to this set are listed in (58). Although the set comprises a rather small number of words, several of them are of very frequent occurrence.

The FOOT vowel has no traditional name, though expressions such as 'short *oo*' are sometimes used. It derives from the same Middle English sources as STRUT, namely short /u/ and shortened /oː/, and represents the other possible outcome of the FOOT–STRUT Split (3.1.7 below). Much as STRUT, it is usually spelt *u* or *oo*, less commonly *o* or *ou*.

Scottish and Ulster accents have no phoneme /ʊ/, the FOOT vowel having merged with that of GOOSE. Elsewhere the quality of /ʊ/ does not vary very greatly, though there are differences in the degree of roundedness, backness, and closeness: a more peripheral and round-ed variety is perhaps generally associated with old-fashioned or rural speech in England, Wales, and Ireland, and more centralized and/or unrounded varieties with innovative or urban speech. In North America, however, the rural hillbilly stereotype is charac-terized precisely by this latter kind, centralized and unrounded. Another typically American variant is a centring diphthong, [ʊə].

Certain of the words listed in (58) are found with /uː/, not /ʊ/, in Ireland and parts of the north of England, e.g. *cook*. Most or all words with *-ook* spelling do the same, e.g. *book, look*.

(58) FOOT *put, puss, bush,*
full,
cuckoo, butcher, cushion, pudding, bullet, ... ;
good, stood, wood, cook, look, shook, wool, ... ;
woman, wolf, bosom,
could, should, would, shouldn't.

2.2.7 BATH

The standard lexical set BATH is defined as comprising those words whose citation form contains the stressed vowel /æ/ in GenAm, but /ɑː/ in RP. That is to say, BATH words belong phonetically with

TRAP in GenAm, but with PALM and START in RP. For a description of the phonetic quality of the BATH vowel, see under TRAP (2.2.3) and START (2.2.20) respectively; it can range from [iə] to [ɒː]. It is noteworthy that qualities closer than [æ] are most commonly found outside Britain – particularly in North America – and that most kinds of British speech use a fully open vowel, [a] or backer.

The terms '**flat A**' and '**broad A**' are sometimes used, particularly in the United States, to refer to the TRAP and PALM vowels respectively, or to their use in the BATH words. (But in Britain the expression 'flat A' tends to be used in a quite different sense, to refer to the use of /ʌ/-like realizations of the TRAP vowel.) We shall extend this convenient terminology by referring to flat-BATH accents (with BATH = TRAP) and broad-BATH accents (with BATH = PALM). It must be noted, though, that in this context the term 'broad' has a quite different connotation from the one we give it in expressions such as 'a broad accent' (= far from standard, 1.1.5 above). In this sense the accents of the south of England, the West Indies, and the southern hemisphere are, generally speaking, broad-BATH accents like RP; those of most of North America are flat-BATH. In the north of England and in New England there is sociolinguistic variation between the two. In some kinds of Scottish and west-of-England speech the question does not arise since there is only one open vowel, TRAP and PALM being merged.

The term 'the *ask* words' has some currency in the United States as a synonym of what I designate 'the standard lexical set BATH'. In this work *bath* has been chosen as the keyword for this set, rather than *ask*, for the reasons stated above in 2.1.4.

The broad-BATH pronunciation, and with it the need to recognize a standard lexical set BATH, derives from the eighteenth-century TRAP–BATH Split (3.2.6 below), which involved a phonemic split in the /æ/ derived from Middle English /a/ or /au/. This led the BATH words to be pronounced with a long vowel, ultimately in RP the present /ɑː/.

Another, more recent, development has caused certain BATH words to be pronounced with a long vowel in North America. This is the BATH Raising discussed in vol. 3, 6.1.4, which involves the change from [æ] to a quality typified by [eə].

In the list (59), words in section (59b) are sometimes said with the TRAP vowel in accents which otherwise have broad BATH

(Australian, West Indian), while those in (59c) typically have the PALM vowel in the otherwise flat-BATH accents of the north of England; words in (59a) are subject to neither of these reservations. The appendix, (59'), comprises words which have /æ/ in GenAm, but in RP fluctuate between /æ/ and /ɑː/, hovering therefore between our standard lexical sets TRAP and BATH. It should be noted that although most of the obvious derivatives of BATH words also have the BATH vowel (e.g. *staffing, pathway, underpass, passing, passable, classy*), there are a number which have the TRAP vowel instead (e.g. *classic, classify, passage*, all with /æ/ in RP).

(59) BATH (a) *staff, giraffe,*
        path, lath,
        brass, class, glass, grass, pass,
        raft, craft, graft, daft, shaft, aft, haft, draft,
        clasp, grasp, rasp, gasp,
        blast, cast, fast, mast, aghast, last, past, contrast, vast, avast,
        ask, bask, mask, flask, cask, task,
        after, rafter, Shaftesbury,
        master, plaster, disaster, castor, pastor, nasty, disastrous,
        basket, casket, rascal,
        fasten, raspberry, ghastly, castle,
        laugh, laughter, draught;
      (b) *dance, advance, chance, France, lance, glance, enhance,*
        prance, trance, entrance v.,
        grant, slant, aunt, chant, plant, advantage, vantage,
        chantry, supplant, enchant,
        branch, blanch, ranch, stanch, stanchion,
        demand, command, remand, slander, chandler,
        commando, Alexander, Sandra, Flanders,
        example, sample,
        chancel, chancellor, Frances, Francis, lancet, answer;
      (c) *calf, half, calve, halve, rather, Slav,*
        shan't, can't,
        Iraq, corral, morale, Iran, Sudan, banana.

(59')   *chaff, graph, alas, hasp, Basque, masque,*
        plastic, drastic, elastic, gymnastic, (Cornish) *pasty, en-*
        thusiastic, bastard, paschal, pastoral, masculine, mas-
        querade, exasperate, blasphemy, masturbate, Glasgow,
        lather, stance, askance, circumstantial, intransigent, sub-
        stantial, transit, transport, transfer, transform, tran-
        sitory, transient, transept, and other words in *trans-;*
        contralto, alto, plaque, Cleopatra.

2.2.8 CLOTH

The standard lexical set CLOTH is defined as comprising those words whose citation form contains the stressed vowel /ɔ/ in GenAm, but /ɒ/ in current mainstream RP. That is to say, CLOTH words belong phonetically with THOUGHT in GenAm, but with LOT in RP. For a description of the phonetic quality of the CLOTH vowel, see under THOUGHT (2.2.12) and LOT (2.2.4) respectively; it ranges from [ɑ] to [oː]. Words belonging to this set are listed in (60).

The CLOTH set falls into three subsets. In the first, (60a), a more conservative kind of RP agrees with GenAm in using the vowel of THOUGHT, /ɔː/, rather than the /ɒ/ of LOT: see discussion in 3.2.6 below. The second and third subsets of CLOTH appear never to have had /ɔː/ in RP or its forerunner. The distinction between these two subsets is based on phonetic environment: in (60c) the following consonant is intersyllabic /r/.

There seems to be no popular terminology referring to the use of one vowel or the other in CLOTH words, although in Britain – where the prestige accent has switched from /ɔː/ to /ɒ/ in these words within the memory of many people – the question arouses a degree of popular interest; but it tends to be formulated in terms such as 'saying *crawss* instead of *cross*'. There seems to be no reason to object to an extension of the flat/broad terminology used for discussing BATH: one could speak of flat-CLOTH accents (using the LOT vowel in CLOTH) and broad-CLOTH accents (using the vowel of THOUGHT).

The broad-CLOTH pronunciation reflects the seventeenth-century Pre-Fricative Lengthening (3.1.9 below). The flat-CLOTH pronunciation retains or restores the historically short LOT vowel, Middle English /ɔ/.

There is considerable variability in the United States as far as the words in (60b and c) are concerned. With words containing a following velar, such as *mock, fog*, it is so great that they have not been included in any standard lexical set; see discussion in vol. 3, 6.1.3.

(60) CLOTH (a) *off, cough, trough, broth, froth, cross, across, loss, floss, toss,*
       fosse, doss,
       soft, croft, lost, oft, cost, frost, lost,
       often, soften, lofty,

Australia, Austria, Austen, Austin,
gone;

(b) *moth, boss, gloss, joss, moss, Ross,*
long, strong, wrong, gong, song, thong, tongs, throng,
accost, coffee, coffer, coffin, offer, office, officer, glossy,
    foster, Boston, Gloucester, sausage;
wash;

(c) *origin, Oregon, oratory, orator, orange, authority,*
borrow, categorical, correlate, coroner, coral,
florid, Florida, florist, florin, historic(al),
horrid, horrible, majority, horrify, horror,
    metaphoric(al), morrow,
Morris, moral, Norwich,[1] porridge, rhetorical, sorrel,
    moribund, . . . ;
sorrow, tomorrow, sorry,
Laurence/Lawrence, laurel, laureate,[2]
quarrel, quarry, warrant, warren, warrior, Warwick.[1]

[1] as English place-names or surnames: RP /'nɒrɪdʒ/, /'wɒrɪk/.
[2] RP also with /ɔː/.

2.2.9 NURSE

The standard lexical set NURSE is defined as comprising those words whose citation form contains the stressed vowel /ɜ:/ in RP and /ɜr/ = [ɝ] in GenAm. The two accents agree substantially in the lexical incidence of this vowel. Phonetically, it is a relatively long unrounded mid central vocoid, [ə:]; in GenAm, though not in RP, it is r-coloured. Both the r-coloured and the non-r-coloured vowel types are extremely uncommon as stressed syllabics in the languages of the world other than English; they are thus one of the striking features of English pronunciation to the foreign ear. Distributionally, /ɜ: ~ ɜr/ occurs both in checked and free position (*turn, fur*). It does not occur immediately before a vowel except across a morpheme boundary, as *stirring (stir # ing)*, RP /'stɜ:rɪŋ/, GenAm /'stɜrɪŋ/. Some of the words belonging in the standard lexical set NURSE are listed in (61).

The NURSE vowel has no traditional name, having been in the language for only a few centuries. There are three common Middle English sources for it: short /i/, /ɛ/, and /u/, all only when followed by a final or preconsonantal /r/. This is the reason for the variedness of our spellings for this vowel: *ir* and *yr*, generally speaking, reflect the first, *er* and *ear* the second, and *ur* or *or* (the latter after *w, wh*) the third. (Current spelling is not, however, an infallible guide to the Middle English pronunciation: *virtue* and *firm*, for instance, had /ɛr/ rather than /ir/, and were indeed formerly spelt *vertue*, *ferm*; while *gherkin* is believed on etymological grounds to have had /ur/.) From these Middle English origins the NURSE vowel reached its present quality through the developments described in 3.1.8 below: the NURSE Merger, R Coalescence, and (for RP and other non-rhotic accents only) R Dropping.

As discussed in 3.1.8, many Scottish and Irish accents reflect a failure to undergo the NURSE Merger, so that they lack the NURSE vowel as a distinct phonological entity. Even among the accents that have undergone it, the merged vowel is not necessarily distinct from the sequence consisting of the STRUT vowel plus /r/. Thus *furry* and *hurry* usually rhyme in GenAm, /ˈfɜri, ˈhɜri/, but not in RP, /ˈfɜːri, ˈhʌri/. Compare also *stir it* vs. *turret*, *occurring* vs. *occurrence*. Where no distinction is made in pairs of this kind, the question arises how best to phonemicize the vowel common to both: in a rhotic accent /ɜr/ or /ʌr/, in non-rhotic accent /ɜːr/ or /ʌr/ (or with /ər/ rather than /ʌr/ where the STRUT vowel and schwa are not in opposition). A decision may be possible only on phonetic grounds. Thus *PEAS* regards NURSE words as having a unit vowel phoneme in all parts of the eastern United States except western Pennsylvania; there, it recognizes instead /ʌr/, 'articulated as [ər ~ ɜr], the /r/ being an alveolar tongue tip consonant as after other vowels in this area' (*PEAS*: 109). Following this line of argument, we could classify *furry* and *hurry* types as follows: (i) [ˈfɝi, ˈhɝi], typical of GenAm, of Canadian, and of most rhotic accents of the west of England; (ii) [ˈfɜːri, ˈhɜːri], typical of eastern New England and most of the American south; (iii) [ˈfʌri, ˈhʌri], typical not only of western Pennsylvania but also of Scotland, Ireland, and the West Indies; (iv) [ˈfɜːri, ˈhʌri] typical of non-rhotic accents of England and Wales (with /ˈhəri/ rather than /ˈhʌri/ in the popular speech of most areas other than south-east England, or /ˈhʊri/ in the north); this last type, (iv), is characteristic also of southern-hemisphere English.

The realization of /ɜː ~ ɜr/ varies most obviously in respect of rhotacization (r-colouring), with r-coloured variants, [ɝ:] etc., being used not only in almost all rhotic merged-NURSE accents, but also in some accents which do not otherwise have non-prevocalic /r/ as such. This is the case in the *SED* records for areas such as Cambridgeshire and north-eastern Lincolnshire in eastern England; it is also the commonest situation reported by *PEAS* for Virginia. The yod-diphthong type [ɜɪ] in checked syllables, familiar from old-fashioned New York City speech, is also common in the American south; it does not occur in the British Isles. The non-r-coloured mid central [ɜ:] type, as in RP, is overwhelmingly the commonest variant in England and Wales and the southern-hemisphere accents, and in the States is the traditional realization in eastern New England; subtypes include lip-rounded variants, common in south Wales and in New Zealand, and rather closer qualities, approaching [ɪ:], associated with some English midland urban accents (Birmingham, Stoke-on-Trent) and with the south-ern-hemisphere accents. A front half-open quality, [ɛ̈:], is one of the variants common on Merseyside, where the NURSE vowel has merged with SQUARE, as also in an area of the east midlands of England. In the West Indies, NURSE is on the whole merged with STRUT in basilectal speech (creole), being realized as [ɔ]. In the Jamaican accent of Standard English it is distinct, but often still rounded while usually being r-coloured, [ɵ˞:]: other West Indian territories are split between GenAm-type and RP-type realizations.

(61)   NURSE   *usurp, hurt, lurk, church, turf, purse,*
curb, curd, urge, curve, furze,
turn, curl, spur, occurred,
burnt, burst, murder, further, ... ;
shirt, irk, birch, birth, bird, dirge,
firm, girl, fir, stirred, first, circus, virtue, ... ;
myrrh, myrtle, Byrne;
twerp, assert, jerk, perch, serf, berth, terse,
verb, erg, emerge, nerve,
term, stern, deter, err,[1] preferred,
certain, person, immersion, emergency, kernel, ... ;
Earp, earth, dearth, hearse, rehearse, search,
heard, earn, yearn, earl, pearl,
rehearsal, early, earnest;
wort, work, worth, worse, word, worm, whorl,

worst, Worthing, worthy, whortleberry;
scourge, adjourn, courteous,[2] journal, journalist, journey;
attorney, colonel, liqueur,[3] masseur,[3] connoisseur.[3]

[1] occasionally with the vowel of DRESS.
[2] occasionally with the vowel of FORCE.
[3] also sometimes with the vowel of CURE.

2.2.10 FLEECE

The standard lexical set FLEECE is defined as comprising those words whose citation form in RP and GenAm has the stressed vowel /i(ː)/. (The fact that we use a length-mark in the symbolization of RP /iː/ but not of GenAm /i/ does not reflect any important difference in this particular vowel, though it does suggest that vowel length in general retains a somewhat greater importance in RP than in GenAm; but in both accents the general phonetic nature of this vowel could be adequately represented as /i/, as /iː/, or indeed as /ɪi/, /ɪj/, or even /iːj/ etc.) The two accents agree substantially in the lexical incidence of this vowel in stressed syllables. Phonetically, /i(ː)/ is a relatively long close front vocoid, often with some degree of diphthongization of the [ɪi] type, particularly in free syllables. Distributionally, this vowel occurs in both checked and free syllables. Some of the words belonging to this set are listed in (62).

The FLEECE vowel has the traditional name 'long E'. It derives in most cases via the Great Vowel Shift (3.1.1 below) from Middle English /eː/ or /ɛː/, the distinction between the reflexes of which was lost by the FLEECE Merger (3.1.6 below). These two origins correspond to (62a) and (62b) respectively. Various French borrowings in Middle English had /ɛː/, and are included in (62b). Other words with this vowel have entered the language more recently; this is the case with the words in (62c). Typical spellings associated with these three subcategories are *ee*, *ea*, and *i* (or *iCe*) respectively. Words in which a vowel historically identical with that of FLEECE occurs before historical /r/ are dealt with in section 2.2.19 below, as the standard lexical set NEAR.

In other accents we find qualities for this vowel ranging from monophthongal cardinal 1, [iː], in more conservative accents such as those of the Celtic countries and the West Indies, to a closing diphthong of the [əɪ] type, such as in Australia. Most accents lie between these two extremes.

(62)   FLEECE   (a)   *creep, meet, seek, beech, reef, teeth,*
seed, sleeve, seethe, cheese,
seem, green, feel,
see, tree, agree,
needle, feeder, sweeten, ... ;
grebe, these, Peter, even, ... ;
shriek, brief, piece, believe, field, ... ;
ceiling, Keith, Sheila, ... ;
be, me, ... ;
key, people;

(b)   *reap, meat, speak, teach, leaf, beneath, peace, leash,*
bead, league, leave, breathe, please,
team, mean, deal,
sea, tea,
feast, reason, weasel, easy, Easter, ... ;
metre, equal, decent, legal, penal,
complete, scene, ... ;
deceive, receive, seize, ... ;
Caesar, an(a)emic, Aesop, ... ;
phoenix, subpoena, f(o)etus, ... ;
quay;

(c)   *police, unique, machine, prestige, elite,*
mosquito, casino, visa, trio, ski, chic, ...

2.2.11 FACE

The standard lexical set FACE is defined as comprising those words whose citation form in RP and GenAm has the stressed vowel /eɪ/. The two accents agree substantially in the lexical incidence of this vowel. Phonetically, /eɪ/ is a front narrow closing diphthong or, less commonly, a front half-close monophthong; in either case, it is unrounded. The monophthongal variant is found particularly in GenAm in unstressed syllables, so that *vacation* may have a monophthong in the first syllable but a diphthong in the second. In RP the monophthongal variant arises chiefly through Smoothing (3.2.9), thus ['pleːɪŋ] *playing*. The qualitative difference between the starting-point of FACE and DRESS may be lost in RP. Distributionally, FACE occurs in both checked and free position. Some of the words belonging to this set are listed in (63).

The FACE vowel has the traditional name 'long A'. It derives in most cases via the Great Vowel Shift (3.1.1 below) from Middle English /aː/ or, in consequence of the FACE Merger (3.1.5), from

/ɛi ~ æi/. These two origins correspond to (63a) and (63b) respectively. The words in (63c) had /ɛː/, and are discussed in 3.1.6 below. Typical spellings associated with these three subcategories are (a) *a*, *aCe*, (b) *ai, ay, ei, ey, aig(h), eig(h)*, and (c) *ea*. Words in which a vowel historically identical with that of FACE occurs before historical /r/ are dealt with in section 2.2.20 below, as the standard lexical set SQUARE.

In other accents we find two other main types of quality for this vowel: monophthongs in the [eː] area, and wide diphthongs such as [ɛɪ, æɪ, ʌɪ]. The use of a monophthong reflects the absence of Long Mid Diphthonging (3.1.12 below), and is a generally northern pronunciation both in England and in the United States, as well as characterizing the Celtic countries and the West Indies. Wide diphthongs are southern, whether in the United States or, as a consequence of Diphthong Shift (3.4.2 below), in England: they also belong to the English accents of the southern hemisphere. A centring diphthong, [eə], is found in Tyneside speech, while an opening diphthong, [ɪɛ] etc., is typical of popular West Indian accents.

(63) FACE (a) *tape, late, cake, safe, case,*
              babe, fade, vague, age, wave, bathe, craze,
              name, mane, vale,
              change, waste, . . . ;
              taper, bacon, nature, station, lady, raven, invasion,
                  April, . . . ;
              bass (in music), *gauge, gaol/jail,*
              crêpe, fête, bouquet;
         (b) *wait, faith, plaice, aitch, raid, nail, main, faint, . . . ;*
              day, play, way, grey/gray, . . . ;
              rein, veil, beige, feint, . . . ;
              they, whey, obey, . . . ;
              weigh, weight, eight, straight, . . . ;
              reign, campaign, deign, . . . ;
         (c) *great, steak, break, yea.*

2.2.12 PALM

The standard lexical set PALM is defined as comprising those words whose citation form has the stressed vowel /ɑː/ in RP, /ɑ/ in GenAm, excluding cases where this vowel is followed by /r/ in

GenAm. (The latter are treated under START, 2.2.21. For comments on the use of the length-mark in RP but not GenAm, see 2.2.10: the PALM vowel is relatively long in both accents.) PALM words thus belong phonetically with START (and BATH) in RP, but with LOT in GenAm. For a description of the quality of the PALM vowel, see under START (2.2.21) and LOT (2.2.4) respectively. In all cases it is a fully open unrounded vocoid. It occurs in both checked and free syllables.

The membership of this lexical set is unusual and difficult to circumscribe. No more than a handful of really common everyday words belong to it unambiguously, e.g. *father*. Most of the PALM words are recent borrowings from foreign languages in which the foreign [a]-type vowel is rendered as the PALM vowel, e.g. *sonata*, *rajah*. But uncertainty arises through the fact that the TRAP vowel is also used to render foreign-language [a]. Thus for example *pasta* and *Nicaragua* usually have stressed /æ/ in Britain, but /ɑ/ in the United States, while conversely *morale* and *Iran* usually have /ɑː/ in Britain and /æ/ in the United States. (Words such as the last-mentioned have been appropriately included in the standard lexical set BATH.)

Two words which are well-known and therefore useful for testing this vowel in British speech are *tomato* and *lager*. In the United States, however, *tomato* belongs with FACE while *lager* fluctuates between PALM and THOUGHT. Several other words assigned to PALM on the strength of their pronunciation in cultivated speech have variants with other vowels in popular speech: *PEAS* shows *calm* with /æ/ very widely in the midland and southern states along the Atlantic (though the *Linguistic atlas of the upper midwest* (*LAUM*) shows that this pronunciation does not extend to the upper midwest).

Insofar as it occurs in native English words, the PALM vowel derives from Middle English /au/ or /a/ with lengthening. This lengthening is essentially the same as that in BATH words (2.2.7), and it has not been satisfactorily explained how GenAm comes to have /ɑ/ in *father*, *palm*, etc., but not in *calf*, *halve*, and the other BATH words. In stressed final free syllables, e.g. *spa*, *pa*, an earlier pronunciation had the vowel of THOUGHT, which persists to some extent in old-fashioned and rural speech, as do various other pronunciations (see for example *PEAS*: 164–5). This reflects the fact that the use of a fully open vowel in a free syllable is a phonotactic innovation for any rhotic accent.

(64) is an attempt at an exhaustive listing of generally known PALM words. (64a) comprises the few words, other than *palm* itself, which are thoroughly native, while (64b) lists words relatively recently borrowed from foreign languages. The appendix, (64′), comprises words which have /ɑː/ in RP but fluctuate in GenAm between /ɑ/ and /æ/, hovering therefore between our standard lexical sets BATH and PALM.

(64) PALM (a) *calm, balm, psalm, alms, father,*
bra, ma, pa, mamma, pappa, aha,
ah, ha(h), blah, hurrah;[1]

(b) *baht, Bach, façade, couvade, roulade, raj, taj,*
salaam, Brahms, Kahn, Afrikaans, kraal, Transvaal, Taj Mahal,
spa, Shah, Pooh-Bah, Armagh, schwa,
cantata, inamorato, legato, sonata, staccato, pizzicato, Lusaka, Karachi, mafia,[2]
Dada, bravado, incommunicado, Mahdi, Mikado, laager, lager,[1]
Zhivago, (maha)rajah, kava, guava, Java, Swazi,
Dali, Mali, Guatemala, Somali(a),
lama, llama, Yokohama, swami, Brahmin, guano, piano ('softly'), *marijuana, iguana, Botswana, (maha)rani,*
ha-ha, Malawi, Bahai, Sumatra, candelabra.[3]

[1] GenAm also with /ɔ/.
[2] RP also with /æ/.
[3] also with other vowels.

(64′) *baa, bah,*
Koran, khan, Pakistan, Shan, chorale, rationale, locale,
khaki, pasha, Nazi,
Colorado, enchilada, Nevada, aubade, lava, palaver, plaza,
almond, drama, pajama/pyjama, panorama,
Ghana, nirvana, sultana, soprano, piranha, Bali, finale.

2.2.13 THOUGHT

The standard lexical set THOUGHT is defined as comprising those words whose citation form in RP and GenAm has the stressed vowel /ɔ(ː)/, excluding cases where this vowel is followed by non-prevocalic /r/ in GenAm. (The latter are treated under NORTH,

2.2.22. For comments on the use of the length-mark in RP but not GenAm, see 2.2.10; the THOUGHT vowel is relatively long in both accents.) This constitutes only a subset of words with /ɔ(ː)/; other words with RP /ɔː/ belong to NORTH (2.2.22) or FORCE (2.2.23), while other words with GenAm /ɔ/ belong to CLOTH (2.2.8) or, with following /r/, to NORTH (2.2.22). Phonetically there is a considerable difference in quality between RP /ɔː/ and GenAm /ɔ/, in spite of the use of the same phonetic symbol to represent them. In present-day mainstream RP, /ɔː/ is a back closely-rounded mid vocoid, lying therefore between cardinals 6 and 7 (though old-fashioned RP has an opener quality). GenAm /ɔ/ is opener, namely between cardinals 5 and 6, and has only open lip-rounding. This vowel occurs in both checked and free syllables. Some of the words belonging to this set are listed in (65).

The THOUGHT vowel has various origins. Among them are Middle English /au/ and /ɔu/ followed by a velar fricative (3.1.3–4 below) and /au/ alone. The spellings *augh*, *ough*, and *au/aw/al* correspond to these different possibilities.

Most accents agree with the standard ones in having a mid to open back rounded monophthong for this vowel. In some forms of North American English, though, it has lost its roundedness and fallen in with the /ɑ/ of PALM and LOT (THOUGHT–LOT Merger, vol. 3, 6.1.2). Closing diphthongs are found in two regional accents: an [ɒo] type in much of the American south, and (in checked syllables only) an [ɔo] type in Cockney. A centring diphthong, [ɔə], is characteristic of New York speech and, in free syllables, of Cockney.

Within the list (65), the words in (65b) have variants with /ɒ/ in RP and also in the north of England. As can be seen, they are cases where the vowel is followed by /l/ plus a consonant.

(65) THOUGHT (a) *taught, caught, Maugham, Vaughan, Waugh,*
naughty, haughty, slaughter, daughter,
ought, bought, wrought, brought, fought, nought,
    sought,
taut, auk, debauch, sauce,
applaud, cause, faun, haul, Paul,
autumn, author, taunt, laundry, gauntlet,…;
gawp, hawk, crawl, shawm, awn, yawn,
jaw, law, saw, draw, awe,…;
chalk, talk, walk, stalk, caulk,

> *all, fall, small, wall, appal, instal, Raleigh,*[1] ...;
> *bald, water, broad;*
>
> (b) *halt, salt, malt, false,*
> *alter, also, alderman, walrus,* ...;
> *fault, vault.*

[1] RP also with /æ, ɑː/.

2.2.14 GOAT

The standard lexical set GOAT is defined as comprising those words whose citation form has the stressed vowel /əʊ/ in RP and /o/ in GenAm. The two accents agree substantially in the lexical incidence of this vowel. Phonetically, GenAm /o/ is a back half-close rounded monophthong or narrow closing diphthong, [o ~ oʊ], whereas RP /əʊ/ is now typically a diphthong with a mid central unrounded starting-point (similar to the quality of RP /ɜː/) moving towards a somewhat closer and backer lightly rounded second element [ʊ]. Distributionally, this vowel occurs in both checked and free syllables. Some of the words belonging to it are listed in (66).

The GOAT vowel has the traditional name 'long O'. It derives in most cases via the Great Vowel Shift (3.1.1 below) from Middle English /ɔː/, or, in consequence of the GOAT Merger (3.1.5 below), from /ɔu/. These two origins correspond to (66a) and (66b) respectively. Typical spellings associated with (66a) are *o, oCe, oa,* and with (66b) *ow, o* before *l.* Words in which a vowel historically identical with that of GOAT occurs before historical /r/ are dealt with in section 2.2.23 below, as the standard lexical set FORCE.

This vowel is particularly variable both regionally and socially, and may be found with a variety of monophthongal and diphthongal qualities ranging from [oː] to [eɤ], [ɐʊ] and [ʊə]. The use of a monophthong reflects the absence of Long Mid Diphthonging (3.1.12 below), and is a generally northern pronunciation both in England and in the United States, as well as characterizing the Celtic countries and the West Indies – being thus a kind of mirror image of FACE. The diphthongal variants, though, are not symmetrical with those of FACE. In particular, GOAT Advancement (3.2.8 below) has given central or front starting-points to the diphthong in much of England, in the southern hemisphere, and in the 'middle Atlantic' area of the eastern United States. As a consequence of Diphthong Shift (3.4.2 below) this starting-point may also be relatively open. A half-close central rounded vowel, [ɵ:], and a centring diphthong, [oə], are found in Tyneside speech, while an opening diphthong, [ʊɔ] etc., is typical of popular West Indian accents. In London and elsewhere, a following /l/ triggers an allophonic variant, e.g. s[ɒʊ]*l* but s[əʊ]*p*.

(66)   GOAT   (a)   *soap, boat, oak, roach, loaf, oath,*
                     road, loathe, coal, roam, loan, boast, coax, . . . ;
                     note, rope, joke, both, gross,
                     robe, code, rogue, grove, clothe, rose,
                     hole, home, tone,
                     so, no, toe, foe, don't, host,
                     noble, ocean, explosion, holy, . . . ;
                     brooch, beau, gauche, mauve;
            (b)   *bowl, own, tow, know, grow, owe, Owen, . . . ;*
                     soul, poultry, mould/mold, shoulder, . . . ;
                     colt, holster, old, bold, soldier, . . . ;
                     roll, scroll, control, . . . ;
                     sew, dough, though, although.

2.2.15 GOOSE

The standard lexical set GOOSE is defined as comprising those words whose citation form in RP and GenAm has the stressed vowel /u(:)/. (For comments on the use of the length-mark in RP but not GenAm, see 2.2.10 above; in both accents the general phonetic nature of this vowel could be adequately represented in either way, or indeed as /ʊu/, /ʊw/, /u:w/, etc.) The two accents agree substantially in the lexical incidence of this vowel. Phonetically, /u(:)/ is a relatively long close back vocoid, often with some degree of diphthongization of the [ʊu] type, particularly in free position. It is often somewhat centralized from fully back. Distributionally, this vowel occurs in both checked and free position. Some of the words belonging to this set are listed in (67).

This vowel is frequently preceded by a palatal semivowel /j/ (or, as it may conveniently be called, a **yod**). When this is the case the sequence /ju(:)/ has the traditional name 'long U'. Where the GOOSE vowel is not preceded by yod it has no traditional name, though expressions such as 'long *oo*' are sometimes used. It derives in most cases via the Great Vowel Shift from Middle English /o:/ or, after Early Yod Dropping, from /iu/ or /ɛu/; where no Yod Dropping occurred these Middle English diphthongs correspond to current /ju(:)/. Words exemplifying the GOOSE vowel with historically no preceding yod are listed in (67a), words which had or still have a preceding yod in (67b). For a discussion of the circumstances under which the yod was lost or alternatively retained, see under Early Yod Dropping (3.1.10 below) and Later Yod Dropping (3.3.3 below). GenAm reflects more widespread Yod Dropping than RP and most other British accents.

The usual spellings for this vowel are *oo* (67a) and *ue, uCe, u, eu, ew* (67b). Words in which a vowel historically identical with that of GOOSE occurs before historical /r/ are dealt with in section 2.2.24 below, as the standard lexical set CURE.

Many accents have a definitely central rather than back quality for GOOSE – e.g. most English popular urban speech, that of Scotland and Northern Ireland, that of the southern hemisphere and the southern United States. In general, a back quality may be seen as indicative of a conservative type of accent, e.g. southern Irish, West Indian. Elocutionary norms of beauty prescribe a fully back [u:] and may thus conflict with the wish to avoid markedly old-fashioned speech habits. Overall, centralling clearly occurs more readily after /j/, less readily before dark /l/; with the further development of L Vocalization (3.4.4 below), this may give rise to a phonemic split of the type *two* vs. *tool*, with [ʉ:] and [u:] etc. respectively. The degree of diphthongization also varies considerably in different accents. It is most marked, [əʉ ~ əʊ], in Cockney and Australian.

(67) GOOSE (a) *loop, shoot, spook, smooch, proof, tooth, loose, tarboosh, boob, mood, Moog, groove, smooth, choose, boom, spoon, fool, too, boost, schooner, booty,...; move, prove, lose, whose,...; tomb, do, who, two,...; group, youth, ghoul, you, Vancouver, through,...;*

          (b) *dupe, mute, duke, truth, obtuse, cube, rude, fugue, huge, amuse, plume, tune, mule, blue, funeral, lucre, prudent,...; flu, duty, pupil, mucus, lucid, crucial, confusion, ludicrous, music, human, lunatic,...; sleuth, deuce, feud, neutral, feudal, eunuch,...;*

newt, lewd, few, knew, pewter, sewage,...;
fruit, juice, cruise, nuisance,...;
view, review,
beauty, beautiful.

2.2.16 PRICE

The standard lexical set PRICE is defined as comprising those words whose citation form in RP and GenAm has the stressed vowel /aɪ/. The two accents agree substantially in the lexical incidence of this vowel in stressed syllables. Phonetically, it is a wide diphthong with a starting-point which is open, unrounded, and most usually centralized-front, [aɪ], though front and central variants, [aɪ ~ ɑ+ɪ] are also common within the standard accents. The diphthong glide is in the direction of [ɪ]. Distributionally, this vowel occurs in both checked and free position. Some of the words belonging to this set are listed in (68).

The PRICE vowel has the traditional name 'long I'. It derives in almost all cases from Middle English /iː/ via the Great Vowel Shift (3.1.1 below). The usual spellings are *iCe, ie, i*, and *y*. This vowel enters into morphological alternations with KIT, as *decide–decision, write–written*.

In other accents we find four main types of variation: in the degree of advancement of the starting-point, in the degree of openness of the starting-point, in the quality of the second element, and in the 'speed' of the diphthong. Very back starting-points, [ɑɪ ~ ɒɪ] are characteristic of the urban south of England, the southern hemisphere, and New York speech (Diphthong Shift, 3.4.2 below); front ones, [aɪ] etc. are typical of the north of England, and less open [ɛɪ] (in certain environments) of Tyneside and Northern Ireland. A starting-point that is not fully open, [ɐɪ ~ ʌɪ ~ əɪ], is typical of the rural south of England, of Barbados, and of parts of the north-eastern United States. In Canada, Virginia, and coastal South Carolina there is marked allophonic differentiation, with a narrower diphthong [ɐɪ ~ ʌɪ ~ əɪ] before a voiceless consonant and a wide one, [ɑɪ] etc., in all other environments. Some degree of allophonic differentiation of this kind is also found in upstate New York speech.

A 'slow' diphthong, with a prolonged first element, is often associated with a reduction in the extent of the diphthongal glide, so that the second element is no closer than [ɛ] or [ə], giving a diphthong of the type [aːɛ ~ aːə], or an outright monophthong, [aː]. These variants are particularly characteristic of the American south. But diphthongs with a weakened second element also occur more widely as optional variants; they are found in London speech, in Manchester and Leeds, in South Africa, in Australia, and in Jamaica.

In Scotland, Ulster and Tyneside it is common to find two diphthongs, perhaps phonologically distinct, in PRICE words (see vol. 2, 4.4.11, 5.2.4, 5.3.14).

The PRICE vowel is particularly subject to Smoothing (3.2.9 below), e.g. in words such as *science, fire*.

(68) PRICE (a) *ripe, write, like, knife, ice,*
tribe, side, arrive, writhe, rise,
time, fine, mile, fire, die, tried, ... ;
Friday, tiger, silent, violent, liar, science,
indict /ɪnˈdaɪt/, *isle* /aɪl/, *child, pint, find, ninth, Christ,*
viscount /ˈvaɪkaʊnt/, *bicycle, island,*
hi-fi, chi, ... ;
type, try, Cyprus, hybrid, dye, Glynde, ... ;
eider, kaleidoscope, eye, height, aisle, buy, choir
/ˈkwaɪə(r)/.
(b) *fight, high, sign,* ... .

2.2.17 CHOICE

The standard lexical set CHOICE is defined as comprising those words whose citation form in RP and GenAm has the stressed vowel /ɔɪ/. The two accents agree substantially in the lexical incidence of this vowel. Phonetically, it is a wide diphthong with a starting-point which is back, rounded, and approximately half-open, gliding towards a closer and fronter unrounded second element, [ɪ]. Distributionally, this vowel occurs in both checked and free position. Some of the words belonging to this set are listed in (69).

The CHOICE vowel has no traditional name. It derives in most cases from Middle English /ɔi/ or /ui/. All these words are believed to be ultimately loan-words, mainly from Old French. A few words with Middle English /iː/ also became CHOICE words, as discussed in

3.1.11 below. The usual spellings for all these categories are *oi, oy*.

The historical interaction of the CHOICE and PRICE sets is discussed in 3.1.11 below. Some conservative rural accents reflect a merger or partial merger of the two diphthongs – in parts of the south of England, where a diphthong of the [ɒɪ] type is used in both PRICE and CHOICE, and in parts of Ireland, the United States, and the West Indies, where diphthongs of the [aɪ ~ ɑɪ] type are encountered.

The diphthong of CHOICE is not everywhere clearly distinct from the sequence /ɔ(:)/ plus /ɪ/ (THOUGHT plus KIT). This sequence, however, arises only across a morpheme boundary, as *rawest* (compare *moist*), *cawing* (compare *coin*). Where they are distinct, as in the standard accents, transcriptional confusion may arise unless (i) length-marks are used, as /'rɔːɪst/ vs. /mɔɪst/, or (ii) the morphological boundary is indicated explicitly, as /rɔ#ɪst/.

Where NURSE has the variant [ɜɪ], as in New York City, this may not always be distinct from CHOICE. Then homophones such as *earl – oil* [ɜɪl] result.

(69) CHOICE (a) *boy, toy, joy, annoy, oyster...*;
                    noise, voice, choice, rejoice,
                    void, moist...;
            (b) *coin, join, oil, boil, soil, spoil, toil,*
                    poison, ointment...;
                    buoy, employ...;
            (c) *groin, hoist, joist.*

2.2.18 MOUTH

The standard lexical set MOUTH is defined as comprising those words whose citation form in RP and GenAm has the stressed vowel /aʊ/. The two accents agree substantially in the lexical incidence of this vowel. Phonetically, it is a wide diphthong with a starting-point which is open, unrounded, and most usually central, about halfway between cardinals [a] and [ɑ]; though centralized-front and centralized-back variants, [a̘−ʊ ~ ɑ̟+ʊ], are also common within the standard accents. The diphthong glide is in the direction of [ʊ], though so close and back a point is not always achieved. Distributionally, this vowel occurs in both checked and free position. There are, nevertheless, phonotactic constraints on the consonants it may precede: it does not occur before labials or velars (if we disregard names, as *Cowper*, and traditional-dialect words, as *gowk*). Some of the words belonging to this set are listed in (70).

The MOUTH vowel has no traditional name. It derives in almost all cases from Middle English /uː/ via the Great Vowel Shift (3.1.1 below). The usual spellings are *ou* and *ow*.

In other accents we find four main types of variation: in the degree of advancement of the starting-point, in the degree of openness of the starting-point, in the quality of the second element, and in the 'speed' of the diphthong. Very back starting-points, [ɑ ~ ɔ], are characteristic of southern Africa and the West Indies; very front ones, [æ ~ ɛ ~e], of the south of England and (in the case of [æ]) of the American south. A half-open or even closer starting-point, [ɐ ~ ʌ ~ ə], is associated particularly with old-fashioned and rural speech, and also with Scotland (where it may be seen as a compromise between Scots [u] and standard [aʊ]).

In several areas there is marked allophonic differentiation, with a narrower diphthong, [ʌʊ ~ əʊ], used before a voiceless consonant, and a wider one, [aʊ] etc., used elsewhere: this is characteristic of Virginia and of coastal South Carolina in the United States, and one of the striking features of Canadian speech in general.

The second element of the MOUTH diphthong is usually relatively close, back, and rounded. A front and unrounded, or barely rounded, second element is found in some parts of the south of England, [ɛɪ] etc., and in Ulster, [ɑɨ ~ aʉ] etc. A mid central second element, [æə], is one of the variants common in London Cockney, as is a monophthong, [æː ~ aː].

Markedly 'slower' diphthongs, with a prolonged first element, are characteristic of the American south.

The MOUTH vowel is particularly subject to Smoothing (3.2.9 below), e.g. in words such as *power, hour*.

(70) MOUTH   *out, pouch, south, house,*
                 loud, gouge, mouth v., *rouse,*
                 noun, foul, thou,
                 count, round, pronounce, oust,
                 flour, sour, trousers, mountain, council, boundary, . . . ;
                 crowd, browse, owl, down, cow, allow,
                 dowry, flower, coward, towel, powder, . . . ;
                 bough, plough/plow, doughty, . . . ;
                 MacLeod.

2.2.19 NEAR

The standard lexical set NEAR is defined as comprising those words whose citation form contains the stressed vowel /ɪə/ in RP (with or without a following intersyllabic /r/) and the sequence /ɪr/ in GenAm. Only certain instances of RP /ɪə/ do in fact correspond to GenAm /ɪr/, and most of them are listed in (71); many others correspond to the sequence /iə/, as exemplified in (71'), though this is rare in stressed syllables. Neither do all instances of GenAm /ɪr/ belong in NEAR; a relatively small number of words such as *spirit*, where it corresponds to the same /ɪr/ sequence in RP, are appropriately assigned to KIT (2.2.1). Phonetically, RP /ɪə/ is a centring diphthong with a starting-point that is unrounded and fairly close and front, [ɪ], moving towards a mid central [ə] quality. GenAm /ɪ/ before non-prevocalic /r/ may in practice often have a rather similar, [ɪə]-type realization, though this is only an allophonic variant of /ɪ/. RP /ɪə/ is most commonly found in free position, as in (71a), or before tautosyllabic /r/, as in (71c); it is rare in syllables checked by other consonants, as in (71b), except where the consonant is an inflectional /d/ or /z/, as in *cheer # ed* /tʃɪəd/ or *cheer # s*. Other inflectional endings yield many further instances of the NEAR vowel before tautosyllabic /r/, as *cheer # ing* /'tʃɪərɪŋ/, *near # er*.

The NEAR vowel has no traditional name, although of course in GenAm it is seen as an instance of 'short I'. Some dictionaries treat it as a 'long E', or as a sequence of 'long E' plus schwa, which reflects not only historical fact but also synchronic morphological alternations such as *severe–severity*, RP /sɪ'vɪə, sɪ'verətɪ/, compare *serene –serenity*. Its origin is indeed most usually Middle English /eː/ or /ɛː/, identical with that of FLEECE, but in the environment of a following /r/ (now lost in RP except prevocalically), as discussed in 3.2.1–2 below. Corresponding spellings are used for NEAR: *eer, ere, erV, ier, eir, ear*.

The opposition between KIT and NEAR in the environment of a following prevocalic /r/, although lost in GenAm, remains in certain regional American accents and in all accents outside North America. It is, however, not an easy opposition to demonstrate. It appears most tangibly in a pair such as *mirror* vs. *nearer*, which rhyme in GenAm (/'mɪrər, 'nɪrər/) but not in RP (/'mɪrə, 'nɪərə/). The closest approach to a minimal pair is *spirit* vs. *spear it*; although the latter is orthographically two words, it behaves as one since *it* is an enclitic. There is no minimal pair with identical morphological composition. Other possible test pairs are not minimal, and are usually open to the further objection of including relatively rare or learned words or proper names: *spirit* vs. *experience, myriad* vs. *period, Syria* vs. *Liberia, hysteria*, or *inferior.* The pair *delirious* vs. *mysterious*, which on historical grounds ought to exemplify the opposition, often fails in Britain because of the recent spread of a new pronunciation /dɪˈlɪərɪəs/ alongside the traditional /dɪˈlɪrɪəs/. The dog-star *Sirius* (vs. *serious*) is sometimes pronounced with PRICE rather than KIT. Even where these pairs are distinct there is the further problem of deciding what the appropriate phonemicization is of the NEAR vowel which contrasts with /ɪ/. For RP and many other accents it seems appropriate to recognize a diphthong phoneme /ɪə/; but elsewhere phonemic identification can be made with the /i(ː)/ of FLEECE (Scotland, Ireland, some American southern and New England, some parts of England, Wales), or perhaps with other vowels.

In environments other than that of a following prevocalic /r/ all accents retain the opposition between KIT and NEAR, so that *bid* is everywhere distinct from *beard.* Again, though, the opposition is not necessarily one of /ɪ/ vs. /ɪr ~ ɪə/: the vowel of *beard, fear* is sometimes to be identified with the /i(ː)/ of FLEECE, as above, but also sometimes with a disyllabic sequence of /i(ː)/ plus /ə/ (non-rhotic British and northern US accents) or with a sequence of /j/ plus the /ɜː ~ ɜr/ of NURSE (Virginia and adjacent parts of the American south, west of England, south Wales). NEAR words may also have a diphthong phoneme best symbolized /eə/, on the grounds of its phonetic quality (much American southern) and/or its having merged with SQUARE (some East Anglia and New Zealand). In the West Indies /iː/ may be used in the environment of a following prevocalic /r/, as *serious*, but /e: ~ eə/ otherwise, as *beard, fear.*

Many non-rhotic accents have a NEAR diphthong with a less centralized starting-point than that of RP /ɪə/, namely a diphthong of the type [iə]. This is true of London speech, for example. Southern-hemisphere accents, on the other hand, tend to smooth the diphthong into a monophthongal [ɪː]. In free position, as *here, dear*, the /jɜː/ variant with a shift of prominence to the second element may sometimes be accompanied by a noticeable opening of this second element, giving [hjʌː ∼ çɑː], [djʌː ∼ djaː] etc. Such pronunciations have often been considered to fall within RP, although they clearly do not belong in its mainstream. Gimson characterizes them (1980: 7.28) as belonging to 'some kinds of advanced and conservative RP', and the openest [ɑː] forms as 'an affectation'. Indeed, to me they suggest the special accent either of an aristocratic Bertie Wooster (the model of an upper-class twit) or else of an army sergeant-major.

It is, however, very usual in RP and similar accents to have an allophonic alternation with /ɪə/ involving a rather opener second element in word-final (and particularly utterance-final) environments than elsewhere.

(71)   NEAR   (a)   *beer, deer, career, . . . ;*
                    here, mere, sincere, interfere, . . . ;
                    bier, pier, cashier, . . . ;
                    weir;
                    fear, ear, appear, yearling, . . . ;
             (b)   *fierce, pierce;*
                    weird, Deirdre;
                    beard;
             (c)   *serious, mysterious, period, serum, diphtheria, hero,*[1] *. . . ;*
                    eerie, peerage, Madeira, dreary, weary.

(71′)[2]   *idea, Korea, diarrh(o)ea, Galatea, . . . ;*
                    European, Jacobean, Crimean, . . . ;
                    ratafia, Maria, Sophia, . . . ;
                    museum, Colosseum, Te Deum, . . ;
                    real, ideal.

[1] GenAm also /ˈhiro/.
[2] several of these words also have RP variants with /iːə/. See 3.2.9 below.

2.2.20 SQUARE

The standard lexical set SQUARE is defined as comprising those words whose citation form contains the stressed vowel /ɛə/ in RP (with or without a following intersyllabic /r/) and the sequence /ɛr/ (or, alternatively, /ær/) in GenAm. Almost all instances of RP /ɛə/ do correspond to GenAm /ɛr ∼ ær/ (on the question of the choice between these two GenAm possibilities, see vol. 3, 6.1.5). But not all instances of GenAm /ɛr ∼ ær/ belong in SQUARE; a number of words such as *merry*, where it corresponds to RP /ɛr/, and a number of words such as *barrow*, where it corresponds to RP /ær/, are appropriately assigned to DRESS (2.2.2) and TRAP (2.2.3) respectively. Phonetically, RP /ɛə/ is a centring diphthong with a starting-point which is front, unrounded, and approximately half-open (ranging in fact from the phonemic norm of /e/ in DRESS to that of /æ/ in TRAP), moving towards a mid central quality, thus [ɛə]. GenAm /ɛ/ before non-prevocalic /r/ may in practice often have a rather similar, [ɛə]-type realization, though this is only an allophonic variant of /ɛ/. RP /ɛə/ is most commonly found in free position, as in (72a), or before tautosyllabic /r/, as in (72c); it is extremely rare in syllables checked by other consonants, as in (72b), except where the consonant is an inflectional /d/ or /z/, as in *share # d* /ʃɛəd/ or *share # s* /ʃɛəz/. Other inflectional endings yield many further instances of the SQUARE vowel before tautosyllabic /r/, as *shar # ing* /ˈʃɛərɪŋ/, *fair # er* /ˈfɛərə/.

The SQUARE vowel has no traditional name, although of course in GenAm it can be seen as an instance of 'short E' (or 'short A'). Some dictionaries treat it as a 'long A', or as a sequence of 'long A' plus schwa; this does in fact reflect not only historical fact but also synchronic morphological alternations (though few in number), thus *compare – comparison*, RP /kəmˈpɛə, kəmˈpærɪsn̩/, parallel with *sane – sanity*. Its origin is indeed most commonly Middle English /aː/ or /ai/, like FACE, in the environment of a following /r/ (now lost in RP except prevocalically), as discussed in 3.2.1–2 below. Other SQUARE words had Middle English /ɛː/ in the same environment. Corresponding spellings are used for SQUARE: *are, ar*V, *air, ear* plus occasional further possibilities.

The opposition between SQUARE and DRESS in the environment of a following prevocalic /r/ is easily tested by pairs such as *Mary–merry, fairy–ferry, bearer–error*. Although typically lost in GenAm, this opposition remains in all accents outside North America. Within the United States the distinction is found only in parts of the east and south. The same is true of the opposition between SQUARE and TRAP in the same environment, easily tested by pairs such as *Mary–marry, hairy–Harry, rarity–parity, a parent– apparent*. For discussion of the partial or complete loss of this triple distinction in North America see 3.3.1 below and vol. 3, 6.1.5. Where the oppositions are maintained there is still the question of deciding what is the appropriate phonemicization of the SQUARE vowel. In some accents, such as most Scottish and some Irish, it is clearly to be equated with FACE, as /e(ː)/. This is also right for most American southern and New England speech. Elsewhere, as in RP, it seems appropriate to recognize an additional vowel phoneme (diphthongal in RP and New York, otherwise quite often monophthongal), as RP /ɛə/.

In environments other than that of a following prevocalic /r/ all accents retain the opposition between SQUARE and DRESS (and TRAP), so that *shared* is always distinct from *shed* (and *shad*). In much English and southern-hemisphere speech, and in Wales, the opposition exemplified by *shed* vs. *shared* is one of duration rather than quality, [ʃɛd] vs. [ʃɛːd] etc. Elsewhere the vowel of *scarce, fair* etc. is sometimes to be identified with /e(ː)/ (in rhotic accents, as above) and sometimes to be regarded as a distinct phoneme /ɛə/.

The opposition of NEAR and SQUARE is lost categorially in the West Indies and variably in certain other areas (East Anglia, New Zealand, the American south). In some parts of the north of England the opposition of SQUARE and NURSE is lost, so that [ɜː]-like qualities may be heard in SQUARE words.

RP /ɛə/ often involves very little diphthongal movement. As with the other centring diphthongs, it typically has a rather opener second element in word-final (sentence-final) position than elsewhere.

(72) SQUARE   (a) *care, share, bare*, . . . ;
              air, fair, pair, . . . ;
              bear, pear, wear, swear, . . . ;
              heir, their, there, where, Ayr, Eyre, prayer, mayor;[1]
  (b) *scarce*;
  (c) *vary, canary, Mary, aquarium, various, rarity, area, Pharaoh*, . . . ;
              dairy, prairie, fairy, . . . ;
              aerial, [2] *Dun Laoghaire, Eire.*

[1] GenAm also /ˈmeɪər/, rhyming with *player*.
[2] GenAm also /eɪˈɪriəl/, rhyming with *imperial*.

2.2.21 START

The standard lexical set START is defined as comprising those words whose citation form contains the stressed vowel /ɑː/ in RP (with or without a following intersyllabic /r/) and the sequence /ɑr/

in GenAm. Although this covers many instances of RP /ɑː/, others belong in BATH (2.2.7) or PALM (2.2.12). Almost all instances of GenAm non-prevocalic /ɑr/ belong in START.

Phonetically, the /ɑː/ of RP START–BATH–PALM is a fully open unrounded vowel lying between back and central, [ɑ̟ː]. In GenAm, START words have the vowel of LOT followed by /r/: for a phonetic description, see under LOT (2.2.4). RP /ɑː/ is common in free position (73a) and checked by a consonant other than /r/ (73b); it is rare in the environment of a following /r/ (73c), except where a morpheme beginning with a vowel follows an item such as might be included in (73a), e.g. *starring* /ˈstɑːrɪŋ/, *starry* /ˈstɑːrɪ/, *a st*[ɑːr] *is born*, all from *star* /stɑː/.

The START vowel has no traditional name, although in GenAm it can be seen as an instance of 'short O'. Its origin is usually Middle English /ar/, via Pre-R Lengthening (3.1.8 below) and, in the case of RP and other non-rhotic accents, R Dropping (3.2.2 below). The usual spelling is accordingly *ar, arC.*

The most important phonetic variation with START concerns the degree of advancement of the vowel. Both RP and GenAm have central to back qualities, as already mentioned. Front realizations, in the vicinity of cardinal 4, [aː], are characteristic of many parts of the north of England, of Australia and New Zealand and of eastern New England. Particularly back qualities are found in New York City and in South Africa.

In a few places START is merged with NORTH. In Jamaica, Guyana, and the Leeward Islands this is the case in popular speech, with [a-ː]-type vowels in both sets; so also in some rural speech of Hampshire and Wiltshire. In the Delmarva peninsula of the United States, and in some rural southern and midwestern speech, they are merged into a back rounded quality, [ɒ ~ ɔ]. The West Indian accents where this applies are non-rhotic or semi-rhotic, the American ones rhotic. It can be tested by pairs such as *barn–born, farm–form, chart–short.*

(73) START (a) *far, star, bar,...;*
                    bazaar, Saar;
             (b) *sharp, part, bark, arch, scarf, farce, harsh,*
                    garb, card, large, carve, parse,
                    farm, barn, snarl, Charles,

party, *market, marvellous,* . . . ;
heart, hearken, hearth;
sergeant;
aardvark;

(c) *sari, Bari, safari, cascara, curare, Mata Hari*[1], *aria*[1],
scenario[1], *Sahara*[1], *tiara*[1].

[1] GenAm also /ær ~ ɛr/.

2.2.22 NORTH

The standard lexical set NORTH is defined as comprising those
words whose citation form contains the stressed vowel /ɔː/ in RP
and the sequence /ɔr/ in GenAm, or rather in that variety of GenAm
which retains the opposition between /ɔr/ and /or/. This covers only
a minority of words with RP /ɔː/; others belong in THOUGHT (2.2.13)
or FORCE (2.2.23) perhaps also in CURE (2.2.24) or CLOTH (2.2.8). In
the variety of GenAm in question most words containing the sequence /ɔr/ belong in the set NORTH, except where /ɔr/ is followed by
a vowel; in the latter case the corresponding RP vowel is usually /ɒ/,
so that such words are appropriately included in the set CLOTH. For
the variety of GenAm which does not distinguish /ɔr/ and /or/ (e.g.
horse = hoarse), many words containing the merged /ɔr/ belong in
the set FORCE.

The phonetic quality of the NORTH vowel has been treated under
THOUGHT above (2.2.13). Distributionally, there are very few
NORTH words in which the /ɔː ~ ɔr/ is word-final, (74a), or pre-
vocalic, (74c); usually a consonant follows, as (74b).

The NORTH vowel has no traditional name. Historically it usually
derives from Middle English short /ɔ/ plus /r/ via Pre-R
Lengthening (3.1.8 below). Prevocalically, this sequence remained
short in RP, giving contemporary /ɒ/; the words in (74c) are thus
exceptional. To them can be added the only word formed by adding
a suffix beginning with a vowel to a stem from (74a), namely
warring.

The usual spellings are *or*, and *ar* where the preceding sound is
/w/. The *or* spelling is ambiguous as between NORTH and FORCE;
since NORTH and FORCE are merged in very many accents, comprehensive lists of the membership of these sets are supplied below.

Regionally, there is not a great deal of variation in the NORTH vowel other than what has been described already under THOUGHT (2.2.13), with which NORTH is in any case merged in non-rhotic accents. The rural START – NORTH merger mentioned above (2.2.21) usually results in [ɑː]-type qualities in England and the West Indies but rounded [ɒ]-type qualities in the United States. Those American accents in which THOUGHT has become unrounded and merged with PALM–LOT (vol. 3, 6.1.2) retain a rounded, [ɔ]-type vowel in NORTH.

(74)   NORTH   (a)   *or, for, nor, Thor;*
        war;

        (b)   *Thorpe, assort, cavort, consort, distort, exhort, resort, re-*
              tort, short, snort, tort, cork, fork, stork, torque, York,
              scorch, torch, morph, gorse, horse, remorse,
              orb, absorb, accord, chord, cord, lord, re'cord, George,
              gorge,
              corm, form, reform, storm, adorn, born, corn, horn, morn,
              porn, scorn, shorn, thorn, corpse,
              porpoise, torpid, torpor, fortify, fortunate, fortune,
              important,[1] *corporal, importunate, mortal, mortar,*
              shorten, tortoise, orchestra, orchid, Dorking, torture,
              forfeit, morpheme, morphia, morphine, orthodox,
              torso,
              orbit, order, border, ordinary, organ, organism, organize,
              Morgan,
              dormer, Mormon, normal, ornament, corner, forward,
              fortress;
              quart, quarter,[2] *quartz, sward, swarm, swarthy, warble,*
              ward, warden, wardrobe, warlock, warm, warmth,
              warn, warp, Warsaw, wart;

        (c)   *aura, aural, Laura, Taurus.*

[1] in accents other than GenAm usually a FORCE word.
[2] GenAm also /ˈkwɒtər/.

2.2.23 FORCE

The standard lexical set FORCE is defined as comprising those words whose citation form contains the stressed vowel /ɔː/ in current mainstream RP and the sequence /or/ in GenAm, or rather in that variety of GenAm which retains the opposition between /ɔr/ and /or/. These qualifications are necessary because in both standard accents the FORCE words, historically distinct from NORTH words, have now become or are now in the process of becoming merged with them. In RP this process is generally complete; some older speakers, though, may retain /ɔə/, distinct from /ɔː/, in some of the FORCE words. (This [ɔə] must not be confused with the London [ɔə], essentially a morpheme-final allophone of /ɔː/, now perhaps achieving phonemic status as discussed in vol. 2, 4.2.5.) In GenAm the FORCE–NORTH opposition (e.g. *hoarse* vs. *horse*) has by no means wholly disappeared, though it is obviously recessive.

The set FORCE covers only a minority of words with RP /ɔː/; others belong in THOUGHT (2.2.13) or NORTH (2.2.22), perhaps also in CURE (2.2.24 below) or CLOTH (2.2.8). In the variety of GenAm which retains the opposition almost all /or/ words belong in FORCE; in the variety which does not, FORCE words contain the same merged /ɔr/ as NORTH.

The phonetic quality of the FORCE vowel has been treated under THOUGHT (2.2.13) for RP, and under GOAT (2.2.14) for GenAm. Before /r/, though, GOAT is often not diphthongal: so GenAm [oʊ] *owe* but [or] (i.e. [oə], itself phonetically a diphthong) *ore*. Distributionally, FORCE occurs readily in word-final position, (75a), preconsonantally (75b), and prevocalically (75c). Subset (75b) is subdivided in accordance with the lexical incidence of /ɔː, ɔə/ in old-fashioned RP: /ɔː/ in (75b i), /ɔə/ in (75b ii).

The FORCE vowel has no traditional name, except insofar as it remains an instance of 'long O'. Historically it usually derives from Middle English long /ɔː/, the same vowel as GOAT, via the Great Vowel Shift (3.1.1 below), in the environment of a following /r/, now lost in RP and other non-rhotic accents except prevocalically. Less commonly it derives from Middle English /oː/ or /uː/, also before /r/. The usual spellings are *or*, *ore*, *oar*, and sometimes *oor*, *our*. The spelling *or*, as noted in 2.2.22, is ambiguous as between NORTH and FORCE.

Regionally, it is obviously important to distinguish the accents which have undergone the FORCE–NORTH Merger (3.2.7 below and vol. 3, 6.1.5) from those which have not. For the former, see discussion in the previous section, 2.2.22. In the latter (where FORCE and NORTH remain distinct) FORCE almost invariably has a vowel phonemically identical with that of GOAT. Thus in Scottish English, for instance, the principal difference between *court* and *coat*, both phonologically and phonetically, is just the presence vs. the absence of [r]. There may of course be allophonic differences dependent on the pre-/r/ environment, as in GenAm, where /o/ is not diphthongal before /r/. In a non-rhotic accent the possibility arises of homophony between FORCE and GOAT, e.g. *court* and *coat* both [kɔːt]. This may indeed be the case in parts of Wales, the American south, and the West Indies; but in all these places a more prestigious accent seems to require that the distinction be preserved in such pairs, either by the use of [oə] in FORCE words or by the actualization of the historical /r/.

(75)   FORCE (a)   *ore, adore, afore, before, bore, chore, core, crore, deplore, explore, fore, galore, gore, ignore, implore, more, ore, pore, restore, score, shore, snore, sore, spore, store, swore, tore, whore, wore, yore;*
                          boar, hoar, oar, roar, soar;
                          floor, door;
                          four, pour;

              (bi)   *deport, export, fort, import, port, report, sport, support, pork, porch, forth, divorce, afford, ford, horde, sword, forge, borne, shorn, sworn, torn, worn, portent, porter, portrait, proportion, Borneo;*

              (bii) *coarse, hoarse, board, hoard, boarder; court, fourth, course, resource, source, mourn,*[1] *courtier, mourning;*[1]

              (c)   *oral, adorable, angora, aurora, borax, boron, choral, Dora, fedora, flora, floral, glory, gory, moron, Nora(h), porous, story, thorax, torus, Tory, censorious, euphoria, gloria, glorious, Gregorian, historian, laborious, memorial, meritorious, moratorium, notorious, pictorial, pretorian, stentorian, thorium, uxorious, Victoria(n),* other words in *-orial, hoary, uproarious.*

       [1] also sometimes with RP /ʊə/, GenAm /ʊr/.

2.2.24 CURE

The standard lexical set CURE is defined as comprising those words whose citation form contains the stressed vowel /ʊə/ in conservative RP and the sequence /ʊr/ in GenAm. The qualification 'conservative' RP is necessary in view of the fact that traditional /ʊə/ is now increasingly being replaced by /ɔː/ in RP (3.2.7 below, CURE – FORCE Merger). A phonetically identical [ʊə] also arises in RP from the sequence /uːə/ through the process of Smoothing e.g. *fewer* (3.2.9 below) [fjʊə]; thus only a proportion of words containing the RP diphthong [ʊə] belong in the set CURE. All GenAm /ʊr/ words belong in it.

Phonetically, RP /ʊə/ is a centring diphthong with a starting-point that is weakly rounded, somewhat close and back, [ʊ], moving towards a mid central [ə] quality. In the varieties of RP where, as is now usual, there is no contrastive /ɔə/, the starting-point may alternatively be rather opener, namely about mid [ǫ +]. GenAm /ʊ/ has been discussed above under FOOT (2.2.6); but in this environment, namely before /r/, there is no opposition /ʊ/ vs. /u/, and in consequence rather [u]-like qualities are occasionally encountered.

Distributionally, the /ʊə(r) ∼ ʊr/ of CURE most commonly occurs in free position (76a) or before a vowel (76c); it is rare preconsonantally (76b).

Like GOOSE, the CURE vowel is frequently preceded by a yod, /j/. Subsets (a) and (c) are further subdivided, into those items (i) which historically had no preceding yod, and those (ii) which had or still have a preceding yod. It so happens that no items in (b) had one. The historical yod was in many cases lost as discussed elsewhere (3.1.10 below, Early Yod Dropping; 3.3.3 below, Later Yod Dropping). GenAm reflects more widespread Yod Dropping than RP and most other British accents.

The CURE vowel has no traditional name, although in GenAm it can be seen as an instance of 'short *oo*'. When preceded by yod, it can be interpreted as a 'long U'. Its origin is the same as that of GOOSE, in the environment of a following /r/ (now lost in RP except prevocalically), namely in most cases Middle English /oː/, /iu/ or /ɛu/. Common spellings are *oor*, *our*, *ure*, *urV*, *eur*.

The opposition between FOOT and CURE in the environment of a following prevocalic /r/, although lost in GenAm, remains in many other accents. It is an opposition of an unusual kind, however: its functional load approaches zero, since there are virtually no words containing [ʊr] in accents which have prevocalic [ʊər] in CURE words. (In my own speech one such word is *courier* ['kʊrɪə], which therefore does not rhyme with *curia* ['kjʊərɪə].) The justification for identifying the vowel of CURE words as something other than that of FOOT in such accents is primarily phonetic: a word such as *insurance* typically has the [ʊə ∼ uː ∼ ɔə ∼ ɔː] of *sure*, not the short [ʊ] of *sugar*.

As with [ɪə], so with [ʊə]: for RP and many other accents it seems appropriate to recognize a diphthong phoneme /ʊə/, although elsewhere phonemic identification can be made with the /u(ː)/ of GOOSE, e.g. Scottish /'fjure/ *fury*. This applies in Scotland, Ireland, some parts of England and Wales, and perhaps in some American eastern speech. But everywhere in England the vowel used in CURE words, whatever it has been till now, is tending to be levelled to the [ɔː] of NORTH–FORCE, just as in RP: ['muːə] *moor* yields to ['mɔː] etc.

In environments other than that of a following prevocalic /r/ all accents retain the opposition between FOOT and CURE so that *should* is everywhere distinct from the end of *insured*. The opposition is not necessarily one of /ʊ/ vs. /ʊr ~ ʊə/: the vowel of *insure, tour* is sometimes to be identified with the /u(ː)/ of GOOSE, as above, plus – in non-rhotic accents – the vowel /ə/, giving a disyllabic sequence. In some places this is levelled, variably or possibly even categorically, with the [ɜː] of NURSE, so that *sure* is [ʃɜː], etc., with a vowel identifiable with that of *shirt*. In yod-dropping East Anglia (vol. 2, 4.3.4) this process can yield several new homophones such as *pure – purr* [pɜː]. Elsewhere, though, this process seems to be restricted to items where RP [ʊə] follows a palatal or palato-alveolar consonant, as [pjɜː] *pure*, [mə'tjɜː ~ mə'tʃɜː] *mature*, but not *[tɜː] *tour*. So *surely* may merge with *Shirley*, and *your* with *year* (if pronounced [jɜː]), but otherwise new homophones are rare. I have the impression that the pronunciation ['ʃɝli] for *surely*, making it homophonous with *Shirley*, is not uncommon in the United States, though works of reference scarcely record it. (*LAUM* records [ʃɝ] for *sure* sporadically in Iowa, Nebraska, and Minnesota; *PEAS* contains no examples of it.)

(76) CURE (ai) *boor, moor, Moor, poor, spoor;*
               amour, dour,[1] *tour, your;*
         (aii) *abjure, adjure, allure, assure, con'jure, demure, endure,*
               ensure, immure, insure, inure, lure, McClure, manure,
               mature, obscure, procure, pure, secure, sure;
         (b) *bourse, gourd, Bourbon,*[2] *bourgeois,*[3] *gourmand, gourmet,*
               tournament,[2] *tourney,*[2] *tourniquet;*[2]
         (ci) *boorish, houri, tourism, tourist;*
         (cii) *Ural, angostura, assurance, bravura, bureau,*[3] *c(a)esura,*
               Huron, incurable, insurance, mural, plural, rural,
               Truro,
               anthurium, centurion, curious, furious, injurious, luxu-

rious, Muriel, penurious, spurious, Uriel,
curate, during, fury, futurity, jury, lurid, maturity, ob-
scurity, purify, purity, security, sulfuric/sulphuric, tel-
lurium, thurible;
Europe, neural, neuron/neurone, pleurisy.

[1] GenAm also /daʊr/.
[2] GenAm also with NURSE vowel.
[3] alternatively stressed on the final syllable.

2.2.25 Weak vowels: *happ*Y, *lett*ER, *comm*A

Although it is convenient to include them in tables of lexical incidence, *happ*Y, *lett*ER, and *comm*A are not really standard lexical sets
in the sense of 2.1.4. They do, though, have indexical and diagnos-
tic value in distinguishing accents.

These are weak (unstressable) vowels occurring word-finally.
Their phonemic identification with strong vowels will usually be
debatable; though it may often be possible to equate *happ*Y with
FLEECE or KIT (occasionally even with FACE), *lett*ER with NURSE, and
*comm*A with STRUT (or non-rhotic NURSE).

The set *happ*Y is exemplified in (77). They include words with
orthographic *-y*, *-ie*, and *-i* (the latter being loanwords from other
languages), as in (77a); and also words with orthographic *-ee*, *-ey*,
-ea (77b). This latter group used once to have the FACE vowel,
although now they have the ordinary *happ*Y vowel; compounds of
day, such as *holiday, yesterday, Sunday, Monday*, still fluctuate, as
spelling pronunciation contends with the normal development.

Until the seventeenth century there existed the possibility, often
exploited in verse, for *happ*Y (type 77a) to have the vowel of PRICE
(at that time a diphthong of the type [əi]). Prior to the Great Vowel
Shift, this involved merely an alternation between short and long
/i(ː)/ (on this see Dobson 1968: §§275, 350).

Most RP, and conservative varieties of GenAm, have [ɪ] for
*happ*Y. This quality is also found in the centre of the north of
England (Manchester, Leeds), in Jamaica, and in the American
south. Rather opener qualities, approaching [ë], are found in
Nottingham and in certain varieties of RP (particularly that associated with army officers). Some English northerners, some RP
speakers, and some Americans have a context-sensitive variation
between [i] (used finally before a vowel, as *happier, tidy it*) and [ɪ]
(used finally before a consonant and in absolute final position: *tidy*

them, tidy‖). Consistent final [i] is found in much of the south of England, as well as in the peripheral north (Liverpool, Newcastle, Hull, Birmingham). It is now the most usual quality in GenAm and Canadian, and also in the southern hemisphere. Qualities similar to FACE, i.e. [e], are typically Scottish.

Many accents show fair leeway in the realization of *happ*Y, since the opposition between FLEECE and KIT is in effect suspended in weak syllables (pairs such as *stele* vs. *steely*, *Carrhae* vs. *carry*, American *trustee* vs. *trusty* are marginal).

Clitic pronouns *me, he, she* often adopt the same quality as *happ*Y, so that *would he* is homophonous with *woody* (RP ['wʊdɪ]).

(77) *happ*Y   (a) *copy, city, inky, baby, ready, foggy,*
                    fluffy, heavy, breathy, fussy, busy, fishy,
                    tetchy, edgy, gloomy, penny, sorry, lily,
                    canopy, vanity, strategy, economy, . . . ;
                    scampi, spaghetti, khaki, corgi, Nazi,
                    taxi, hibachi, salami, macaroni, sari, chilli, . . . ;
                    sortie, talkie, birdie, boogie, movie,
                    lassie, budgie, stymie, prairie, calorie, . . . ;
              (b) *committee, coffee;*
                    hockey, abbey, covey, curtsey, jersey,
                    money, comfrey, valley, . . . ;
                    Chelsea, Swansea.

The set *lett*ER is exemplified in (78). All include orthographic final *r* or *re*. They are regularly pronounced with /ər/ (usually realized as [ɚ]) in rhotic accents (Scottish /ɪr/ where no /ə/ is present), and with plain /ə/ in non-rhotic accents (except when subject to linking /r/ before a word or suffix beginning with a vowel).

The clitic pronoun *her* often adopts the same quality as *lett*ER, so that *tell her* is homophonous with *teller*. Where it does not, such pairs furnish evidence of the phonemic distinctiveness of *lett*ER vis-à-vis NURSE.

(78) *lett*ER   *paper, better, whisker, rubber, order, tiger,*
               offer, cover, leather, dresser, cruiser,
               usher, teacher, soldier, customer, liner,
               scorer, dealer, tower, . . . ;
               metre, centre/center, acre, fibre/fiber, ogre, . . . ;
               calendar, sugar, polar, liar, . . . ;
               stupor, indicator, anchor, Tudor, camphor, survivor,

author, professor, razor, major, tremor,
donor, error, pallor, . . .;
succo(u)r, harbo(u)r, odo(u)r, vigo(u)r,
flavo(u)r, armo(u)r, humo(u)r, colo(u)r, . . .;
martyr, satyr, zephyr;
figure, pressure, measure, feature, perjure, tenure,
failure, . . .

The set *comm*A is exemplified in (79). These words, with orthographic final *a*, have all entered English in the last half millenium:
Middle English had no /ə/ in final position. *Comm*A words are
regularly pronounced with /ə/ (but /ʌ/ in Scottish accents having no
/ə/). Certain rhotic accents, however, preserve the Middle English
phonotactic constraint against /ə#/ by pronouncing them with /ər/
[ɚ] instead: this is found in parts of the west of England and in
southern mountain speech in America.

Words like *yellow, window, piano* are not separately treated here.
In educated accents their final vowel can be equated with GOAT
(although in old-fashioned RP and American southern reduced to
[o ~ ʊ ~ ɵ], unlike the diphthong of strong syllables); in popular
speech it often joins *comm*A, as [ə ~ ɚ].

(79) *comm*A *catalpa, quota, vodka, am(o)eba, panda, saga,*
       sofa, saliva, Bertha, balsa, visa, acacia,
       dementia, neuralgia, drama, arena, opera,
       Cinderella, phobia, . . .

In non-final environments weak vowels may be rather different.
There are accents which have a clear opposition between [ɪ] and [ə]
before a final consonant, as RP *Lenin* /ˈlenɪn/ vs. *Lennon* /ˈlenən/,
rabbit /ˈræbɪt/ vs. *abbot* /ˈæbət/. There are other accents where no
such contrast is available, so that *Lenin* and *Lennon* are pronounced
identically, while *rabbit* and *abbot* rhyme. In yet other accents the
contrast is variable, since speakers have it potentially available but
not necessarily made. Traditional RP, along with West Indian and
American southern accents, can be considered conservative in this
respect; southern-hemisphere accents are innovative, having
generally undergone what may be called the **Weak Vowel Merger**
and thus lost the contrast; and GenAm and Irish, along with many
accents of England including some which could perhaps be considered to fall within RP, occupy the intermediate, variable,
position.

Several further examples to test the possible contrast in weak vowels arise through the clitic pronouns: thus *pig it* /'pɪgɪt/ vs. *bigot* /'bɪgət/, *sell it* /'selɪt/ vs. *zealot* /'zelət/. Some RP speakers have *dye it* and *diet* as homophones /'daɪɪt/, but most nowadays pronounce *diet* /'daɪət/. Compare also *a massive cloud* vs. *a mass of cloud*. RP *it* and *at* are never homophonous, but in Australia they share the weak form /ət/; the same applies to (*h*)*im* and (*th*)*em*, *in* and *and*, as can be seen from the fact that *tell 'im* and *tell 'em* are distinct in RP but not in Australian.

Although /ən/ is an input to the Syllabic Consonant rule (→ [ṇ]), /ɪn/ is not. Hence RP *Barton* is ['bɑːtṇ], but *Martin* is ['mɑːtɪn], not ['mɑːtṇ]. (But in Southampton, Dublin, Sydney, and Chicago, *Martin* does have [-tṇ].)

2.3 Systems; a typology

2.3.1 Part-system A

It is convenient to subdivide vowel systems of English into four part-systems. Part-system A comprises the traditional stressable short vowels. These are the vowels phonotactically restricted to occurrence in checked syllables (at least in the case of stressed monosyllables): where /e/ and /æ/ are members of part-system A, there is no possible word of the shape *⋆/be/ or *⋆/sæ/.

In RP part-system A has six members: the vowels KIT, DRESS, TRAP, LOT, STRUT, and FOOT respectively. In 2.1.2 above, we arranged them as in (80a), which is phonetically realistic but asymmetrical. They can alternatively be arranged as in (80b), which is symmetrical but not phonetically realistic (since /ʌ/ is nowadays not a mid back vowel).

(80a)	ɪ		ʊ		KIT		FOOT
	e	ʌ			DRESS	STRUT	
	æ		ɒ		TRAP		LOT
(80b)	ɪ		ʊ		KIT		FOOT
	e		ʌ		DRESS		STRUT
	æ		ɒ		TRAP		LOT

(80c)	e	ɪ	ʊ	DRESS	KIT	FOOT
	æ	ʌ	ɒ	TRAP	STRUT	LOT

(80c) represents a rearrangement which is justified on phonetic grounds in a New Zealand accent (where KIT might more realistically be written /ɪ/ or /ə/).

Systemically equivalent notational variants appropriate in particular cases include /ɛ/ for DRESS, /a/ for TRAP, /ɑ/ for LOT, and /ə/ for STRUT.

This six-term part-system is to be found not only in RP and the accents of the south of England but also in those of southern Ireland, New York City, Australia, and New Zealand.

The part-system may be reduced in various ways.

(i) If LOT is merged with the /ɑ/ of PALM–START, or with the /ɔ/ of THOUGHT–NORTH, then it is no longer a checked vowel of part-system A, but moves to part-system D. This gives the five-term A-system (81), characteristic of GenAm and Canadian.

(81)	ɪ	ʊ	KIT	FOOT
	ɛ		DRESS	
		ʌ		STRUT
	æ		TRAP	

Again one can argue for various alternative arrangements of this pattern, particularly in respect of the place of STRUT.

(ii) Where STRUT is not distinct from FOOT, we have the five-term A-system (82), characteristic of popular accents of the midlands and north of England.

(82)	ɪ	ʊ	KIT	FOOT–STRUT
	ɛ		DRESS	
	a	ɒ	TRAP	LOT

(iii) Where TRAP is merged with LOT, we have the five-term A-system (83), characteristic of certain types of popular West Indian speech, including that of Jamaica.

(83)	ɪ	ʊ	KIT	FOOT
	ɛ	ʌ	DRESS	STRUT
	a		TRAP–LOT	

(iv) Where FOOT is merged with GOOSE, it is no longer a checked vowel of part-system A, but moves to part-system C. This gives the five-term A-system (84), a Scottish possibility.

(84) ɪ   KIT
     ɛ   ʌ   DRESS   STRUT
     a   ɒ   TRAP   LOT

In Scottish or Ulster speech the part-system may be further reduced by the loss of LOT to part-system D, through its merger with THOUGHT, and/or by the loss of TRAP to part-system D through its merger with PALM. If just one of these applies, a four-term part-system will result; if both apply, we arrive at the three-term A-system (85).

(85) ɪ   KIT
     ɛ   ʌ   DRESS   STRUT

This appears to be the minimum size for part-system A. If /ɛ/ (DRESS) transfers to part-system B (or D?) through being used in *day* etc., as in some Ulster accents, then its place in part-system A is taken by the now always checked /e/ of *face* etc.

Part-system A may also be augmented in various ways.

(v) Where a phonemic split has taken place within the KIT set, as arguably in South African English, the part-system is increased by the extra /ə/ (notational variant: /ɪ/), giving a seven-term A-system, (86).

(86) ɪ   ʊ   KIT[1]   FOOT
   e ə ʌ   DRESS KIT[2] STRUT
   æ   ɒ   TRAP   LOT

(vi) Where the 'New England short *o*' is phonemically distinct from all other vowels, the part-system is augmented by the extra /ɵ/ of certain GOAT words. New Englanders who have /ɵ/ usually have LOT merged with THOUGHT as a member of part-system D, so that their part-system A has six terms, (87).

(87) ɪ   ʊ   KIT   FOOT
   ɛ   ɵ   DRESS (GOAT)
   æ   ʌ   TRAP   STRUT

(vii) Some Scottish people have a vowel /ë/ distinct from the ordinary /ɛ/ of DRESS, though used in certain words of the set DRESS. This co-occurs only with one of the smallish part-systems discussed in (iv) above, giving at the most a six-term A-system.

(viii) Some Americans have a phonemic split in TRAP, giving a /eə/ distinct from /æ/. Although /eə/ is a phonetically rather long and tense vowel, it does not occur in free syllables (unless in a non-rhotic SQUARE etc.), and so arguably ought to be included in part-system A. Similar arguments apply if there are Americans or others who use a vowel in (some) BATH words intermediate between their /æ/ of TRAP and their /a ~ ɑ/ of START. There is a similar problem for some English southerners who have a long /æː/ in *bad* etc., contrasting with the /æ/ (TRAP) of *lad*. At most these will be sub-systemic additions, restricted to a small range of phonetic environments.

2.3.2 Part-system B

Part-system B comprises those of the traditional long vowels and diphthongs which have a front mid to close quality or (if diph-thongal) endpoint. The phonotactics permits them to occur in free syllables (but see reservations on this point below).

In the reference accents and many others, part-system B com-prises four members: FLEECE, FACE, PRICE, and CHOICE. They can be arranged as (88a), or alternatively as (88b). Phonetically, one could say that RP has over the last century been moving from (88a) to (88b).

(88a)	iː		FLEECE	
	eɪ		FACE	
	aɪ	ɔɪ	PRICE	CHOICE

(88b)	iː		FLEECE	
	eɪ	ɔɪ	FACE	CHOICE
		aɪ		PRICE

Systemically equivalent notational variants which may be appro-priate in particular instances include /i, ɪi, əi/ for FLEECE, /e, eː, ʌɪ, æɪ, əɪ/ for FACE, /ɑi, ɒɪ, ʌi, əi/ for PRICE, and /ɒɪ, oɪ, œe/ for CHOICE.

The part-system is reduced by one member in accents where PRICE does not contrast with CHOICE, as in some rural speech in England, Ireland, and the West Indies. This gives the three-term B-system (89).

(89a)·	iː	(89b)	əi	FLEECE
	eː		aɪ	FACE
	aɪ		ɔɪ	PRICE–CHOICE

Notation (89a) would be appropriate for Jamaica, notation (89b) for rural Essex.

There are various ways in which part-system B may be augmented.

(i) Some accents distinguish the vowel of *eight* etc. from that of *late* etc., with /ɛɪ/ in the former and /eː/ in the latter. (See discussion in 3.1.5 below.) This gives the five-term B-system (90), found in some provincial accents of England and Wales.

(90) i: FLEECE
     e: FACE[1]
     ɛɪ   ɔɪ   FACE[2]   CHOICE
        aɪ   PRICE

(ii) In Scotland there is often a split, arguably phonemic, within the PRICE set, /ae/ being distinct from /ʌi/. This gives the five-term B-system (91).

(91) i   FLEECE
    e   FACE
    ae   ʌi   ɔe   PRICE[1]   PRICE[2]   CHOICE

There may also be Scottish accents in which CHOICE has a disyllabic vowel sequence rather than a diphthong, so that it no longer belongs to part-system B.

(iii) In some American accents (New York City, South Carolina), NURSE has a diphthongal variant of the type [ɜɪ]. If this is regarded as sufficient grounds for including an /ɜɪ/ in part-system B, a five-term part-system results. Against this it must be said that [ɜɪ] does not occur in free syllables (*fur* [fɜ ~ fɝ], not *[fɜɪ]). Another American southern diphthong which is a prima facie case for inclusion in part-system B is the [æɪ] of certain TRAP and BATH words. But [æɪ], too, is excluded from free syllables. It is true, however, that /æɪ/ may have contrastive status vis-à-vis /æ/. If we abandon the free-syllable criterion and admit both of these diphthongs, a six-term B-system results, as in (92).

(92) i: FLEECE
    eɪ   ɜɪ   FACE   (NURSE)
    æɪ   aɪ   ɔɪ   (BATH)   PRICE   CHOICE

2.3.3 Part-system C

Part-system C comprises those of the traditional long vowels and diphthongs which have a back mid to close quality or (if diphthongal) endpoint. The phonotactics normally permits them to occur in free syllables.

In the reference accents and many others, part-system C comprises three members; GOOSE, GOAT, and MOUTH. They can be arranged and symbolized in various ways: (93a, b) are appropriate for RP and GenAm respectively.

(93a)	uː	(93b)	u	GOOSE
	əʊ		o	GOAT
	aʊ		aʊ	MOUTH

(One can also argue for arranging the three in a vertical straight line in current RP or near-RP, given the tendency to centre GOOSE to [ʉː].)

Systemically equivalent notational variants which may be appropriate in particular instances include /ʊu, ʉ(ː), əu/ for GOOSE, /oː, uː, ʌʊ, oʊ, ɔʊ/ for GOAT, and /æʊ, æʉ, ɛɪ, ʌu, əu/ for MOUTH.

It appears that part-system C never has fewer than three terms. It may, however, be augmented in various ways.

(i) Some accents have a diphthong /ɪu/ used in certain GOOSE words. It contrasts with /uː/ of GOOSE, e.g. [θrɪu] *threw* vs. [θruː] *through*. This contrastive /ɪu/ is found in various conservative accents of England, Wales, and North America. It results in a four-term C-system, (94).

(94)	ɪu	uː	GOOSE¹	GOOSE²
		oː		GOAT
	aʊ		MOUTH	

(ii) Some accents distinguish the vowel of *knows*, *mown*, etc., from that of *nose*, *moan*, etc., with /ɔʊ/ in the former but /oː/ in the latter (or systemically equivalent notational variants of these). (See discussion in 3.1.5 below.) This gives a four-term C-system (95), found in some provincial accents of England; if combined with additional /ɪu/, the five-term C-system (96) results, found in some Welsh accents.

(95)	ʉː		GOOSE	
	ʌʊ	oː	GOAT¹	GOAT²
	æʊ		MOUTH	

173

(96)	ɪu	uː	GOOSE[1]	GOOSE[2]
	ɔʊ	oː	GOAT[1]	GOAT[2]
	əu		MOUTH	

(iii) In some accents THOUGHT has what is phonetically a closing diphthong, [ɔʊ]. This is found in American southern speech, and also in London, where there also exists a variant with a half-close monophthong, virtually [oː]. If this vowel is included in part-system C, a four-term system results, (97).

(97)		u		GOOSE
		o		GOAT
	æʊ	ɔʊ	MOUTH	THOUGHT

(iv) Through L Vocalization (3.4.4 below) there arise a number of new phonetic diphthongs. If these are analysed as additional unit phonemes (rather than as /Vl/), then a considerably augmented C-system may result. This new-phoneme analysis is particularly persuasive in cases where allophonic differences in vowels (__ɫ vs. other environments) are phonologized as a consequence of L Vocalization. This has happened in London's local accent (vol. 2, 4.2.6), where GOAT has arguably split into two phonemes which may be written /ʌʊ/ and /ɒʊ/, e.g. *polar* vs. *roller*. Combined with the /ɔʊ/ of THOUGHT discussed in (iii) above, this gives a five-term C-system, (98).

(98)	ʉː		GOOSE	
	ʌʊ	ɔʊ	GOAT[1]	(THOUGHT)
	æʊ	ɒʊ	MOUTH	GOAT[2]

If we admit a wider range of diphthongs deriving from historical /Vl/, we easily achieve a C-system of nine or more terms. A case can be made out for (99) in some types of Cockney; this does not include the ordinary MOUTH vowel (where no historical /l/ follows), since it typically has a realization [æə ~ æː] and can therefore be considered to belong to part-system D.

(99)	ɪʊ	ʉː	ʊu	*field, build*	*too*	*tool*
	ɛʊ	ʌʊ	ɔʊ	*shelf*	*toe*	*fall, sort*
	æʊ	ɑʊ	ɒʊ	*fail, foul*	*snarl, smile*	*doll, dole*

(v) In American southern accents there is often a stressable syllabic velar lateral monophthong, [ɫ], as in *full* [fɫ], which could conceivably be included in part-system C.

2.3.4 Part-system D

Part-system D comprises those of the traditional long vowels and diphthongs which have a relatively open quality or (if diphthongal) endpoint, including under 'relatively open' the mid central quality [ə]. The phonotactics normally permits them to occur in free syllables.

In GenAm part-system D has three members: PALM–START, THOUGHT–CLOTH, and NURSE. They can be arranged as in (100). This presupposes an analysis of [ɝ] as either an independent phoneme /ɝ/ or else a sequence /ɜr/. In many subvarieties of GenAm, however, it is possible to consider it a realization of the sequence /ʌr/; if so, then the D-system has only two members, (101). Most Scottish accents have no /ɝ/; their D-system, too, is the simple two-term (101).

(100) 3 ~ ɝ   NURSE
       ɑ ɔ   LOT–PALM   THOUGHT–CLOTH

(101) ɑ ɔ   (LOT–)PALM–START (LOT–)THOUGHT–CLOTH

D-systems (100) and (101) are perhaps those most typical of rhotic accents.

Systemically equivalent notational variants which may be appropriate in particular cases include /3(ː), ɚ/ for NURSE, /ɑː, a(ː)/ for (LOT–)PALM, and /ɔː/ for THOUGHT(–CLOTH).

Part-system C may be reduced to one member (plus the uncertain /ɝ/). This arises in several subvarieties of GenAm, where pairs such as *don* and *dawn*, *cot* and *caught*, etc., are not distinguished. Associated by *PEAS* with western Pennsylvania, this one-member D-system, (102), is becoming increasingly common in the United States. It is also the usual Canadian system.

(102) ɑ   LOT–PALM–THOUGHT–CLOTH

A systemically equivalent notational variant writes this merged vowel /ɒ/ rather than /ɑ/.

There are several ways in which part-system D may be augmented. Nearly all arise through the phonologization of what were previously allophonic effects in the environment of a following /r/.

(i) Old-fashioned RP (perhaps now obsolete) adds four centring

diphthongs /ɪə, ɛə, ɔə, ʊə/ (NEAR, SQUARE, FORCE, CURE). This gives a
seven-term D-system, (103).

(103)	ɪə		ʊə	NEAR		CURE
	ɛə	ɜː	ɔə	SQUARE	NURSE	FORCE
	ɑː	ɔː			START—PALM	THOUGHT—NORTH

(ii) The disappearance of /ɔə/ as an independent phoneme
reduces this to the six-term system (104), characteristic of contemporary RP and many other accents, including most non-rhotic
accents of England and those of the southern hemisphere. If the
present trend towards the disappearance of /ʊə/, too, as an
independent phoneme continues, then the five-term D-system
(105) will prevail.

(104)	ɪə		ʊə	NEAR		CURE
	ɛə	ɜː	ɔː	SQUARE	NURSE	FORCE—THOUGHT—NORTH
		ɑː			START—PALM	

(105)	ɪə			NEAR		
	ɛə	ɜː	ɔː	SQUARE	NURSE	FORCE—THOUGHT—NORTH
		ɑː			START—PALM	–CURE

Systemically equivalent notational variants for /ɛə/ include /æə/,
/eə/, /ɛː/ and /eː/.

(iii) There is not always a distinct phoneme for SQUARE. In some
parts of midlands and north of England, SQUARE is merged with
NURSE in a long monophthong which may be either front or central,
[ɛː ~ ɜː]. In this kind of accent *stare* is homophonous with *stir*, and
the D-system may comprise only the four terms /ɪə, ɜː, ɔː, ɑː/. An
alternative possibility, found sometimes in East Anglia, New
Zealand, and the American south, as well as regularly in the West
Indies, is the absence of a phonemic opposition between SQUARE
and NEAR (although SQUARE and NURSE remain distinct). Writing
the merged phoneme as /eə/, we have the four-term D-system
(106). (In the West Indies this D-system applies, of course, only to
the non-rhotic accents, such as that of Trinidad.)

(106)	eə	3	NEAR—SQUARE	NURSE	
	ɑ	ɔ		START—PALM	FORCE—THOUGHT—
					NORTH—CURE

(iv) In non-rhotic American southern accents, START usually remains potentially distinct from PALM–LOT, as /ɑə/ vs. /ɑ/ (also written as /a/ vs. /ɑ/). Where SQUARE is not merged with NEAR, it usually has /æə/, which may also contrast with an /ɛə/, e.g. *air* vs. *e'er*. There may or may not be contrasts between NORTH and THOUGHT, NORTH and START, FORCE and GOAT, FORCE and CURE; if all are present, then the system includes independent phonemes /ɔə, oə/. The D-system therefores includes up to eight members, as (107).

(107)	ɪə	ʊə	NEAR¹		CURE
	ɛə	ɜ	oə	NEAR²	NURSE	FORCE
	æə	ɑː	ɔː	SQUARE	START	NORTH

(107)	ɪə	ʊə	NEAR¹		CURE
	ɛə	ɜ	oə	NEAR²	NURSE	FORCE
	æə	ɑː	ɔː	SQUARE	START	NORTH

(v) The long tense /eə/ developing in certain TRAP and BATH words in GenAm (*halve* /heəv/ vs. *have* /hæv/ etc.) could be considered on phonetic grounds to belong to part-system D, even though it does not occur in free syllables. This would increase systems (100), (101), or (102) by one member.

(vi) In RP a case can be made out for recognizing distinct phonemes /aə/ and sometimes also /ɑə/, in words such as *fire, pirate,* and *tower, dowry* (see below, 3.2.9 Smoothing). If added to (104) these would give the eight-term D-system (108).

(108)	ɪə	ʊə	NEAR		CURE
	ɛə	3ː	ɔː	SQUARE	NURSE	FORCE – THOUGHT–NORTH
	aə	ɑː	ɑə	*fire*	START–PALM	*tower*

There is also the question of the possible contrastively long /æː/ in *bad* (vs. short /æ/ in *lad*) in some varieties of RP or near-RP. This /æː/ does not occur in open syllables, but it could be argued on phonetic grounds that it should be included in part-system D.

(vii) Lastly it can be argued on phonetic grounds that Cockney MOUTH, [æə ~ æː], should be included in part-system D; this argument receives important phonological backing from the fact that R Insertion (intrusive /r/), otherwise triggered only by /ə/ and the vowels of part-system D, does occur after Cockney MOUTH /æə/ (['æərɪʔ'ɪz] *how it is*).

PEAS applies a binary analysis of centring diphthongs, treating them as phonemically consisting of /V/ plus /ə̆/. This has two disadvantages: first, it forces false distinctions (since the first ele-

ment in, say, [ɛə] has to be identified as an allophone either of DRESS
or as TRAP, i.e. in RP as /e/ or /æ/, when phonetically it may be
intermediate between them and when they do not contrast in this
environment); and secondly, it is phonetically unreal in accents
where Monophthonging has operated (if [ɛː], too, has to be analysed
as /eɜ/ or /æɜ/). In fact, it is open to just the same objections as the
binary analysis of vowels of part-systems B and C, objections well
summarized by Kurath & McDavid themselves (*PEAS*: see also
1.2.5 above: 3–5). It is on these grounds, then, that I have preferred
to treat centring diphthongs along with other part-system D vowels
as unitary phonemes.

2.3.5 The consonant system

Accents of English do not differ very greatly in their consonant
systems. Those differences that do exist relate principally to /θ, ð/,
/ŋ/, and /h/.

The consonant system as a whole may be divided into part-
systems on the basis of the manner of articulation of the phonemic
norms: plosives, nasals, fricatives, and approximants (liquids,
semivowels, /h/).

(i) Most accents have a six-term plosive system, (109). The
opposition between the upper row and the lower may depend upon
voicing, aspiration, or a combination of the two. These factors, and
perhaps others as well, are subsumed in the labels 'fortis' and 'lenis'
for the upper and lower rows respectively.

(109)	p	t	k	*pin*	*tin*	*kin*
	b	d	g	*bin*	*din*	*give*

This system may be augmented by the inclusion of dental plosives, /t̪,d̪/, in opposition to alveolars /t,d/, as in (110). This applies
most notably in southern Irish English, and also in Indian English;
there are other accents, too, in which dental plosives occur as
sociolinguistically conditioned variants of dental fricatives (e.g. in
New York City). Phonological support for the inclusion of /t̪, d̪/
among the plosives comes from the fact that in the accents in
question they do not occur in clusters with /t, d/, whereas in accents
having fricative /θ, ð/ such clusters do occur (*eighth* in most accents
/-tθ/, but Irish and Indian /eːt̪/).

(110) p ʈ t k   *pin thin tin kin*
       b ḍ d g   *bin this din give*

Although many accents include the glottal plosive [ʔ] among their phonetic plosives, there is nowhere a contrastive phoneme **/ʔ/*. In many popular accents of England, however, the three-way opposition /p/ vs. /t/ vs. /k/ may be optionally neutralized under [ʔ] in certain environments, e.g. ['raɪʔ 'pɛə] *ripe pear* or *right pair*; ['laɪʔ 'braʊn] *light brown* or *like Brown*. Otherwise, [ʔ] is to be regarded either as an allophone of /t/ or else as a prosodic feature inserted by optional rule before certain syllable-initial vowels.

The affricates /tʃ/ and /dʒ/, as in *chin* and *gin* respectively, may be treated either as phonemic clusters or else as independent affricate phonemes (in which case they may alternatively be symbolized unitarily as /č,ǰ/ or as /c, ɟ/). There are arguments for and against both treatments. If they are included with the plosives, the resultant part-system, (111), has eight members (or ten, with dentals).

(111) p t tʃ k   *pin tin chin kin*
       b d dʒ g   *bin din gin give*

The sequences /tr, dr/ are realized as post-alveolar affricates is many accents; but these affricates, it appears, may always be analysed as phonemic clusters of plosive plus liquid.

(ii) Most accents have a three-term nasal system, (112); only /m/ and /n/, however, occur syllable-initially.

(112) m n ŋ   *mat, rum gnat, run rung*

As discussed in 1.2.11 above, arguments exist for denying the velar nasal a place in the system of consonant phonemes. For those who accept these arguments, the nasal system has only two terms. There are certain accents, however, where all would agree that there are only two nasal phonemes: notably in parts of the western midlands and north-west of England, where words like *rung* have final [ŋg], and [ŋ] occurs only before velars. Here [ŋ] is an allophone of /n/, and the nasal system has two terms (113).

(113) m n   *mat, rum gnat, run*

In some Irish or Scottish speech it can be argued that the [ɲ] used in words like *new* [ɲʉː] merits phonemic status, rather than being regarded as a realization of /nj/.

(iii) Most accents have an eight-term fricative system, (114); this is on the assumption that /h/ is treated separately and that [ʍ] and [ç], if present, are analysed as /hw, hj/. As with plosives, the two rows may be classified as fortis and lenis respectively; though in fricatives aspiration has little or no rôle in distinguishing the series.

(114)   f θ s ʃ   *fin*   *thin* *sin* *shin*
         v ð z ʒ   *vivid* *this* *zip* *measure*

The fricatives /ð/ and /ʒ/ have rather sharply restricted phonological distribution. In initial position, /ð/ is found only in words belonging to syntactically minor word-classes (*the*, *thus*, *that*, *then* etc.), while /ʒ/ occurs, if at all, only in loan-words (*gigolo*, *jabot*, *Zhivago*). Medially, in the environment 'V—V, both occur readily (*father*, *vision*). Finally, both occur (*smooth*, *camouflage*), although in some popular accents /ʒ/ is replaced by /dʒ/ in this position.

Accents in which the dentals are plosive (/t̪, d̪/ above) lack /θ, ð/ among their fricatives. All accents have /f, s, ʃ/. There may occasionally be doubts about the status of [v] vis-à-vis [b, w] in the West Indies; otherwise all accents have /v/. Some Celtic-influenced speech may lack contrastive /z/, using [s] (= /s/) instead: this is found among populations where Welsh, Scottish Gaelic, or Irish Gaelic are spoken. The same applies to /ʒ/, with /ʃ/ used in its place. Some West Indians lack /ʒ/ and use /dʒ/ instead. The smallest fricative system in use for English would appear to be (115), applicable in such western Irish accents as have no voiced sibilants.

(115)   f s ʃ   *fin*   *sin, zip* *shin, measure*
         v   *vivid*

The only serious candidate for addition to the eight-term fricative system (115) is /x/, the voiceless velar or uvular fricative. In most accents this is at best a very marginal item used in loan-words and/or proper names; Scots, however, often use /x/ in certain words of Standard English (e.g. *technical* /'tɛxnɪkl̩/). Even in Scottish English, though, /x/ can be regarded as a loan-phoneme from Scots dialect. In the English of Wales, Ireland, and South Africa it can be regarded as a loan-phoneme from Welsh, Irish, and Afrikaans respectively; in that of New York, from Yiddish. (See further 3.1.3 below.)

There are fricative allophones of /l, r, j, w/ in most accents, but these are not to be considered members of the system of fricative phonemes.

The glottal fricative or aspirate, /h/, is phonetically on the borderline between fricatives and approximants. Unlike the regular voiceless fricatives, it is not paired with a voiced counterpart. It is missing from the consonant system of most popular accents of England and Wales (3.4.1 below), but the situation is complicated by its importance as a sociolinguistic variable wherever it is commonly dropped in popular speech.

All accents of English have two liquids, /l/ and /r/, and two semivowels, /j/ and /w/. Together they comprise the non-nasal approximants, (116).

(116)   j   w   l   r   *yet   wet   let   red*

In the analysis of long vowels and diphthongs adopted in this book, /j/ and /w/ occur only syllable-initially (including in syllable-initial clusters). In non-rhotic accents, of which RP is one, /r/ too is subject to severe constraints in its phonotactics, occurring only when the following segment is a vowel (or [l]). One may hypothesize that when L Vocalization, a development currently in progress, is complete (3.4.4 below), and a phonemic restructuring has taken place, then /l/ too will be subject to this constraint.

2.3.6 A typology for accents of English

It seems clear that a suitable typology for accents of English must be based upon vowel rather than consonant characteristics. The one proposed here depends upon two factors: (i) the vowel system, systemic differences in which have been investigated in 2.3.1–4 above; and (ii) the phonological distribution of these vowels as revealed particularly in words of the lexical sets NEAR and SQUARE. On this basis it is possible to recognize four characteristic types of vowel system.

A vowel system which comprises six phonemes in part-system A, four in part-system B, three in part-system C, and two in part-system D, can be conveniently referred to as a 6-4-3-2 system. Similarly, a 5-5-3-2 system is one which has five distinctive vowels in part-system A, five in B, three in C, and two in D.

The most conservative vowel systems are of **Type 1**. They are usually 6-4-3-2 or 6-4-3-3, depending on whether NURSE has (or is analysed as having) a part-system A vowel plus /r/ or a separate part-system D vowel. As an example we take the vowel system of provincial southern Irish English, (117). In this accent *near* is /niːr/ and *square* is /skweːr/.

(117)

I	ʊ	iː		uː	
ɛ	ʌ	eː		oː	
æ	ɒ	aɪ	ɔɪ	aʊ	aː ɔː

A	B	C	D

This type has no centring dipthongs in part-system D; NEAR and SQUARE have vowels from part-system B, normally plus /r/. Vowel length plays an important rôle. Historical /r/ and /l/ are retained.

Other examples of Type I vowel systems are those of Jamaica and Barbados.

RP is a **Type II** accent. Type II accents are distinguished by the presence of an augmented D-system, developed as a consequence of R Dropping (3.2.2 below). In RP the vowel system is 6-4-3-6, as set out in (118). Vowel length retains some importance.

(118)

I	ʊ	iː		uː	ɪə	ʊə
e	ʌ	eɪ	əʊ		ɛə	3ː ɔː
æ	ɒ	aɪ	ɔɪ	aʊ	ɑː	

A	B	C	D

Other examples of Type II accents are those of Australia, New Zealand, and South Africa, and indeed most accents of England and Wales.

GenAm is a **Type III** accent. It has a 5-4-3-3 vowel system, as set out in (119); if NURSE, though, is analysed as having /ʌr/, then the system is 5-4-3-2. The special characteristic of Type III accents is the use of part-system A vowels in the lexical sets NEAR and SQUARE, giving potential rhymes such as *mirror–nearer, herring–sharing*. Vowel length is not important in Type III accents, which accounts for the non-use of length-marks in transcribing the vowels. A characteristic (but not necessary) consequence is that *bother* and *father* rhyme, with the LOT vowel belonging to part-system D.

(119)

I	ʊ	i		u	
ɛ	ʌ	eɪ		o	(3ʻ)
æ		aɪ	ɔɪ	aʊ	ɑ ɔ

A	B	C	D

Another example of a Type III accent is that of Canada. Those of the American south and eastern New England are basically of Type II, but subject to increasing Type III influence from GenAm.

Type IV is represented by the accents of Scotland and Northern Ireland. Vowel length is not important in Type IV, except in signalling certain boundaries; but the consequence here, unlike in Type III, is the absence of certain traditional distinctions between paired long and short vowels, in particular that between FOOT and GOOSE. The vowel system of one Scottish accent is set out in (120).

(120)

I		i			u		
ε	ʌ	e	ʌi		o		
		ae	ɔe	ʌu		ɑ	ɔ
A		*B*		*C*		*D*	

Type IV is not found outside Scotland, northermost Northumberland, and northern Ireland.

I must emphasize that what I am proposing in this section is a typology, not an exhaustive and mutually exclusive classification. Accents may be of mixed type, exhibiting the characteristics of more than one of Type I–IV. This is particularly likely to be the case when a prestige norm belongs to a different type from the low-prestige variety it is influencing.

With the foregoing caveat, table (121) may be of use in assigning accents to types.

(121)

	I	II	III	IV
1. Does *lawn* rhyme with *corn*?	No	Yes	No	No
2. Does *mirror* rhyme with *nearer*?	No	No	Yes	No
3. Does *good* rhyme with *mood*?	No	No	No	Yes

These synchronic characteristics reflect differences in historical phonology. In terms of the developments discussed in chapter 3 below, Type II accents have undergone R Dropping (3.2.2), which had the effect of phonologizing Pre-R Breaking (3.2.1); Type III accents have undergone Pre-R Schwa Deletion (3.3.1), which had the effect of phonologizing Laxing (3.2.1, 3.3.1); and Type IV accents have undergone Aitken's Law and so not developed a FOOT vowel distinct from GOOSE. Type I accents have undergone none of these developments, and it would appear that there are virtually no accents which have undergone more than one of the three.

3

Developments and processes

3.1 Residualisms

In this section we consider various phonological developments – sound changes – which have taken place in the history of the reference accents, RP and GenAm, but not necessarily in other accents of the language. From the point of view of the reference accents, and many others, these developments may be regarded as long since completed and accordingly now of historical relevance only; elsewhere they may sometimes have no relevance at all (not having taken place in the accent in question), or be only partially complete, or be characterized by sociolinguistic variability.

3.1.1 The Great Vowel Shift

Around the fifteenth century the long vowels of English underwent a series of important changes in quality, traditionally known as the Great Vowel Shift. The changes are as shown in (122).

(122)	Middle English (c. 1100–1450)		Early Modern English (c. 1450–1600)	Examples	
	iː	→	ei (or perhaps əi)	*time*, . . .	PRICE
	eː	→	iː	*sweet*, . . .	FLEECE
	ɛː	→	eː	*clean*, . . .	
	aː	→	ɛː	*name*, . . .	FACE
	ɔː	→	oː	*stone*, . . .	GOAT
	oː	→	uː	*moon*, . . .	GOOSE
	uː	→	ou (or perhaps əu)	*house*, . . .	MOUTH

Thus what happened was that the half-close, half-open, and open long vowels moved one step closer (higher): /eː → iː/, /ɛː → eː/, /aː → ɛː/, and /oː → uː/, /ɔː → uː/; and the close long vowels diphthongized (/iː → ei/, /uː → ou/; these diphthongs developed further in due course to yield present-day [aɪ] and [aʊ]). Thus all the vowel contrasts were maintained, though the phonetic qualities altered. Following Jespersen (1909) we can diagram the Great Vowel Shift as (123):

(123)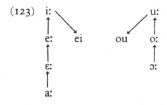

It is a matter of some dispute among scholars which was the precipitating factor in the Great Vowel Shift, the raising of the mid vowels or the diphthongization of the close vowels. Did the raising of the opener vowels trigger off the raising of /eː/ and /oː/, which by their raising in turn pushed /iː/ and /uː/ aside into diphthongization (the 'push-chain' theory)? Or did the close vowels diphthongize first and thus facilitate or entail the raising of the mid vowels (the 'drag-chain' theory)? Did these changes happen simultaneously or in succession? In any case it is clear that the various parts of the overall shift were interdependent, since no losses of opposition occurred.

By the year 1600 the Great Vowel Shift was completed: although Chaucer in the original must have been pronounced in a pre-GVS way, Shakespeare was not. As far as concerns the description of present-day Standard English, the relevance of the Great Vowel Shift is thus purely historic, with the possible exception of two considerations: the orthography and the facts of derivational morphology. Before turning to these, we consider briefly certain facts about dialectal speech.

As far as the front vowels are concerned, no traditional-dialect of English was exempt from the operation of the Great Vowel Shift. But with the back vowels the shift was regionally restricted. North of a line running from southern Cumbria to the Humber estuary, the present-day dialectal reflex of Middle English /oː/ is a front vowel, e.g. [gɪəs] *goose*, while Middle English /uː/ remains monophthongal, e.g. [huːs] *house*. This is what has usually been called the 'northern' area in English dialectology; it corresponds to what I call the 'far north' of England (vol. 2, 4.4.1). In Scots dialects, too, the back vowels were exempt from the Great Vowel Shift. It seems that what happened north of this Lune–Humber line was that Middle English /oː/ had become fronted to /øː/ some two centuries before the Great Vowel Shift took place. This meant that in these dialects there was no half-close back /oː/ to raise and thus push the close /uː/ aside into diphthongality in the way it did elsewhere (and /eː/ did to /iː/ everywhere) when the Great Vowel Shift came into operation. Hence /uː/ remained as a monophthong, so that the MOUTH words keep [u] to this day (or in some cases have later diphthongized for other reasons, as in southern Scotland). The front /øː/, meanwhile, was susceptible to various further changes as shown in (124) below. The Great Vowel Shift in general raised it to /yː/, though in Scots it typically remains /øː/ before the consonants /r, v, ð, z/ and finally. In England the [yː] has often become partially or completely unrounded, and now appears in traditional-dialect as [ɪʊ], [ju], etc., or – most commonly – as [ɪə]. Nowadays, of course, all of these traditional-dialect pronunciations are sharply recessive in the face of local-accent forms with /uː/. Similarly, the undiphthongized [u(ː)] in MOUTH words is recessive in the face of various diphthongal pronunciations.

(124)

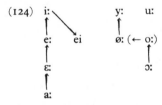

Returning from the dialects of the north-east of England and Scotland to English in general, we observe that one of the ways in which our traditional orthography is odd is in that it takes no cognizance of the Great Vowel Shift, reflecting rather the situation before it occurred. Middle English /iː/ and /i/ were phonetically similar vowels, one long and the other short; it was reasonable to represent both in the spelling by the same letter *i*, as *kite* and *kit*. Today we still use these spellings, but the first of the vowels in question is a wide diphthong, /aɪ/ etc., which phonetically no longer stands in a simple long–short (or tense–lax) relationship to /ɪ/. Similarly with the *e* spelling in *theme* and *them*, the *a* in *rate* and *rat*, the *o* in *note* and *not*, or the *ou* digraph in *doubt* and *double*. In each case we now have two quite different, phonetically unrelated, vowels spelt with the same letters.

It seems likely that KIT words had a short [i] until the seventeenth century, rather than the lowered and centralized [ɪ] qualities found today; and that the short vowel corresponding to long [uː] was similarly [u] rather than [ʊ]. (The first reference to a quality distinction such as exists in current FLEECE vs. KIT, [i(ː)] vs. [ɪ], is in Cooper's grammar written in the 1680s.)

Middle English had certain phonological rules which shortened or lengthened vowels in particular phonetic environments. As we have just seen, a change in quantity probably involved little or no change in quality. One such rule was Trisyllabic Shortening, which made a stressed long vowel short in the environment __CVCV. This accounted for the alternation between long vowel in *divine*, *serene*, *profane*, but short in *divinity*, *serenity*, *profanity*: in Middle English the alternations were between /iː/ and /i/, /eː/ and /e/, /aː/ and /a/. We still have the alternations in present-day English, but as a result of the Great Vowel Shift they are now between (RP) /aɪ/ and /ɪ/, /iː/ and /e/, /eɪ/ and /æ/ – no longer a simple phonetic relationship.

Whether because of a historical fluctuation or because of an uncertainty in reading rules or spelling pronunciation, we still have a number of words in which speakers or accents vary between PRICE and KIT, FLEECE and DRESS, or FACE and TRAP, thus *privacy*, *lever*, *fetid*, *patriot*, *patent*.

Chomsky & Halle (1968: passim) take the view that a rule corresponding to the Great Vowel Shift is still a synchronic rule of English phonology. They would say that a speaker stores the morpheme common to *divine* and *divinity* in the form /dɪviːn/, the one common to *serene* and *serenity* as /sɛreːn/, and the one common to *profane* and *profanity* as /profæːn/. The rule of Trisyllabic Laxing (trisyllabic shortening), also in their view a synchronic rule, then shortens the vowel in the *-ity* forms, while the Vowel Shift rule ensures the correct quality for the stressed vowel in *divine*, *serene*, and *profane* themselves. These and other rules also enable us, they would claim, to store single phonological representations in our mental lexicon for the shared morphemes underlying pairs such as *divide–division*, *conspire–conspiracy*, *bite–bitten*; *recede–recession*, *sphere–spherical*, *keep–kept*; *nation–national*, *compare–comparison*, *mania–manic*. While Chomsky & Halle's approach does lead to considerable simplification in the description of English derivational morphology, it is difficult to see how it can be squared with what we know about language acquisition. It implies that a child who hears everyday words such as *knee, piece, bean* (which have no derivationally related words with other vowels) somehow realizes that he must store them lexically with the phonological representations /neː, peːs, beːn/ (rather than /niː, piːs, biːn/), since otherwise the Vowel Shift rule, needed for pairs of related words which a child mostly does not learn till approaching puberty, would not allow them to have the correct phonetic output.

In the nature of things it is impossible to prove anything one way or the other about the alleged synchronic validity of the Great Vowel Shift. It also has no real bearing on the description of different English accents. Henceforth, therefore, we shall assume that it has no synchronic relevance, and that the various synchronic traces which remain of its historical operation are just that.

3.1.2 NG Coalescence

In most accents words such as *sing, wrong, gang* end in what is phonetically a velar nasal, [ŋ]. As discussed above (1.2.11), one line of argument in phonology leads to the conclusion that this segment is, synchronically speaking, the realization of an underlying sequence /ng/. Other phonologists reject this argument, and recognize a phoneme /ŋ/. Whatever its synchronic analysis, though, there can be no doubt that current [ŋ] results historically from a consonant cluster of nasal plus /g/. The nasal was doubtless always phonetically homorganic with the following plosive, so that words such as those mentioned ended with underlying /ng/, realized phonetically as [ŋg].

About 1600 the final [g] ceased to be pronounced in educated London English. Put another way, rule (19) of 1.2.11 above was added to the grammar: g → Ø / Nasal __ #. The velar nasal was accordingly left exposed in word-final position. Minimal pairs such as *sin* [sɪn] vs. *sing* [sɪŋ] resulted. Once this change was established, a prima facie case existed for the recognition of a third nasal phoneme, /ŋ/.

The result of this sound change is the coalescence of a consonant cluster: two consonants become one. So although we referred in 1.2.11 to Final [g] Deletion, a more appropriate name for the present discussion is NG Coalescence.

There are certain accents where NG Coalescence did not (does not) take place: notably the western part of the midlands and middle north of England, including Birmingham, Manchester, and Liverpool (see discussion and map in vol. 2, 4.4.6). Here *sing* and *wrong* are [sɪŋg], [rɒŋg]. This applies also in some London Jewish speech, as well as sporadically in New York and the south – and in foreign accents – in the United States, thus [lɔŋg] *Island*. Such accents may be termed **non-NG-coalescing**.

Hypercorrection by speakers with non-NG-coalescing accents takes the form of deleting /g/ too generally after the nasal, so that they carefully say not only [sɪŋ], ['sɪŋə], [lɒŋ], but also ['lɒŋə], ['strɒŋə], ['jʌŋɪst] etc. This hypercorrection can be heard in the speech of the speech-conscious not only from the relevant parts of England but also from the American south.

Something similar is found in the local accents of the west of Scotland and Ulster. Here, though, it is a stigmatized characteristic which the speech-conscious would certainly shun. It results from the widening of NG Coalescence to cover all instances of underlying /ng/, yielding such forms as ['fɪŋər] (traditional-dialect ['fæŋər]) for *finger*, as discussed in 1.2.11 above. We may refer to such accents as **generalized-NG-coalescing**.

Pairs such as *finger* and *singer* do not rhyme in RP or GenAm. They do rhyme both in non-NG-coalescing accents, where they both have intervocalic [ŋg], and in generalized-NG-coalescing accents, where they both have plain [ŋ].

There is great variability, in the standard accents as in others, on the question of NG Coalescence in the environment of a following /w/ or non-syllabic /l/, as in *English, language*; the majority probably retain [g]. Before a following /j/ or /r/, as in *singular, angry*, most accents categorically retain [g]. Generalized-NG-coalescing accents constitute an exception; and the *LAE* (map Ph241) shows [-ŋr-] in *hungry* as widespread in the south-west and north of England. These variants can be seen as reflecting minor differences in the specification of the environment for the operation of the [g]-deleting rule.

3.1.3 The velar fricative

The spelling *gh* in current orthography usually indicates that in Middle English the word in question was pronounced with /x/, a voiceless velar fricative (perhaps with a palatal allophone, [ç], if the preceding vowel was front). In the sixteenth century this fricative was still pronounced, in certain circles at least; by the latter part of the seventeenth century it had disappeared in the precursor of RP, except that in some cases /x/ had been switched instead to a labiodental, /f/. Hence the spelling *gh* now either is 'silent', as in *right*, *high*, *eight*, *bough*, *dough*, *daughter*, *through*, or else corresponds to phonological /f/, as in *cough*, *rough*, *laugh*. Both possibilities are exemplified in the same word in the place-name *Loughborough* /'lʌfbərə/. Before it disappeared, the /x/ often exerted some influence on the preceding vowel, such as causing it to lengthen. The resulting multiplicity of pronunciations corresponding to orthographic *-ough* is notorious.

In traditional-dialect of the north of England and Scotland, /x/ may remain in many of the words in which it was found in Middle English. Where it does not remain as such, it often happens that it yielded /f/ in items where standard accents have zero consonant, or vice versa. Hence on the one hand we have the stereotype Scots phrase *bricht moonlicht nicht* /'brɪxt 'munlɪxt 'nɪxt/ (for *bright moonlight night*; compare standard /braɪt/ etc.), and on the other hand occasional relic forms such as [trɒx] for *trough* (RP /trɒf/) and [lɪçt] for *light*, recorded by *SED* in southern West Yorkshire (at localities Y30 and Y21 respectively). In both these cases the local accent (as opposed to traditional-dialect) lacks /x/.

Quite apart from traditional-dialect, a fair number of names in the Celtic countries contain /x/ in the local pronunciation. This is the case with *Buchan* and *Auchtermuchty* in Scotland, *Amlwch* /-lʊx/ and *Loughor* /'lʌxə/ in Wales. A more English, less Celtic pronunciation commonly involves the replacement of this /x/ by /k/: English people and other outsiders call *Buchan* /'bʌkən/. In Ireland /h/ is common corresponding to putative earlier /x/, as in *Donaghadee*, *Haughey*, though some speakers do have a /x/. Thus there is a sense in which the consonant system even of Standard English, as pronounced in the Celtic countries, includes /x/, whether as a residualism going back to Middle English /x/ or as a loan-phoneme from Scottish Gaelic, Welsh, or Irish.

Even in England /x/ can be said to hold a tenuous and marginal position in the consonant system of educated speakers, though certainly no longer found in Standard English in words which contained it in Middle English. Here it is clearly a loan-phoneme.

Everybody knows the word *loch* and its Scots 'guttural sound'. The composer Bach is often called [bɑːx], with a vowel reflecting the German short [a] only poorly but a consonant which is more successful. Some English people, too, will attempt [x] in surnames of Celtic origin such as *MacLachlan*. The hyperforeignism ['mjuːnɪx] for *Munich* (German ['mʏnçən]) is very common; [xl] is also familiar as one of the would-be sophisticated attempts at Welsh [ɬ], as in *Llangollen*.

A velar or uvular fricative /x/ has also been taken into South African English along with Afrikaans words containing it, as *gogga* /'xɒxə/. In the United States it has similarly been borrowed along with Yiddish words such as *chutzpah* /'xʊtspə/.

3.1.4 THOUGHT Monophthonging

In late Middle English words such as *law, ball, taught* had a diphthong /au/: /lau, baul, tauxt/. From around the beginning of the seventeenth century this diphthong gave way to a monophthong, the /ɔ(ː)/ of present-day RP and GenAm.

The THOUGHT vowel can in most cases be traced back to Middle English /au/, with or without a following /x/. In *thought* itself, as well as in other words with orthographic *-ought* and in *daughter*, the Middle English diphthong was /ɔu/, which evidently underwent a merger with /au/ just in the environment __xt. A monophthongal pronunciation of the THOUGHT vowel seems to have been general from about 1600 onwards; but Middle English /au/ may have had a variant [aː] since considerably earlier. It is not clear whether the process involved was one of coalescence, [a] plus [u] yielding the qualitatively intermediate [ɔː], or whether there was an intermediate stage [ɔu], so that one had first a partial assimilation of the first element of the diphthong to the second, [au] → [ɔu], and then a partial assimilation of the second element to the first, [ɔu] → [ɔɔ], i.e. [ɔː]. If the latter, then it would be possible to regard the [ɔu] variants of American southern and/or Cockney as residualisms preserved since the fifteenth century. But this is unlikely: it is virtually certain that these diphthongs are relatively recent developments which have arisen independently in the two accents in question.

Not all words with Middle English /au/ have current pronunciations with /ɔ(ː)/. Where there was a following labial consonant, or a cluster of nasal plus another consonant, the vowel has instead fallen in with that of BATH or, in certain cases, PALM or FACE – as in *laugh*, *calm*, and *ancient* respectively.

A consequence of the disappearance of /x/, discussed above, was the creation of new homophones, such as *taught–taut*, *sight–site*. Occasionally, though, the /x/ had exerted an allophonic effect upon the preceding vowel, and the deletion of the /x/ caused this previously allophonic difference to be phonologized. In the north of England various words which once included /x/ now have non-standard diphthongal forms, e.g. the words commonly spelt *nowt* ('nothing') and *owt* ('anything' – the cognate Standard forms are *nought* ~ *naught* and literary-archaic *aught*). In some areas this diphthong is identical with the /aʊ/ of MOUTH words, so that *owt* and *out* are homophones; but in others, including the urban working-class speech of Leeds (West Yorkshire), it is distinct, and we have [ɒʊt] *owt* opposed to [aʊt] *out*.

North of the Lune–Humber line across the north of England, where local traditional-dialect keeps /uː/ in MOUTH words, it may well be that the inherited [aʊ]-type diphthong of *aught* (*owt*), etc., is what is gradually being reallocated to MOUTH words as /uː/ recedes in the face of standard /aʊ/.

3.1.5 The Long Mid Mergers

Nowadays pairs such as *mane* and *main*, *toe* and *tow* are homophones in most accents. Previously it was not so. A distinction in pronunciation existed up to the seventeenth century, when it disappeared in polite usage through operation of the process we refer to as the Long Mid Mergers. By this sound change the originally monophthongal vowels of *mane* and *toe* fell together with the diphthongs of *main* and *tow*. In various local accents these mergers are not yet complete.

The lexical sets FACE and GOAT thus both reflect mergers of distinct Middle English vowels. Of the FACE words, those in (63a) (2.2.11 above) had a monophthongal vowel, [aː], shifted qualitatively to [ɛː], as we have seen (3.1.1) by about 1600. The words in (63b), on the other hand, had a diphthong in Middle English, [ɛi] or [æi] (the earlier distinction between these two possibilities having been levelled by perhaps the fourteenth century). By the sixteenth or seventeenth century this vowel was losing its diphthongal quality. Hence, although careful speakers may have retained the distinction for some time, the erstwhile diphthong eventually fell in with the [ɛː] resulting from Middle English /aː/, so that the distinction between the vowel of the (63a) words and that of the (63b) words disappeared. Thus pairs such as *pane–pain*, *raze–raise*, *wave–waive*, and *daze–days* came to be identical in pronunciation. We may refer to this development as the FACE Merger. By the eighteenth century the merged (or merging) vowel took on a closer quality, [eː], and around 1800 this diphthongized in polite English usage (as discussed below in 3.1.12), giving a quality similar to the current RP [eɪ].

The back vowels in the lexical set GOAT followed a parallel course. The words in (66a) had a monophthongal [ɔː] in Middle English, whilst those of (66b) had a diphthongal /ɔu/. The former vowel was raised to [oː] by 1600; the latter fell in with it shortly afterwards, in what we may call the GOAT Merger. This left *toe–tow*, *sole–soul*, *nose–knows* as identical in pronunciation. The merged [oː] diphthongized in polite usage around 1800, giving an [oʊ] such as is still current in GenAm and may sometimes be heard in old-fashioned RP, as well as in various other accents.

Both FACE and GOAT Mergers involve the loss of an opposition between a diphthong and a long mid vowel. Hence they may be referred to jointly as the Long Mid Mergers. They are displayed diagrammatically in (125). (It must be pointed out, though, that there is some scholarly disagreement about the precise order and timing of these various developments.)

(125)	*pane, raze, daze*	*pain, raise, days*	*toe, sole, nose*	*tow, soul, knows*
Middle English	aː	ɛi	ɔː	ou
Great Vowel Shift	ɛː	–	oː	–
Long Mid Mergers	ɛː		oː	
Eighteenth-century Raising	eː		–	
Long Mid Diphthonging	eɪ		oʊ	

In local accents there are traces in areas as scattered as the far north of England, East Anglia, south Wales and Newfoundland of the pre-merger pattern. This can be seen from the fact that pairs such as *pane* vs. *pain*, *daze* vs. *days*, or *toe* vs. *tow*, *nose* vs. *knows* are often still distinguished in pronunciation in these places, e.g. as [peːn] vs. [pɛɪn], [noːz] vs. [nɔʊz]. (Trudgill & Foxcroft, 1978, analyse the gradual disappearance of the lexical distinction in GOAT words in East Anglia.)

With minimal pairs of this kind there are, however, one or two complicating factors to be taken into consideration before drawing firm conclusions:

(i) Today's spelling does not always reflect the historical situation accurately. Although the spelling *a-C-e* usually indicates Middle English /aː/ and *ai* or *ay* Middle English /ɛi/, this is not true in, for instance, the words *mail* (post), *gait*, and *waist*, all of which go back to Middle English /aː/ and have hence presumably been homophones of *male*, *gate*, *waste* since long before the Long Mid Mergers. The spelling of *roe* (fish eggs) similarly suggests Middle English /ɔː/, though in fact it had /ɔu/, just like *row* (with oars). *Throe* is thought to be etymologically identical with *throw*.

(ii) Some of the FACE words listed in (63b) formerly contained a velar fricative after the vowel, reflected in a spelling with *gh* (as *weigh*, *straight*). Various words of French origin are spelt with a silent *g* after the vowel (as *reign*): this may have been pronounced at one period as a velar nasal. In most of the north of England these former velars have left a phonetic residue in some or all of such words in the shape of a palatal glide, so that e.g. *weight* [wɛit] may be distinct from *wait* [weːt], even though the latter rhymes perfectly with *late* in consequence of the FACE Merger. (See above, 3.1.3, The velar fricative.)

(iii) The minimal pairs *daze–days*, *nose–knows* may be distinguished in some accents even though the Long Mid Mergers have been carried through, because of morphological considerations: *daze* and *nose* are solid morphemes, while *day#s* and *know#s* include a morpheme boundary between stem and ending. In Belfast, for instance, *days* [dɛːz] is typically distinct from *daze* [deəz], even though *pane* and *pain* are homophonous.

3.1.6 The FLEECE Merger

Pairs such as *meet* and *meat*, *piece* and *peace* are nowadays homophones in most types of English. In Middle English they were distinct. The difference disappeared through a merger which took place in the seventeenth century. Since both sets of words involved belong to the standard lexical set FLEECE, we may refer to this development as the FLEECE Merger. There are various provincial British and Irish accents in which the FLEECE Merger has not applied, or applied only partially.

The phonemically distinct vowels of Middle English were /eː/, used in the words of (62a) (2.2.10 above) (*meet* etc.), and /ɛː/, used in the words of (62b) (*meat* etc.). Both vowels were raised by one stage in the Great Vowel Shift, so that *meet* became [miːt] and *meat* [meːt]; then the FLEECE Merger levelled the distinction between them by about 1700, giving our modern homophones such as *meet–meat, piece–peace, see–sea*. These developments are diagrammed in (126).

(126)

	meet, piece, see, believe	meat, peace, sea, receive
Middle English (fourteenth century)	eː	ɛː
Great Vowel Shift (by 1600)	iː	eː[1]
FLEECE Merger (by about 1700)	iː	

[1] probably [iː, ɛː] in certain types of pronunciation.

There seems to have been a considerable period during which rival pronunciations were current in words of the subset (62b) (*meat* etc.). Indeed, rhymes between these words and those of the lexical set FACE are found well into the eighteenth century, as in the poem *The solitude of Alexander Selkirk* by William Cowper (1731–1800):

> I am monarch of all I sur*vey*,
> My right there is none to dispute,
> From the centre right round to the *sea*,
> I am lord of the fowl and the brute.

Pronunciations reflecting the situation prior to the FLEECE persist in the traditional-dialect of much of the north of England. *SED* shows the vowel of *grease* (I.11.4) as qualitatively distinct from that of *geese* (IV.6.15) in most of (old) Lancashire, Yorkshire and Lincolnshire, with [ɪə] in *grease* but [iː] (or in the Yorkshire Dales [əi]) in *geese*. (These items are mapped in *LAE*, Ph74 and Ph93.)

The use of [eː] or [eɪ] rather than [iː] in words of the subset (62b) is one of the hallmarks of a caricature Irish accent, thus [teː] *tea*, [meːz|z] *measles*. Nevertheless, this pronunciation is sharply recessive in present-day Ireland, and is restricted to conservative rural or working-class urban speech; even there it is inconsistently used and subject to sociolinguistic variation. Mostly a Dubliner pronounces *tea* as [tiː], just as does someone from Cardiff, Edinburgh, Minneapolis, or Montego Bay. Nor is the [eː] form restricted to Irish speech: *SED* records [teː] for *tea* in much of Lancashire, Cheshire, and Shropshire, as well as in patches in Devon, Hampshire and Wiltshire (VII.8.3; map Ph78 in *LAE*). In all of these places the [eː] pronunciation is without any doubt sharply recessive.

The words *break*, *great*, *steak*, and *yea* nowadays belong to the lexical set FACE (constituting, along with certain proper names spelt with *ea*, such as *MacLean* and *O'Shea*, the subset (63c)). Thus *break* is now a homophone of *brake*, and *great* of *grate*. In Middle English they had /ɛː/, the same vowel as used in (62a); so that they might have been expected to end up in the lexical set FLEECE, with *great* pronounced identically with *greet*. Their current pronunciation implies that for some reason they have been exempt from the FLEECE Merger. It is known that their pronunciation fluctuated in the eighteenth century between /iː/ (FLEECE) and /eː/ (FACE); it is only since then that they have settled down among the FACE words. Boswell represents Dr Johnson, in the year 1772, as saying (Hill 1934: ii. 161) that Lord Chesterfield ('the best speaker in the House of Lords') considered that *great* should be pronounced so as to rhyme with *state*, while Sir William Yonge ('the best speaker in the House of Commons') thought it should rhyme with *seat*, claiming that 'none but an Irishman would pronounce it *grait*'. Although Lord Chesterfield's view has prevailed in the standard accents, other pronunciations are still to be encountered in local dialects; indeed a cultivated American southern accent may often give *great* the vowel of DRESS, which implies a Middle English shortening of /eː/ to /e/ in this word (as generally in *deaf* etc.).

3.1.7 The FOOT–STRUT Split

The reference accents, like most accents of English, have /ʊ/ and /ʌ/ as contrastive phonemes, as can be demonstrated by minimal pairs such as *could–cud*, *put–putt*, *look–luck*, *stood–stud*. Middle English had no such distinction among its short vowels. The present situation results essentially from the fact that Middle English short /u/

has split into two phonemes, the current /ʊ/ and /ʌ/. This split, dating from the seventeenth century, has not taken place in the broad accents of the north of England, and only partly so in Ireland. In consequence their local accents may have *put* and *putt*, *could* and *cud*, etc., as homophones.

The situation is complicated by the fact that some words now belonging to the FOOT and STRUT sets derive from a Middle English long vowel, namely /oː/. Some of these underwent shortening early on, and joined the Middle English /u/ category before it split; they typically now have /ʌ/, as *blood, flood, love*. Others, though, shortened rather later, and typically now have /ʊ/, as *good, stood, foot, book*. The lexical incidence of this shortening, though, varied somewhat in different places, with the consequence that in the north of England and in Ireland (for example) pronunciations such as /luːk/ *look*, /buːk/ *book* are still encountered. Even the reference accents vacillate between FOOT and GOOSE in words such as *broom, groom*, and *room* (RP /rʊm ~ ruːm/). Some Americans would distinguish between a square /rut/ in mathematics and digging up old /rʊts/ in the yard. In some parts of England – particularly, it seems, in the west – words such as *hoof, roof, tooth, soon, spoon* are pronounced with short /ʊ/ rather than long /uː/.

Leaving aside this question of words deriving from Middle English /oː/, we find that most FOOT and STRUT words derive from Middle English short /u/. Most commonly this vowel became-opener and unrounded, thus yielding the current /ʌ/. This applies to the words in the standard lexical set STRUT: *cut*, for example, developed from Middle English /kut/ to present-day RP (etc.) /kʌt/. Other words, though, were for some reason exempt from this development. They retained a short vowel, in due course somewhat centralized to yield current /ʊ/. This is the case with words in the standard lexical set FOOT, as for example *put*, which has a current pronunciation /pʊt/ in RP (etc.) only slightly different phonetically from its Middle English form /put/.

The split of the old short /u/ into two distinct qualities seems to have been established by the middle of the seventeenth century. It may well have originated as an allophonic alternation, with unrounded [ɤ], the forerunner of modern /ʌ/, in most environments, but a rounded quality (modern /ʊ/) retained after labials. This explains why we have [kʌt] *cut*, but [pʊt] *put*; [dʌl] *dull*, but [fʊl] *full*. But there are various exceptions which show unrounding of the vowel in spite of a preceding labial – *vulture*, *fun*, *mud* among them. Others have retained a rounded vowel even though the preceding consonant is not labial, for example *sugar*. The influx of words with a vowel arising from the shortening of Middle English /oː/ made the distribution of [ʌ] and [ʊ] even less complementary, particularly by increasing the possibilities of having [ʊ] after a non-labial (*good*, *look*). And so we arrived at the present situation in most accents, in which there are clearly two phonemically distinct vowels, even though there are not a large number of minimal pairs by which to demonstrate this fact.

As mentioned above, there are accents which have never undergone the split of old short /u/ (the FOOT–STRUT Split). Thus in all broad local accents of the north of England there is just a single phoneme /ʊ/ corresponding to the two phonemes, /ʊ/ and /ʌ/, of RP and south-of-England accents. In this kind of accent *put* is a homophone of *putt* and *could* of *cud*. It does not necessarily follow, though, that *book* is homophonous with *buck* in such an accent; instead, it may retain the long vowel of GOOSE, thus [buːk] *book* vs. [bʊk] *buck*. If we consider the triplet *Luke–look–luck*, it will be seen that a broad north-of-England accent cannot have all three different (as they are in RP, [luːk] vs. [lʊk] vs. [lʌk]): *look* must fall in either with *Luke* /luːk/ or with *luck* /lʊk/.

We can diagram the historical development of Middle English /oː, u/ in the reference accents as (127).

(127)

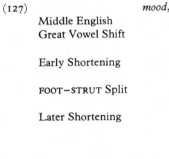
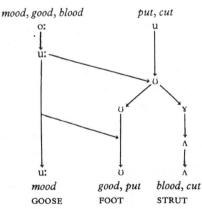

	mood, good, blood	*put, cut*
Middle English	oː	u
Great Vowel Shift		
Early Shortening	uː	
FOOT–STRUT Split		ʊ
Later Shortening		ʊ ʏ
	uː	ʊ ʌ
	mood	*good, put* *blood, cut*
	GOOSE	FOOT STRUT

Another way the same facts can be presented is in tabular form, (128), tracing the five possible paths: *goose* itself followed the same path as *mood*, *foot* the same as *good*.

(128)		*mood*	*blood*	*good*	*cut*	*put*
	Middle English	oː	oː	oː	u	u
	Great Vowel Shift	uː	uː	uː	–	–
	Early Shortening	–	u	–	–	–
	(Quality adjustment)	–	ʊ	–	ʊ	ʊ
	FOOT–STRUT Split	–	ɤ	–	ɤ	ʊ
	Later Shortening	–	–	ʊ	–	–
	(Quality adjustment)	–	ʌ	–	ʌ	–
	Output	uː	ʌ	ʊ	ʌ	ʊ

For accents with unsplit FOOT–STRUT, things are somewhat simpler, (129):

(129)		*mood*	*blood*	*good*	*cut*	*put*
	Middle English	oː	oː	oː	u	u
	Great Vowel Shift	uː	uː	uː	–	–
	Early Shortening	uː	u	–	–	–
	(Quality adjustment)	–	ʊ	–	ʊ	ʊ
	Later Shortening	–	–	ʊ	–	–
	Output	uː	ʊ	ʊ	ʊ	ʊ

Where *look* is /luːk/, it was unaffected by Later Shortening; where it is /lʊk/, it followed the same path as *good*.

3.1.8 The NURSE Merger

In most present-day accents of English, words such as *heard*, *herd*, *stirred*, *bird*, and *word* all rhyme. It was not always so, as the spelling we use suggests: in Middle English these words had various vowels (normally short) followed by the consonant /r/. In the English spoken in Scotland and Ireland this situation has persisted to some extent. Elsewhere, most or all of the vowels in question have undergone two developments: (i) they have merged into a single mid central vowel, and (ii) this vowel has coalesced with the /r/ to yield an r-coloured vocoid. The merged and coalesced vowel has subsequently in many accents lost its r-colouring. Hence for all the words mentioned above we have GenAm /ɜr/ [ɝ], RP /ɜː/.

The merging of these various Middle English vowels seems to have started in northern and eastern dialects of English in the fifteenth century; by the sixteenth it had spread to popular London speech, and by the seventeenth to the precursor of RP. The vowels in question, Middle English /ɪ/, /ɛ/ and /ʊ/, were centred and merged as [ə] in the environment of a final or preconsonantal /r/, as in *sir, bird; err, fern; spur, church*. This development may be referred to as the (**First**) NURSE Merger. It is as a consequence of this merger that the standard lexical set NURSE exists and that we nowadays have homophones in the reference accents such as *serf–surf, tern–turn, birth–berth, pearl–purl*, or perfect rhymes such as *serve–curve, heard–word*. This, too, is how *kernel* came to be a homophone of *colonel*, which had an earlier form /kʊrnɛl/ *cor(o)nel*.

In most Scottish accents the NURSE Merger has not occurred, or has only partially occurred. Indeed, some have as many as five different vowels corresponding to the NURSE set (and this is in an accent of Standard English, not Scots dialect), thus *heard* with [ɛr], *herd* with [ɛ̈r], *stirred* with [ɪr], *bird* with [ər], and *word* with [ʌr] (vol. 2, 5.2.3). This is extreme, but it is commonplace in both Scotland and Ireland to have two contrasting possibilities, so that (for instance) *word* and *bird* have [ər] but *heard* [ɛr]. Minimal pairs may include the *serf–surf, tern–turn, pearl–purl* mentioned above, and also *Beirne–burn, earn* (or *Erne*)–*urn, kerb–curb, Hertz–hurts*. As can be seen, few of these minimal pairs are very satisfactory, since they depend on proper names or rare words; moreover, *kerb–curb*, which is certainly attested in some Irish English as /kɛrb/ vs. /kʌrb/, must depend on a spelling pronunciation of *kerb*, since the two words are etymologically identical (and still spelt the same by Americans). It follows, then, that the presence vs. absence of NURSE Merger is usually best tested by potentially rhyming pairs such as *serve–curve, earth–worth, jerk–work, deterring–occurring*. Alternatively, there is the old music-hall pun, 'What's a Grecian urn?' – 'I dunno, about a hundred quid a week, I suppose.'

When prevocalic, Middle English /ɪ/, /ɛ/, and /ʊ/ plus /r/ were in principle unaffected by the NURSE Merger: thus RP still has a short vowel plus /r/ in words such as *mirror* /'mɪrə/, *very* /'vɛrɪ/, *furrow* /'fʌrəʊ/. Regional pronunciations such as /'vərɪ/ *very*, /ə'mərɪkə/ *America* are, however, by no means uncommon, with [ɛ] centred to [ə] before prevocalic /r/. In American speech *squirrel, stirrup*, and *syrup* (all with RP /-ɪr-/), as well as *furrow, worry*, etc. (RP /-ʌr-/), are very widely pronounced with central vowels (/-ʌr-/ or /-ɜr-/), although other items such as *mirror, spirit* usually have /ɪ/. Merger in the prevocalic environment is thus subject to severe lexical and geographical restrictions.

The [əɹ] regularly resulting from the NURSE Merger was phonetically particularly similar to the [ʌɹ] sequence derived from Middle English /ʊr/ by the FOOT–STRUT Split, as in *furrow, worry, hurry*. In RP and some other accents, nevertheless, theẏ have remained distinct, so that today RP has /ɜː/ in *bird, fur, stirring*, but /ʌr/ in *furrow, worry, hurry*; note also *occurring* /əˈkɜːrɪŋ/ vs. *occurrence* /əˈkʌrəns/. In many other other accents, including most GenAm, the two possibilities merged, yielding present-day /ɜr/ in all the words mentioned and giving rise to new rhymes such as *furry–hurry, stir it–turret*. We may refer to this further merger as the **Second NURSE Merger**.

In RP and similar accents the /ər/ resulting from the NURSE Merger has developed into a long vowel: we have [ɜː] in preconsonantal and absolute-final position (*bird, fur*‖) and [ɜːɹ] in prevocalic position (*stirring, stir it, furry*). The last three examples suggest that this is not some sort of compensatory lengthening linked to the loss of non-prevocalic /r/; rather, we must recognize a **Pre-R Lengthening** of mid and open short vowels in the environment of /r/ plus a consonant or word boundary (including the internal # of *stirring, furry*) – affecting, in fact, just the same environments as the NURSE Merger itself. The input, though, was more general, since /a/ and /ɒ/ were also affected (*start, north*); and of course after the NURSE Merger there were no instances left of other short vowels in this environment. Pre-R Lengthening can be dated to the seventeenth century.

We can now restate the rules we have been discussing as (130–132).

$$(130) \quad \text{ɪ, ɛ, ʏ} \rightarrow \text{ə} \;/\; \_\_r \begin{Bmatrix} C \\ \# \end{Bmatrix} \qquad \text{First NURSE Merger}$$

$$(131) \quad V \rightarrow \text{long} \;/\; \_\_r \begin{Bmatrix} C \\ \# \end{Bmatrix} \qquad \text{Pre-R Lengthening}$$

$$(132) \quad \text{ʌ} \rightarrow \text{ɜ} \;/\; \_\_r \qquad \text{Second NURSE Merger}$$

To be able to trace the developments from Middle English right through to the present day in the words we are considering, we need to recognize four further rules:

(133)

	sir	refer	fur	bird, term, turn, stirring	occurring	start, bar	north, for	mirror	herald	hurry	narrow
Middle English	ɪr	ɛr	ʊr	ɪr	ʊr	ar	ɔr	ɪr	ɛr	ʊr	ar
FOOT–STRUT Split	–	–	ʏr	–	ʏr	–	–	–	–	ʏr	–
First NURSE Merger (130)	ər	ər	ər	ər	ər	–	–	–	–	–	–
Pre-R Lengthening (131)	əːr	əːr	əːr	əːr	əːr	aːr	ɔːr	–	–	–	ær
Quality changes (i)	ɜːr	ɜːr	ɜːr	ɜːr	ɜːr	ɑːr	ɔːr	–	–	ʌr	ær
(RP) R Dropping (ii)	ɜː	ɜː	ɜː	–	–	ɑː	ɔː	–	–	–	–
RP output	ɜː	ɜː	ɜː	ɜːr	ɜːr	ɑː	ɔː	ɪr	ɛr	ʌr	ær
(GenAm) Loss of distinctive length (iii)	ɜr	ɜr	ɜr	ɜr	ɜr	ɑr	ɔr	–	–	ɜr	–
(GenAm) Second NURSE Merger (132)	–	–	–	–	–	–	–	–	–	ɜr	–
(GenAm) R Coalescence (iv)	ɝ	ɝ	ɝ	ɝ	ɝ	ɑr	–	–	–	ɝ	ær
GenAm output	ɝ	ɝ	ɝ	ɝ	ɝ	ɑr	ɔr	ɪr	ɛr	ɝ	ær

(i)   quality changes in certain vowels (lengthened ə, a, ɒ → ɜ, ɑ, ɔ; short ʏ, a → ʌ, æ);

(ii)   (for RP only) non-prevocalic R Dropping (3.2.2 below);

(iii) (for GenAm only) loss of distinctive length (3.3.4 below);

(iv) (now for GenAm only; can be interpreted as an allophonic rule) R Coalescence (ɜr → ɝ).

The developments for GenAm and RP are set out in (133).

There are quite a few instances where preconsonantal or final Middle English /ɛr/ has given a current standard pronunciation with the vowel of START rather than that of NURSE, for example *far*, *star*, *heart*. There seems to have been a period of some fluctuation in such words, with the tendency towards spelling pronunciation perhaps playing a rôle; one consequence is the handful of present-day well-known British/American differences – *clerk*, *Derby*, *Berkeley* with RP /ɑː/ but GenAm /ɜr/. Other variants with START for NURSE or vice versa are still found in conservative regional speech both in England and elsewhere, including Appalachia. In England, both *Derby* and *clerk* are quite often pronounced with /ɜː/ by working-class speakers. In the eighteenth century the novelist Fielding put the pronunciations 'sarvis, sartain, parson' into the speech or writing of characters we are intended to consider vulgar. The last-mentioned form, though obsolescent or obsolete now in the sense 'person', has nevertheless lived on in the doublet word *parson* 'clergyman'; the two words are etymologically identical. We still have *varmin(t)* as a rustic variant of *vermin*. The form *varsity* is still alive in some places as an abbreviation of *university*. And *I'll larn you* remains as a jocular pseudodialectalism meaning 'I'll teach you a lesson you won't forget', a witness to the once widespread usage whereby *learn* had the START vowel – a usage still frequently encountered, for example, in popular Jamaican speech.

3.1.9 Pre-Fricative Lengthening

The environment of a following /r/, as discussed in the preceding section, was not the only one in which the successors of Middle English /a/ and /ɒ/ underwent lengthening. By the end of the seventeenth century these vowels had become subject to lengthening in the environment of a following voiceless fricative (or at least /f, θ, s/). Short /a/ had by now been raised to [æ] in the precursor of the reference accents, and the lengthening to [æː] and [ɒː] respectively was presumably merely allophonic, at least to begin with. It resulted in forms such as *st*[æː]*ff, b*[æː]*th, p*[æː]*ss,* [æː]*sk;* [ɒː]*ff, cl*[ɒː]*th, l*[ɒː]*ss, fr*[ɒː]*st.* Formulaically,

(134)   Open V → long / __ Voiceless fricative

In time, though, the long and short vowels sometimes came to be distinct in quality as well as in length, and these developments were often lexically inconsistent, i.e. did not apply across the board to every word which met their structural description. Thus we now have RP /ɑː/ in *staff, bath, pass, grasp,* as against /æ/ not only in *trap, bat, sack,* etc., but also in *maths, gas,* and *asp;* and we have GenAm /ɔ/ in *off, cloth, loss, frost* as against /ɑ/ in *top, lot,* and also usually in *doff* and *Goth.*

It can be seen that the lengthening of [æ] became phonologized in this manner in RP, though not in GenAm, so establishing the standard lexical set BATH (RP /ɑː/ but GenAm /æ/); while the lengthening of [ɒ] became phonologized in GenAm, so establishing the standard lexical set CLOTH (mainstream RP /ɒ/ but GenAm /ɔ/). (This issue is complicated here by the existence of the rival, now old-fashioned U-RP /ɔː/ in CLOTH words, so that we may in fact rather have to recognize an RP history for *cloth* of Middle English [klɔθ] → sixteenth-century [klɒθ] → seventeenth-century [klɒːθ] → [klɔːθ] → modern mainstream RP [klɒθ], some U-RP [klɔːθ].)

Pre-Fricative Lengthening has accordingly given rise to two phoneme splits: the TRAP–BATH Split (Middle English /a/) and the LOT–CLOTH Split (Middle English /ɔ/). The allophonic lengthening, attested by the end of the seventeenth century, is to be regarded as belonging to the period prior to the divergence of British and American English, although its phonologization may not. It is noteworthy that West Indian accents have long vowels in BATH and CLOTH: in popular Jamaican speech *bath* is [baːt], *cloth* [klaːt] (compare *flat* [flat], *lot* [lat], with short vowels). English became established in the West Indies in the seventeenth century; the stopping of /θ/ (θ → t, see vol. 3, 7.1.3) may well be attributable to African influence and datable to the same period. This shows that the vowels of *bath* and *cloth* must already have been long at that time; because if the lengthening of the vowel in BATH and CLOTH words were a fashion introduced later from England or elsewhere it would have been likely to affect other words ending in [t], such as *flat, lot*, which it did not. In early West Indian speech, in fact, the local development of TH Stopping must have served to phonologize the Pre-Fricative Lengthening earlier than elsewhere.

The north of England remained unaffected by Pre-Fricative Lengthening, hence typical northern [baθ, klɒθ], as against typical southern [bɑːθ, klɔːθ] (the current mainstream RP [bɑːθ, klɒθ], carrying forward the southern development of BATH but the northern conservative form in CLOTH, now gradually displacing the regional rivals). The TRAP–BATH Split made some headway in the United States, probably as a fashionable import from Britain in the eighteenth or nineteenth century: see vol. 3, 6.4.3. But for most American accents the loss of distinctive length (3.3.4 below) meant that BATH words kept the same phonemic vowel as TRAP, /æ/ (at least until the twentieth-century development of a distinctive /eə/, vol. 3, 6.1.4).

Current RP also has /ɑː/ in many words where the vowel is followed by /ns, ntʃ, nt, nd/, such as *dance, answer, branch, grant, demand*. Some of these had Middle English variants with /aʊ/ (which would normally yield present-day /ɔː/); some are loanwords from French. They have /æ/ (or now /ɛə/) in GenAm. See further in 3.2.4 below. There are also many instances where GenAm has /ɔ/ rather than /ɑ/ in environments other than that of a following voiceless fricative or /r/, implying a lengthening of earlier /ɒ/ (an /ɒ/ which still remains in RP): thus *long, dog, gone*. There appears to have been considerable fluctuation and inconsistency in the seventeenth-century (and later) pronunciation of these and other words where /æ/ was followed by a nasal plus obstruent or /ɒ/ by a velar. There was also inconsistency in Pre-Fricative Lengthening where the word was not a monosyllable, though on the whole vowels remained short in polysyllables (hence RP /æ/ in *passage*, GenAm /ɑ/ in *possible*; but note fluctuation still at the present day in *exasperate, blasphemy*, etc., RP /æ ~ ɑː/). For some more details, see above, 2.2.7–8.

Middle English /a/ yields GenAm /ɑ/ principally in the environment of a following non-prevocalic /r/, through Pre-R Lengthening (3.1.8 above) and a later quality change, [aː] → [ɑː].

Also affected were such PALM words as existed in the language at the time (though note variants in rural American speech as /kæm/ *calm*, /mɔ/ *Ma*). One of these was the word *father*; the anomalous development of this everyday word (which might be expected to have kept a short front vowel, like *gather*) has not been satisfactorily explained.

Middle English short /ɔ/ yields GenAm /ɔ/ in three principal environments: before non-prevocalic /r/ in NORTH words (Pre-R Lengthening, 3.1.8), before /f, θ, s/ in monosyllables (Pre-Fricative Lengthening), and before /ŋ/ and to some extent other velars. Examples of the third type are *long* and *strong*, GenAm /lɔŋ, strɔŋ/. This suggests that at least some speakers in eighteenth-century England had long [ɒː] before /ŋ/, even though the short vowel ultimately prevailed (RP etc /lɒŋ, strɒŋ/).

3.1.10 Yod Dropping

Pairs such as *threw–through*, *brewed–brood* used to be distinguished by the use of a diphthong in the former member of each pair as against a monophthong in the latter. The diphthong, of the [ɪ̆u] type, developed into a rising [juː] through the transfer of syllabicity from the first segment to the second; in certain environments the [j] then disappeared, a development we may refer to as **Early Yod Dropping**. The pairs mentioned are accordingly now homophones in most accents. (Scottish people distinguish *brewed* from *brood* in another way–[bruːd] vs. [brud]–and for another reason, namely the morpheme boundary in *brew # ed*: see vol. 2, 5.2.3.)

Certain conservative Welsh, north-of-England, and American accents did not undergo Early Yod Dropping, and thus retain the distinction, e.g. Welsh [θrɪu] *threw* vs. [θruː] *through*.

The GOOSE words in (67a) of 2.2.15 above mostly had Middle English /oː/, which developed into a close /uː/ by about 1500. The remaining GOOSE words, (67b), contained a variety of Middle English vowels (/ɪu, ɛu, yː/ etc.), all of which had merged by the early seventeenth century into a falling diphthong of the [ɪu] type. In the conservative Welsh, northern, and American (southern and New England) accents mentioned above, a diphthong /ɪu/ remains in the vowel system, phonemically distinct from /u(ː)/, giving minimal pairs such as /tʃɪuz/ *chews* vs. /tʃuz/ *choose*, /rɪum/ *rheum* vs. /rum/ *room* (both adduced by Kenyon 1958: §348, a phonetician who had this distinction in his own speech). Some speakers, though not Kenyon, may even retain the distinction after /j/, thus /jɪus/ *use* (n.) vs. /juθ/ *youth*.

In London the falling diphthong [ɪŭ] had by the end of the seventeenth century given way to a rising [ĭu:], phonetically identical with the inherited /juː/ of *youth* etc. This development brought into existence a large number of new initial consonant clusters involving /j/. Several of them were intrinsically awkward to pronounce, so that we find that from the beginning of the eighteenth century the [ĭ] or [j] element disappears in certain environments, leaving a vowel identical with /uː/ and creating new homophones such as *threw–through*.

The environments in which Early Yod Dropping applied most generally are (i) after palatals (including palato-alveolars), as in *chute, chew, juice, yew*; (ii) after /r/, as in *rude, crew, shrew, grew*; and (iii) after consonant plus /l/, as in *blue, flue, flew, glue*. Formulaically, (135):

$$(135) \quad j \to \emptyset \ / \left. \begin{cases} \text{Palatal} \\ \text{r} \\ \text{C l} \end{cases} \right\} \ \underline{\quad}$$

The accents of East Anglia are notable for having extended Yod Dropping to most or all postconsonantal environments, for example in *few, music, cube, Hugh*. This **Generalized Yod Dropping**, in its most extreme form, can be written as (136).

$$(136) \quad j \to \emptyset \ / \ C \ \underline{\quad}$$

Other accents occupy intermediate positions, retaining /j/ after labials, velars, and /h/, but perhaps not after some alveolars. In RP there is variability in the environment of a preceding /θ, s, z, l/, as in /ɪn'θ(j)uːzɪæzm̩/, /s(j)uːt/, /rɪ'z(j)uːm/, /l(j)uːd/ *lewd*; the yod is consistently retained after /n/, as in /njuː/ *new*, and also after /t, d/, as in /tjuːn/, /djuːk/ (where there is the further possibility in casual speech of Yod Coalescence to [tʃuːn], [dʒuːk]). In GenAm, and also in parts of the south and midlands of England, /j/ is lost after alveolars, /t, d, n, l, s, z/, but not after labials or velars: see below, 3.3.3, Later Yod Dropping.

Another possible development is that earlier [ɪu] monophthong-izes to a central [ʉ] which remains in opposition to back [u]. *Brewed* and *brood* are then [brʉd] and [brud] respectively. This form of pronunciation is ascribed by Jones (1962: §732) to 'some forms of American English'; *PEAS* records it only as a rare and recessive variant in northern New England and upstate New York (maps 33, 147).

Although nowadays almost everybody pronounces *yew* and *you* identically, there remains a convention whereby the eye-dialect spelling *yew* can serve to imply a pronunciation of *you* with a particularly central or diphthongal realization of /u(ː)/. An author who writes 'If yew were the only girl in the world ...' is showing that he does not care for the pronunciation of the character into whose mouth he puts it.

The discussion so far relates to stressed syllables (more generally, perhaps, to strong syllables). Where the vowel is subject to weaken-ing, Yod Dropping is more restricted in occurrence. Those who have no /j/ in *lewd* may well have one in *value* and *valuation*; compare also *salute*, *salutation* (for me, /sə'luːt/ but /ˈsæljʊ'teɪʃn̩/). Those who drop the yod of *new* are likely to keep it in *annual* and *monument*.

3.1.11 PRICE and CHOICE

Nowadays most accents, including the standard ones, make a con-sistent distinction in minimal pairs such as *bile–boil, imply–employ*. It was not always so; and there are still accents which do not maintain any such distinction. A further point is that there is considerable phonetic overlap in the range of diphthongs used by different accents in such words, so that – for instance – a Cockney pronunciation of *tie* maybe identical with an RP rendering of *toy*.

The most usual Middle English source of the PRICE vowel is [iː], a long front close monophthong which was converted by the Great Vowel Shift into a diphthong, probably of the [ei] type. In the precursor of the standard accents, this diphthong developed through an eighteenth-century [ʌɪ] type to a modern-style [aɪ]. (This has moved even further away from the Middle English quality, namely to [ɑɪ] or [ɒɪ], in accents which have undergone Diphthong Shift (3.4.2 below). Monophthongization to [aː] is presumably an independent development in the American south, parts of the north of England, and South Africa.)

The PRICE words can be divided etymologically into two groups, (68a) of 2.2.16 above, which did not contain /x/ after the vowel in Middle English, and (68b), which did. In traditional-dialect of the north of England and in Scotland, forms with [i(ː)] may be encountered from both groups, e.g. [diː] *die*, [rit] *right*.

The CHOICE vowel goes back to at least two different diphthongs in Middle English; and all CHOICE words are believed to be ultimately loan-words, mainly from Old French.

The two source types in Middle English were /ɔi/, used in words such as those listed in (69a) of 2.2.17 above, and /ui/, used in words such as those listed in (69b). The latter apparently developed into a variety of [əi] or [ʌi], which led to confusion between these words and PRICE words, so that for instance *boil* (v.) could be a homophone of *bile*, or *joined* rhyme with *find*. The history of the various diphthongs involved is in fact very complex and the subject of some scholarly disagreement; be that as it may, the (69b) words seem to have fluctuated between PRICE and CHOICE in the standard accents until the nineteenth century, when they settled firmly with (69a) CHOICE. Traces of the earlier situation remain in conservative language varieties. A well-known example is in the lyrics of 'Clementine', where the old-time gold-miner is represented as saying 'jine' for *join*:

> Then the miner, forty-niner,
> Soon began to peak and pine;
> Thought he oughta jine his daughter.
> Now he's with his Clementine.

A few words with Middle English /iː/, which ought regularly to have developed like the other PRICE words, got attracted in this confusion into the CHOICE set. They include those listed in (69c) and also the word *boil* 'inflamed swelling', which became homophonous with *boil* (v.) 'seethe'; also *employ*, which in this way became distinct from *imply* (with which it is etymologically identical). Current spelling reflects the newer pronunciations.

The CHOICE vowel seems to have merged with PRICE in the popular speech of parts of the south of England, where a diphthong of the [ɒɪ] type may be used for both. The influence of RP, though, and of the spelling, exert constant pressure to keep the two diphthongs distinct. The same merger can be found in Newfoundland, the West Indies and Ireland (with details varying from place to place). In popular Jamaican speech, for example, *vice* and *voice* are homophones, [vaɪs], and similarly *grind–groin*, *tie–toy*; but cases where there is a labial before the diphthong remain distinct through the appearance of a labial-velar glide in CHOICE words but not in PRICE words, thus *boy* [bwaɪ], but *buy* [baɪ]. Traces of this inserted [w] are also found in the *SED* records for Wiltshire and Dorset (*poison* iv.11.4, *boiling* v.8.6; *LAE* map Ph185a).

3.1.12 Long Mid Diphthonging

The most recent development included in tabulation (125) of 3.1.5 above was the change in FACE from [eː] to [eɪ] and in GOAT from [oː] to [oʊ]. This development may be referred to as Long Mid Diphthonging, involving as it does the addition of a closing offglide to the long mid vowels. In the precursor of RP it seems to have happened around 1800, and was purely a realizational change, involving no alteration in the system as such.

As far as the FACE words are concerned, Long Mid Diphthonging was preceded by a raising to [eː] of what had previously been [ɛː]. This raising appears to have happened during the eighteenth century in educated speech, though well before 1700 in 'vulgar, or at least careless, speech' (Dobson 1968: §102). Then [eː] gave way to diphthongal [eɪ] at the beginning of the nineteenth century; it is intrinsically likely that the diphthongal quality developed earliest in free monosyllables (*day*) and only later in certain other environments (*gate*, *vacation*). It remains something of an open question how far diphthongal FACE and GOAT constitute part of the shared history of RP and GenAm before the two traditions diverged; it may well be that [eɪ] and [oʊ] arose from the shared inheritance of [eː] and [oː] independently in England and America, although diphthongs as vulgar or careless variants of standard-speech monophthongs may date from the early eighteenth century. American speech had presumably become established as a distinct accent by 1750, although the influence of new fashions from England (of pronunciation, as of other matters) certainly continued to be felt even after 1776.

In local accents Long Mid Diphthonging has in some places happened only variably or not at all. It may well be a development for which the Long Mid Mergers are a precondition, so that from those who distinguish between *pain* and *pane* we should always expect a monophthong, [eː ~ ẹː], in the latter, or – as in Lincolnshire and Tyneside – a centring diphthong of the [eə] type. Even where the Long Mid Mergers have been carried out, we find monophthongs in many conservative accents, [eː ~ ẹː] in FACE and [oː ~ ọː] in GOAT. Qualities such as these are found quite widely: in rural and conservative urban working-class accents of the north of England; rather more generally in Wales and Ireland; very generally in Scotland, where diphthongs may even be perceived as a mark of the anglophile; in cultivated West Indian speech, where it is often in sociolinguistic variation with a lower-prestige opening diphthong; and in the northernmost part of the midwest of the United States (Michigan, Wisconsin, Minnesota), particularly in the environment of a following voiceless consonant, thus *gate* [geˑt], *soap* [soˑp]; more widely in GenAm in unstressed pretonic syllables, as in the first syllables of *vacation, chaotic, donation*, and *oasis*; and lastly in Indian English and often in African and some other kinds of Third World English.

3.1.13 The great divide

We are now in a position to infer the approximate state of polite English pronunciation in the early or mid eighteenth century. It seems reasonable to fix the date 1750 as marking the end of the shared development of the forerunners of present-day RP and GenAm. Later RP innovations (3.2 below) either had no effect at all on American pronunciation, or had an effect that was sharply limited, geographically or otherwise. Likewise, later American innovations (3.3 below) have had little or no influence on British pronunciation patterns.

There are several sound changes along the path from Middle English to the present day which we have not considered in this chapter. This is because they have applied to all accents of current English (though not necessarily to all traditional-dialect speech), without leaving pockets of unchanged patterns (residualisms) in particular geographical areas. Examples of such sound changes include Consonant Singling (double /dd/ in *ladder* becomes single /d/, and likewise other doubled consonants); the deletion of an initial velar before /n/, as in *know, gnat*; and the backing and rounding of /a(ː)/ after /w/, as *wasp, swan, squat* (though not before a velar, as *quack, wag*).

For this period, then, we can infer a vowel system (137). We assume that /aː/ had by now achieved independent phonemic status, although the long [æː] of BATH was still an allophone of /æ/. Diphthongal /ɪu/ already sounded old-fashioned in London, where the sequence /juː/ was by now usual in its place. The diphthongs /aɪ/ and /aʊ/ were still realizationally [ʌɪ, ʌʊ] for many speakers.

(137)

ɪ	ʊ	iː				(ɪu)	uː
ɛ	ʌ	eː			3ː		oː
æ	ɒ	aɪ	ɒɪ	aː	ɒː	aʊ	

    checked   *free*

Mid long /eː/ and /oː/ probably had diphthongal allophonic variants by now, [eɪ] and [oʊ]; before /r/ they may have retained older, opener qualities, [ɛː] and [ɔː]. Long /3ː/ was always followed by /r/, and was in all likelihood subject to a realization rule of R Coalescence, /3ːr/ → [ɝː].

The table of lexical incidence looked like this, (138):

(138)

KIT	ɪ	FLEECE	iː	NEAR	iːr
DRESS	ɛ	FACE	eː	SQUARE	eːr
TRAP	æ	PALM	aː	START	aːr
LOT	ɒ	THOUGHT	ɒː	NORTH	ɒːr
STRUT	ʌ	GOAT	oː	FORCE	oːr
FOOT	ʊ	GOOSE	uː (, ɪu)	CURE	uːr (, ɪur)
BATH	æ [æː]	PRICE	aɪ	*happ*Y	ʔiː
CLOTH	ɒː	CHOICE	ɒɪ	*lett*ER	ər [ɝ]
NURSE	3ːr [ɝː]	MOUTH	aʊ	*comm*A	ə

3.2 British prestige innovations

In this section we consider certain phonological developments in the history of RP which took effect after the GenAm mainstream had separated off. Some of these developments applied also to the majority of accents in England; others had a more restricted application. Some, at least, originated in popular accents and spread from there to 'polite English' and RP; they are thus innovations which have come to characterize RP, rather than innovations which necessarily first arose in RP. Mostly they apply also to the accents of the south-east of England and (perhaps with the exception of Smoothing) to those of the southern hemisphere, where English speakers first settled after these changes had taken place in England.

3.2.1 Vowels before /r/

In a Scottish accent the words *beer, chair, more,* and *sure* are pronounced [biːr, tʃeːr, moːr, ʃuːr]. In quality these vowels agree with those of FLEECE, FACE, GOAT, and GOOSE respectively, and are unhesitatingly assignable to the same respective phonemes. This accent is conservative in this respect, in that it has preserved the historical situation. The corresponding forms in RP are [bɪə, tʃɛə, mɔː, ʃʊə ~ ʃɔː], with vowels sharply distinct not only phonetically but also phonologically from those of FLEECE, FACE, GOAT, and GOOSE. The loss of final /r/ we shall deal with in 3.2.2, R Dropping; here we are concerned with the other changes. They are conveniently described under two heads, **Pre-R Breaking** and **Pre-Schwa Laxing**. The first of these must logically have preceded R Dropping; the second may be later.

We mentioned in 3.1.13 that in the eighteenth century /eː/ and /oː/ may have retained older, opener qualities, [ɛː] and [ɔː], in the environment of a following /r/, as in *chair* and *more*. According to this view, which is forcefully maintained by Dobson (1968: §§205–10), these words were phonemically /tʃeːr, moːr/ but phonetically [tʃɛːɹ, mɔːɹ], the usual raising from half-open to half-close quality being regularly inhibited before /r/. A difficulty with this view is that half-close, [eː, oː]-type qualities are to be found today in such words in accents spread quite widely around the world: in Scottish, Irish, West Indian, and some New England and American southern accents. If these accents do not represent the continuation of an English use of [eː] and [oː] qualities in the environment of a following /r/, then they must all separately have innovated the raising from half-open to half-close before /r/, which seems unlikely.

Be that as it may, the first development with which we are here concerned is Pre-R Breaking, which involves the epenthesis of a schwa between any of the vowels /iː, eː, oː, uː/ and a following /r/. This is a very natural kind of phonetic development. To pass from a 'tense' close or half-close vowel to the post-alveolar or retroflex posture associated with /r/ requires considerable movement of the tongue. If this is somewhat slowed, an epenthetic glide readily develops as the tongue passes via the [ə] area. This glide is non-syllabic, and can generally be regarded as a non-distinctive transition phenomenon: /iː/ and /uː/ acquire the pre-/r/ allophones [iːə] [uːə], and /eː, oː/ the allophones [eːə, oːə], (or, if Dobson is right, [ɛːə, ɔːə]). In its basic form, then, Pre-R Breaking is a low-level allophonic rule, statable as (139) and with effects as (140).

(139) $\emptyset \rightarrow ə$ / [−low, +long V] __ r

(140)

	beer	*chair*	*more*	*sure*
Input	biːr	tʃeːr	moːr	ʃuːr
Pre-R Breaking	biːər	tʃeːər	moːər	ʃuːər

Pre-R Breaking also applied to the diphthongs of PRICE and MOUTH, which end in closish qualities. In this environment, in fact, there is evidence for the epenthetic [ə] as early as the fifteenth or sixteenth century (Dobson 1968: §218). Examples are *fire, tower*, as in (141); whether the diphthongs were of the type [ʌɪ, ʌʊ] or [aɪ, aʊ] at the time is not relevant to this development.

(141)

	fire	*tower*
Input	faɪr	taʊr
Pre-R Breaking	faɪər	taʊər

The next stage, Pre-Schwa Laxing, involves the switch from a long ('tense') vowel to the corresponding short and lower ('lax') vowel in the environment of the following non-syllabic schwa inserted by Pre-R Breaking. Thus [iː, eː, oː, uː] become [ɪ, ɛ, ɔ, ʊ]. (Compare the very similar phenomenon of Smoothing in contemporary RP, vol. 2, 4.1.3 and 3.2.9 below). This development, like Breaking, can be seen as merely realizational (allophonic), since the diphthongs [ɪə, ɛə, ɔə, ʊə] which result are restricted to the environment __r, an environment from which the phonemic norms [iː, eː, oː, uː] are excluded. These complementary distributions will be upset only if (i) new instances of [ɪə], etc., arise from other sources in environments other than ___r, or (ii) the /r/ which furnishes the conditioning environment itself disappears. In the history of RP both of these things happened, which is why the centring diphthongs achieved phonemic status.

There were various words in which one of the long close or half-close vowels /iː, eː, oː, uː/ was stressed and followed by an ordinary syllabic /ə/. Many of these were and are comparatively learned or specialist words, as *pyorrhoea, protozoa, skua*. But at least one is an everyday word, namely *idea*. Whereas the learned words fluctuate in their pronunciation through the uncertain influence of the spelling, *idea* is firmly /aɪˈdɪə/ in current RP, and is a word of two syllables only. Previously it must have been trisyllabic, /aɪˈdiː.ə/; hence we must conclude that its earlier final syllabic /ə/ became non-syllabic at some time, and that its earlier /iː/ participated in the Pre-Schwa Laxing process. Thus we have the developments shown in (142), where, for clarity, non-syllabic schwa is written explicitly as [ə̆].

(142)		*beer*	*idea*	*chair*	*more*	*sure*
	Input	biːr	-diːə	tʃeːr	moːr	ʃuːr
	Pre-R Breaking	biːə̆r	-diːə	tʃeːə̆r	moːə̆r	ʃuːə̆r
	Syllabicity Loss	–	-diːə̆	–	–	–
	Pre-Schwa Laxing	bɪə̆r	-dɪə̆	tʃɛə̆r	mɔə̆r	ʃʊə̆r

This **Syllabicity Loss** of /ə/ after long vowels is also responsible for the fact that *theorem* now rhymes with *serum* (RP /ˈθɪərəm, ˈsɪərəm/) and for the old-fashioned pronunciation of *boa* (RP occasionally /ˈbɔə/, now usually /ˈbəʊə/).

Given these forms [bɪər] *beer*, [aɪˈdɪə] *idea*, etc., one could already begin to argue for an independent phoneme /ɪə/. Nevertheless a theory of phonology allowing even a modicum of abstraction would still prefer a phonemicization corresponding to the top line of (142). It was the loss of final /r/ which triggered the restructuring of all the words in which historically /iː, eː, oː, uː/ had been followed by /r/, i.e. the lexical sets NEAR, SQUARE, FORCE, and CURE. The outcome was that one or more of the centring diphthongs, /ɪə, ɛə, ɔə, ʊə/, were added to the inventory of vowel phonemes in the various non-rhotic accents.

Breaking and Laxing were not restricted to the environment of a final /r/; they applied also before preconsonantal and prevocalic /r/.

In the environment __rC we have the examples set out in (143), and in the environment __rV, those of (144). Older /ɔə/ has now usually given way to monophthongal /ɔː/ in RP, and /ʊə/ is following the same path (3.2.5 below).

(143)

		beard	*scarce*	*force*	*gourd*
	Input	biːrd	skeːrs	foːrs	guːrd
	Pre-R Breaking	biːərd	skeːərs	foːərs	guːərd
	Pre-Schwa Laxing	bɪərd	skeərs	fɔərs	gʊərd
	(R Dropping	bɪəd	skeəs	fɔəs	gʊəd)

(144)

		dreary	*vary*	*glory*	*jury*
	Input	driːrɪ	veːrɪ	gloːrɪ	dʒuːrɪ
	Pre-R Breaking	driːərɪ	veːərɪ	gloːərɪ	dʒuːərɪ
	Pre-Schwa Laxing	drɪərɪ	veərɪ	glɔərɪ	dʒʊərɪ

There is no need to assume the extension of Breaking and Laxing to open vowels (START and NORTH).

Both Breaking and Laxing are foreign to Scottish accents, and also to Irish accents (though here there are some reservations, at least at the phonetic level). In England and Wales, though, Breaking seems to have taken place virtually throughout the country, though not always in the __rV environment exemplified in (144); it is perhaps possible to regard it as allophonic in rhotic accents, though in non-rhotic accents (including RP) it is clearly phonemic.

Laxing without Breaking, which for example makes *vary* a homophone of *very*, is restricted to North America. It is discussed in 3.3.3 below.

Pre-schwa Laxing is not universal in accents which have undergone Breaking. Pronunciations such as *beer* [biːə, bɹiə, biə] (whether monosyllabic or disyllabic) are not uncommon. Laxing seems to occur most readily in SQUARE, rather less readily in FORCE, and least readily in NEAR and CURE words.

A possible subsequent development is **Monophthonging**, which changes a centring diphthong [ɪə, ɛə, ɔə, ʊə] into a long monophthong [ɪː, ɛː, ɔː, ʊː]. Again, this seems to occur most readily in SCARCE and FORCE words (yielding the forms [skɛːs] *scarce*, [fɔːs] *force*). It is found, sometimes allophonically or variably, in many regional accents of England and Wales, and also in the southern hemisphere. In RP it is applicable to FORCE, but only as a minority pronunciation to SQUARE.

The following set of data (bottom line of 145), from a Cumbrian informant born around 1955, nicely reflects the operation of Laxing and Monophthonging in SQUARE and FORCE but not in NEAR and CURE. This informant, an undergraduate, considered the pronunciations [bɪə] *beer* and [ʃʊə] *sure* 'posh', and said she would have felt out of place using them.

(145)	beer	weary	sure	jury	fair	fairy	store	story
Early Modern								
English input	biːr	wiːrɪ	ʃuːr	dʒuːrɪ	feːr	feːrɪ	stoːr	stoːrɪ
Breaking	biːər	wiːərɪ	ʃuːər	dʒuːərɪ	feːər	feːərɪ	stoːər	stoːərɪ
Laxing	n.a.	n.a.	n.a.	n.a.	fɛər	fɛərɪ	stɔər	stɔərɪ
R Dropping	biːə	–	ʃuːə	–	fɛə	–	stɔə	–
Monophthonging	n.a.	n.a.	n.a.	n.a.	fɛː	fɛːrɪ	stɔː	stɔːrɪ
Happy Tensing								
(3.4.3)	–	wiːəri	–	dʒuːəri	–	fɛːri	–	stɔːri
Data = output	biːə	wiːəri	ʃuːə	dʒuːəri	fɛː	fɛːri	stɔː	stɔːri

(Note, by the way, that I would deprecate any suggestion that the top line of (145) necessarily constitutes the underlying synchronic representation of these words for this speaker; (145) is rather a display of the route by which the present stage developed historically from Early Modern English.)

Since the /aɪ/ and /aʊ/ in words such as *fire* and *tower* are diphthongs ending in relatively close vowel qualities, we naturally expect Pre-R Breaking in such words. Adding non-syllabic [ə] to what are already diphthongs, [aɪ̆] and [aʊ̆], produces triphthongs consisting of a first element [a] plus two successive non-syllabic components, thus [aɪ̆ə, aʊ̆ə]. It is hardly surprising that the option has existed since at least the sixteenth century of avoiding the phonetic intricacy of monosyllabic *fire* and *tower* by pronouncing them as disyllables, ['faɪ.ər, 'taʊ.ər]. The process whereby non-syllabic [ə̆] becomes syllabic [ə] (or in GenAm non-syllabic [ɹ] becomes syllabic [ɚ]) may be termed **Syllabicity Gain**.

Disyllabic sequences of PRICE plus /ə/ naturally occur in words such as *Jeremiah, pliant, higher*. If Syllabicity Gain allows monosyllabic *hire* to become homophonous with disyllabic *hire*, the converse process allows *higher* to become homophonous with monosyllabic *hire*. (This is a case of the Syllabicity Loss referred to above.)

Where PRICE or MOUTH is followed by /r/ plus a vowel, Breaking is evidenced in the usual RP forms /'aɪərɪʃ/ *Irish*, /'paɪərət/ *pirate*, /'maʊərɪ/ *Maori*. Phonetically, these words normally have two syllables only; triphthongal /aɪə, aʊə/ may, just as in *fire* and *tower*, be subject to Smoothing (3.2.9 below) and monophthonging to give [aə], [aː] etc. Most accents of English, however, including some 'near-RP', retain unbroken PRICE and MOUTH, giving /ˈaɪrɪʃ, ˈpaɪrət, ˈmaʊrɪ/ etc.

3.2.2 R Dropping

RP has eliminated historical /r/ except in the environment of a following vowel. This came about in the eighteenth century, when /r/ disappeared before a consonant or in absolute final position. We shall refer to the development deleting /r/ in this way as **R Dropping**.

R Dropping had no effect on initial or intervocalic /r/, as in *red, thread, arrive, story, marry*, RP /red, θred, əˈraɪv, ˈstɔːrɪ, ˈmærɪ/. Nor did it affect the /r/ in words such as *fearing* /ˈfɪərɪŋ/, *barring* /ˈbɑːrɪŋ/, though it did affect *feared* /fɪəd/ and *barred* /bɑːd/.

A first approximation to the formulation of the rule of R Dropping is (146), which deletes /r/ in the environment of a following consonant or word boundary.

$$(146) \quad r \to \emptyset \ / \ \_ \begin{Bmatrix} C \\ \# \end{Bmatrix}$$

Considering first the environment __C, we have consequences such as (147), where the input assumes that Breaking and Laxing have already occurred; the vowels of *start* and *north* have undergone Pre-R Lengthening (3.1.8 above).

(147)	*beard*	*scarce*	*start*	*north*	*force*	*gourd*
Input	bɪərd	skɛərs	stɑːrt	nɒːrθ	fɔərs	gʊərd
R Dropping	bɪəd	skɛəs	stɑːt	nɒːθ	fɔəs	gʊəd

Quality adjustments (aː → ɑː, ɒː → ɔː, ɔə → ɔː) later applied, to give current RP /bɪəd, skɛəs, stɑːt, nɔːθ, fɔːs, gʊəd/.

This development made pairs such as *laud–lord, stalk–stork, taught–tort* homophonous and made *lawn* a rhyme of *corn* (i.e. merged THOUGHT and NORTH); also *father–farther, calve–carve*, etc. (i.e. merged PALM and START).

R Dropping also applied after the mid central vowels, /ɜː/ and /ə/, with consequences such as (148). If, as suggested in 3.1.13 above, sequences of these vowels plus /r/ had until now been subject to a realization rule of R Coalescence, it is clear that R Dropping supervened to inhibit this process, bleeding it in fact of all possible inputs. Syllabic [l], too, must be treated as /əl/ for purposes of R Dropping, which does not occur before it: *barrel* keeps /r/.

(148)		*nurse*	*standard*	*barrel*	
	Input	nɜːrs	stændərd	bærəl	
	R Dropping	nɜːs	stændəd	–	} = current RP
	Later rule	–	–	bærl̩	

R Dropping also involves the deletion of /r/ at the end of a word spoken in isolation, as in (149).

(149)	*near*	*square*	*far*	*or*	*four*	*cure*	*stir*	*letter*
Input	nɪər	skwɛər	faːr	ɒːr	fɔər	kjʊər	stɜːr	lɛtər
R Dropping	nɪə	skwɛə	faː	ɒː	fɔə	kjʊə	stɜː	lɛtə
Other changes	–	–	fɑː	ɔː	fɔː	–	–	letə
Output = current RP	nɪə	skwɛə	fɑː	ɔː	fɔː	kjʊə	stɜː	letə

However, words are not usually spoken in isolation. In connected speech, where a word ending in historical /r/ occurs before another word beginning with a consonant, R Dropping operated as usual. But where the next word begins with a vowel, the /r/ usually remains, now as the special liaison feature known as 'linking /r/'. We have results as in (150).

(150)		*near me*	*near us*	*far gone*	*far away*
	Input	nɪər miː	nɪər ʌs	fɑːr gɒn	fɑːr əweɪ
	R Dropping	nɪə miː	–	fɑː gɒn	–

In this way the R Dropping innovation caused items which historically ended in /r/ to exhibit an alternation: where the word was said in isolation, or before another word or morpheme beginning with a consonant (including where a consonant-initial suffix was attached to it), the /r/ was deleted, i.e. had zero realization, as in *fear‖*, *fear death*, *fearful*, *fears*; but where a vowel followed, whether across a morpheme or word boundary or not, /r/ retained its usual phonetic realization, as in *weary*, *fear anything*, *fearing*. Thus *fear* acquired the alternating forms [fɪər] and [fɪə], *stare* the alternating forms [stɛər] and [stɛə], and likewise *car*, *for*, *store*, *pure*, *fir*, and *better*.

We can revise (146), therefore, to read as (146′) where $\#_0$ stands for 'zero or more major morpheme boundaries', i.e. an optional morpheme or word boundary; ‖ stands for the end of an utterance, a pause, or a major syntactic boundary, such as the boundary between two sentences.

$$(146') \quad r \rightarrow \emptyset / — \left\{ \begin{matrix} \| \\ \#_0 C \end{matrix} \right\}$$

Note, by the way, that there is no justification for positing a rule of straightforward R Vocalization ($r \rightarrow ə$) in place of Breaking plus R Dropping. This would work for *fears*, *near me*, etc., but not for *fearing*, *near us*, etc., where both [ə] and [r] are required in the output. Unlike many Americans, English people do not say *[fɪrɪŋ] or *[nɪr ʌs]. It follows that words such as *fire* and *tower* must be assumed to be underlyingly disyllabic by the time R Dropping occurred (since historical /faɪr, taʊr/ never give */faɪ, taʊ/); they retain the option of a monosyllabic (triphthongal) realization through the principle of Syllabicity Loss (3.2.1 above).

Accents which have undergone the change expressed in (146') are termed **non-rhotic**; accents which have not undergone (146'), but have retained /r/ in all environments where it occurred historically, are termed **rhotic**. (An alternative terminology is **r-less** and **r-ful**; the difficulty with these words is that they are confusing if spoken in a non-rhotic accent, where *r-ful* may readily be mistaken for *awful*.)

Non-rhoticity is found not only in RP and in the local accents of the east and north of England, but also in most accents of Wales and New Zealand, in all native-English-speaking accents of South Africa and Australia, and also in some of New England and much of the south of the United States. The pattern of non-rhoticity in the United States attests its origin as an importation of a new pronunciation fashion from England: the non-rhotic accents are found in the areas around the major Atlantic seaports (Boston, New York, Norfolk, Charleston, Savannah). The pioneers who had already pushed westwards remained unaffected by the new development; rhoticity has prevailed as the American norm.

Non-rhoticity is the prestige norm in England and Wales, so that middle-class accents and, increasingly, working-class accents of the traditionally rhotic areas of the west and north-west of England now tend to exhibit no more than variable rhoticity. Variable rhoticity is also typical of the traditionally non-rhotic areas of the United States (eastern New England, the coastal south, black speech), but in the United States of course it is rhoticity which tends more and more to be the prestige norm. Scotland and Ireland are fairly solidly rhotic, except for a relatively small number of speakers having close class connections with England and RP. West Indian accents vary from island to island, with for instance Trinidad and the Leewards being non-rhotic, but Barbados firmly rhotic.

Intermediate varieties also exist. It is not uncommon for R Dropping to have applied preconsonantally but not finally, i.e. in accordance with the simpler rule (146″)

(146″) $r \rightarrow \emptyset \: / \: \_\_ \: C$

With this restricted version of R Dropping, /r/ is lost from *beard, scarce, start, north, force, gourd*; but not from *near, square, far, or, four, cure*. The mid central vowels seem to behave idiosyncratically in respect of their influence on the retention or otherwise of a following /r/; many Americans whose speech is otherwise non-rhotic retain (or reacquire) /r/ in NURSE words and perhaps also in weak syllables (the *lett*ER words). Similarly in England: the *LAE* shows a patch of East Anglia as having /r/ in *worms* (map Ph58) but not in *darn* (map Ph19), while in North Yorkshire and Humberside there are localities with /r/ in *butter* (map Ph244) but not in *flour* or *four* (maps Ph155, Ph193). In Jamaica, /r/ is much more consistently present in *far* and *near* than in *start, beard,* and *letter.* Accents of this kind, if historical /r/ is retained consistently in some non-prevocalic environments but lost consistently in others, may be referred to as **semi-rhotic.**

Middle English had no native words ending in /ə/. All *comm*A words (2.2.25 above) are borrowings from other languages, many of them belonging to specialist or learned vocabulary. It is not surprising, then, that rustic folk speech in rhotic areas of both England and America tends to make them conform to the very large number of native words in /-ər/ (the *lett*ER words). This produces pronunciations of the type *comma* /-mər/ (phonetically usually [-mɚ], *Cuba* /-bər/, *Samantha* /-θər/, etc., in all phonetic environments (contrast the possibility of identical forms arising in non-rhotic accents by R Insertion, 3.2.3 below). If, as commonly happens, GOAT is weakened to /ə/ in words such as *yellow, window,* then this schwa too may be regularized to /ər/, giving forms such as [ˈjɛlɚ ~ ˈjælɚ], ['wɪndə]. This phenomenon may be referred to as **hyper-rhoticity**. It is nowhere standard.

An earlier, and quite separate, loss of /r/ before certain instances of /s/, /ʃ/, and occasionally other consonants, had already taken place by the sixteenth century (perhaps as early as 1300; see Dobson 1968: §401(c); also Hill 1940). It is this earlier development which is responsible for the standard pronunciation /'wʊstə(r)/ for the name spelt *Worcester*; also for the by-forms *cuss* (*curse*), *bust* (*burst*), *hoss* (*horse*) and the less widespread *passle* (*parcel*) and *catridge* (*cartridge*); and for the fact that Americans write as *ass* the word which the British write as *arse* ('backside'; on this see Sprague de Camp 1971).

3.2.3 R Insertion

Sometime after R Dropping had become established in the precursor of RP and in many other accents of England, a related development took place: there occurred a rule inversion. Instead of these alternations being produced by an R Dropping rule operating on underlying forms containing /r/, a new generation of speakers came to infer underlying forms without /r/, a phonetic /r/ (i.e. [ɹ] etc.) being introduced in the appropriate intervocalic environment by a rule of R Insertion. Instead of (150), the alternations were accounted for as in (151).

(151)		*near me*	*near us*	*far gone*	*far away*
	New input	nɪə miː	nɪə ʌs	fɑː gɒn	fɑː əweɪ
	R Insertion	–	nɪər ʌs	–	fɑːr əweɪ

This restructuring had the advantage of rendering the new underlying form identical with the form used in isolation (in this example /nɪə, fɑː/).

The R Insertion rule which superseded (146') is expressed formulaically in (152). It inserts /r/ after certain vowels before a following vowel, optionally across a morpheme or word boundary.

(152) $\emptyset \rightarrow r / [ɜː, ə, ɑː]$ ___ # $_0$ V

The [ə] in the left-hand environment of the structural description allows the rule to operate after the centring diphthongs /ɪə, ɛə, ɔə, ʊə/, as well as after /ɜː/, /ɑː/, and /ə/; but not after /iː, ɪ, eɪ, aɪ, ɔɪ, ɔː, uː, əʊ, aʊ/. Thus (152) correctly inserts /r/ in *fearing, near us, fairest, square up, boring, four-all, curing; sure enough, stirring, stir up, barring, far away, lettering, better off*, but not in *seeing, tee off, greyer, say it*, etc.

What is the evidence for this rule inversion? In brief, the justification for positing the replacement of the R Dropping rule (146′) by the R Insertion rule (152), together with appropriate restructuring of phonological representations in the lexicon, is the well-known phenomenon of 'intrusive /r/' (e.g. Jones 1956: §361; Gimson 1980: 208). This is the occurrence of /r/ (i.e. [ɹ], [ɾ], etc.) in phrases such as *the idea isn't* /ðiː aɪˈdɪər ɪznt/, *Ada ought* /ˈeɪdər ˈɔːt/. This /r/ is unetymological; it is apt to occur in RP and most other non-rhotic accents in the environment specified in (152), i.e. after /ɪə, ə/ and certain other vowels at a word boundary when the next word begins with a vowel.

The citation form of *beer* in RP is /bɪə/, while that of *idea* is /aɪˈdɪə/. The citation form of *trader* is /ˈtreɪdə/, while that of *Ada* is /ˈeɪdə/. Intrusive /r/ arises essentially from the natural tendency to give identical treatment to words with identical endings. Since /bɪə/ has an inherited prevocalic variant /bɪər/, it is reasonable to furnish /aɪˈdɪə/ with a parallel prevocalic variant /aɪˈdɪər/. Since /ˈtreɪdə/ has an inherited prevocalic variant /ˈtreɪdər/, it is reasonable to furnish /ˈeɪdə/ with a parallel prevocalic variant /ˈeɪdər/. As shown in (153), 'linking /r/' and 'intrusive /r/' are distinct only historically and orthographically.

(153)	beer isn't	idea isn't	trader ought	Ada ought
Inherited forms	ˈbɪər ˈɪznt	aɪˈdɪə ˈɪznt	ˈtreɪdər ˈɔːt	ˈeɪdə ˈɔːt
New citation forms taken as underlying	ˈbɪə ˈɪznt	aɪˈdɪə ˈɪznt	ˈtreɪdə ˈɔːt	ˈeɪdə ˈɔːt
R Insertion	ˈbɪər ˈɪznt	aɪˈdɪər ˈɪznt	ˈtreɪdər ˈɔːt	ˈeɪdər ˈɔːt
	linking /r/	intrusive /r/	linking /r/	intrusive /r/

Other examples include *Africa/r/ and Asia, Kenya/r/ and Uganda, Cuba/r/ is, if Libya/r/ attempts, put a comma/r/ in, the dilemma/r/ appears, ratafia/r/ and brandy, Edna/r/ O'Brien, guerrilla/r/ organization, Cana/r/ of Galilee, Lufthansa/r/ officials, visa/r/ application, Obadiah/r/ is the shortest, Nineveh* /ˈnɪnɪvər/ *is laid waste, the Messiah/r/ is born, in Judaea/r/ again; Korea/r/ and*

Vietnam, India/r/ *and Pakistan, an area*/r/ *of agreement, put my tiara*/r/ *on, the Victoria*/r/ *Embankment, a diarrhoea*/r/ *attack, gonorrhoea*/r/ *and syphilis.* (Some speakers apparently have the R Insertion rule blocked if the immediately preceding consonant is /r/, as in the last few examples.)

Across word boundaries, R Insertion is usually not a categorical rule: typically it is sometimes applied, sometimes not, depending on speech rate, contextual style, and no doubt also random factors. Literacy adds the complication that intrusive /r/, unlike linking /r/, is widely regarded as incorrect or slovenly ('pronouncing a letter which isn't there'); so that the speech-conscious may make some effort to avoid it. Usually, though, such an effort leads to the suppression of all sandhi /r/s, i.e. of every /r/ inserted by (152), whether 'intrusive' or merely 'linking'. One widespread tactic is the use of a glottal stop instead of /r/, thus *the* [bɪəʔ] *isn't, the* [aɪˈdɪəʔ] *isn't*, etc. This seems to be particularly common in South African English. In order to succeed in suppressing intrusive /r/ while retaining linking /r/, as a few do succeed in doing, the speaker must consult his knowledge of the spelling as the only guide to distinguishing the two cases. Given that even university students often write things like *the uvular is situated...*, *the Peninsula War* (instead of *the uvula, the Peninsular War*), it is clear that the average speaker is hardly going to be able to achieve the supposed goal of avoiding intrusive /r/ while keeping linking /r/.

R Insertion also applies word-internally. Even in accents where *fear* is /fɪə/, *fearing* is almost invariably /ˈfɪərɪŋ ~ ˈfɪərɪn/; so also *batter* /ˈbætə/ but *battering* /ˈbætərɪŋ/, *sober* /-bə/ but *soberer* /-bərə/, *cater–caterer, slender–slenderish, tender–tenderize, sculpture–sculpturesque*. Hence also the occasional instances of 'internal intrusive /r/' such as *polkaing* /-kərɪŋ/, *magenta-ish* /məˈdʒentərɪʃ/, *subpoenaing* /-nərɪŋ/, *propaganda-ize* /-dəraɪz/, *Kafkaesque* /ˈkæfkərˈesk/.

Words from certain lexical sets other than those considered so far may be involved in analogical R Insertion. In RP the vowels of PALM and START have fallen together as a consequence of R Dropping (*father* and *farther* are homophones), which means that the smallish number of PALM words ending in /ɑː/ become candidates for R Insertion. Just as *far* has the alternants /fɑː/ and /fɑːr/, so *Ma* acquires the alternant /mɑːr/ alongside its inherited /mɑː/, as in the sentence *Is Ma*/r/ *at home?* Newsreaders on the BBC very generally referred to the (former) *Shah*/r/ *of Iran*. Television advertising proclaimed that *this bra*/r/ *is made of. . .* Other examples include *the Omagh*/r/ *area, an awful fracas* /'fræka:r/, *isn't it?, bourgeois* /'bɔːʒwɑːr/ *ideas*, and (as I have sometimes described Breaking) *schwa*/r/ *insertion*. Word-internally, we have *cha-cha*/r/*-ing*.

The falling together of the FORCE and THOUGHT vowels opens up the large number of THOUGHT words ending in this vowel to R Insertion. As long as *store* /stɔə ~ stɔər/ had a different vowel from *law* /lɔː/, there was no reason for the latter to develop a prevocalic variant with /r/. As soon as FORCE and THOUGHT merge in free syllables (3.2.5 below), *store* (now /stɔː/, prevocalically /stɔːr/) ends identically with *law*, which therefore tends to come into line as /lɔː/, prevocalically /lɔːr/, as in *law and order* /'lɔːr ən 'ɔːdə/. Other examples of intrusive /r/ after /ɔː/ include *the Jackdaw*/r/ *of Rheims, I saw*/r/ *in the paper, the jaw*/r/ *opens, Shaw*/r/ *as a dramatist, a saw*/r/ *attachment, awe*/r/*-inspiring, the Whitelaw*/r/ *administration, some raw*/r/ *apple*. Word-internally, R Insertion is frequently to be observed in England in words such as *gnawing* /'nɔːrɪŋ/, *draw*/r/*ing*, *withdrawal* /wɪð'drɔːrəl/. There is, however, rather more sentiment against intrusive /r/ in this environment than in those previously mentioned, due no doubt partly to the fact that it constitutes a more recent development (since *manna–manner, Korea–career, Ma–mar* became homophonous before *law–lore* did); perhaps also to the fact that a large number of common monosyllables are potentially affected.

Speakers (such as myself) who without making any effort naturally pronounce an /r/ in the phrase *I store it* but not in the phrase *I saw it*, while *store them, saw them* rhyme at the phonetic level, and who have *soar* and *saw* as homophones but not *soaring* and *sawing*, have a slightly complicated phonology at this point. Either, we must assume, FORCE words have underlying /ɔə/ which is monophthonged to [ɔː] by a realization rule which also happens to make it identical with the realization of the /ɔː/ of THOUGHT words; or, alternatively, both FORCE and THOUGHT words have underlying /ɔː/ in the speaker's mental lexicon, but THOUGHT words are specially marked as exceptions to the rule of R Insertion. (In popular London speech, FORCE and THOUGHT are merged as [ɔə] rather than [ɔː] in word-final position, but this does not affect the general argument.)

Once R Insertion applies (categorically or variably) to /ɔː/, so that *core* and *jaw*, say, are equally likely to have or not have /-ɔːr/ forms before a following vowel, then the R Insertion rule can be expressed as (154) rather than as (152):

(154) Ø → r / [-high V] ___ #₀ V

The class of non-high vowels (i.e. mid and open vowels) is more satisfactory as a natural class than the [ɜː, ə, ɑː] of (152); no difficulty arises in connection with the non-high short vowels /e, æ, ʌ, ɒ/, since in any case they never occur word-finally. (It is arguable whether the truncated form of *yes*, usually spelt *yeah*, should be represented phonemically as (RP etc.) /je/ or /jɛə/, since its phonetic range seems to cover both possibilities. In any case, it certainly triggers R Insertion in England, as in *yeah*/r/ *it is*.)

The view that R Sandhi results from an insertion rule (rather than from underlying forms containing /r/) is supported by the readiness of speakers of the relevant accents to intrude /r/ when speaking other languages and in foreign names and expressions. In language classes in London I have often heard instances such as *j'étais déjà*/r/ *ici, ich bin ja*/r/ *auch fertig, tio estas interesa*/r/ *ideo, ʃe wela*/r/ *i rywbeth*. Choirmasters have to admonish against *alpha*/r/ *es et O, gloria*/r/ *in excelsis*, and *viva*/r/ *España*. When it is a matter of foreign words in an English sentence, examples I have noted in scholarly or intellectual discussions include *Degas* /'deɪɡɑːr/ *and Sickert, Dada*/r/*ism, the social milieu* /miːˈljɜːr/ *of Alexander Pope, the junta* /ˈxʊntər/ *in Chile*. R Insertion also applies after acronyms, as in the typical and authentic RP examples *as far as BUPA*/r/ *is concerned*; *we shall hear about Rosla*/r/ *again in a few months* (i.e. British United Provident Association; raising of the school leaving age). Given that these instances can only reflect an insertion rule, it is reasonable to conclude that all sandhi /r/ in contemporary RP and other non-rhotic accents reflects the same insertion rule.

Particular developments in phonetic realization may mean that in certain accents vowels of other lexical sets come to trigger sandhi /r/. In particular, the GOAT vowel in weak syllables is widely reduced to [ə] in working-class accents. In England, at any rate, the automatic consequence is /r/ before a following vowel, as in *to-mato*/r/ *and cucumber production, the window*/r/ *isn't clean, eye-*

shadow/r/ and make-up, Last Tango/r/ in Paris, even *I 'don't know
/'dʌnər/ if he 'is.* (The reason this does not happen in RP is that RP
/əʊ/ does not weaken in this way, but either remains [əʊ] or at most
becomes [o] or [ʊ].)

In Cockney (working-class London speech) MOUTH can phonetically be [æə] or [æː]. In accordance with (154), this characteristically
triggers /r/ in phrases such as *how/r/ are you?*; *now/r/ 'e's done it!*

In many accents the pronoun *you* has a weak form /jə/ (conventionally spellable *ya* in the United States, but *yer* in non-rhotic-
oriented England). This form tends to be eschewed in Mainstream
RP, and in U-RP is even excluded, I think, from prevocalic position
(where only /juː ∼ jʊ/ occur). Those working-class accents which
allow the /jə/ form prevocalically naturally tend, if non-rhotic, to
insert /r/ after it; hence pronunciations such as [jəɹ 'ɑːʔ] *you aren't,
I'll tell you how* [... jəɹ 'æː] (these examples both Cockney). In
such cases, in fact, weakened *you* and *your* become homophonous,
whatever their environment. *To*, too, has /tə/ as one of its weak
forms; parallel considerations lead RP /tʊ 'iːt/ or /tuː 'iːt/ to compete
with not only [tə 'ʔiːt] but also a popular /tər 'iːt/. The contractions
sometimes written *wanna, gotta, hafta, oughta, gonna* follow the
same pattern: as a scholarly syntactician of my acquaintance put it,
'in certain circumstances *want to* becomes /'wɒnər/ and *got to* becomes /'gɒtə/'. The /v/-less form of *of* has a prevocalic alternant
/ər/, to my knowledge, in at least London, Norwich (Trudgill
1974a: 162), and West Yorkshire. So does the /v/-less form of
weakened *have*, underlying Trudgill's Norwich example *he have
often said* [hɛːɹ 'ɒfən 'sɛd] (1974a: 163); and *by* has a Norwich
prevocalic weak form /bər/, as in *run over by /bər/ a bus*. R Insertion
is in fact one of the most productive phonological rules in contemporary English English.

The earliest reference to intrusive /r/ of which I am aware dates
from 1762, when T. Sheridan mentions it as a characteristic of
London speech. It has probably characterized RP since the early
nineteenth century, though no doubt regularly disapproved of and
avoided by the speech-conscious. By now it is found very widely in
non-rhotic British speech, as well as in New York and New
England (to some extent) and in the southern hemisphere (though
not much, I think, in South Africa, where R Insertion of all kinds
seems relatively uncommon).

3.2.4 Glide Cluster Reduction

Pairs such as *whine* and *wine* are homophonous in many accents of English. In others they are distinct, as they were historically: /hwaɪn/ vs. /waɪn/ etc. The loss of /h/ from the cluster /hw/, which gives *whine* the same pronunciation as *wine*, may be referred to as **Glide Cluster Reduction**. Although in a sense this is a kind of H Dropping, its very different social evaluation makes it convenient to distinguish /hw/ reduction from generalized H Dropping (3.4.1 below).

The phonetic realization of /hw/, in accents not subject to Glide Cluster Reduction, may be a sequence representable as [hw], or alternatively a single segment [ʍ], a voiceless labial-velar fricative. In Scottish English, for example, [ʍ] seems to be the norm. An alternative phonemicization is then possible: we can recognize an additional phoneme /ʍ/ in the system, rather than admitting the phonological cluster /hw/, and /ʍ/ is then paired with /w/ in parallel with /p/ and /b/, /f/ and /v/, etc. Under this analysis, we should describe the change we are here discussing not as a cluster reduction (a phonotactic change) but as the loss of the phoneme /ʍ/ (a systemic change). In the remainder of this section, we shall assume the /hw/ analysis.

Glide Cluster Reduction characterizes most accents of England and Wales, the southern hemisphere, and the West Indies, and also some American speech; but not the accents of Scotland or Ireland. The only local accents in England which retain /hw/ are those of Northumberland and nearby.

Glide Cluster Reduction seems to have started in the south of England early in the Middle English period (Jordan 1934: §195), but for a long time it remained a vulgarism; educated speech retained /hw/. The plain [w] pronunciation became current in educated speech in the course of the eighteenth century, and was usual by 1800.

Present-day RP usage could be described as schizophrenic. For most RP speakers /hw/ is not a 'natural' possibility. The usual RP form of *whine* is /waɪn/; similarly *what* /wɒt/, *which* /wɪtʃ/, *whether* /weðə/, *whisper* /wɪspə/, *wheel* /wiːl/. Other RP speakers use /hw/, and say /hwaɪn, hwɒt, hwɪtʃ, hweðə, hwɪspə, hwiːl/, and this usage is widely considered correct, careful, and beautiful. But I think it is true to say that those who use it almost always do so as the result of a conscious decision: persuaded that /hw-/ is a desirable pronunciation, they modify their native accent in this direction. Thus /hw/ is nowadays in England found principally among the speech-conscious and in adoptive RP (vol. 2, 4.1.3). It is often taught as correct for verse-speaking and dramatic declamation. Women seem to be more open to persuasion towards /hw/ than men.

Both Strang (1970: §34) and Gimson (1980: 216) imply that the decline of /hw/ is a current or recent phenomenon in RP. This is true, I think, only in the sense that ever fewer people are receptive to the puristic view that one ought to make the effort to use it. It has not been usual in unstudied RP for two centuries (Dobson 1968: §414).

In *who, whom, whose, whole,* and *whore*, the spelling *wh* corresponds to a pronunciation with simple /h/. In *whoop* there is now competition between /huːp/ and a spelling pronunciation /(h)wuːp/. Otherwise, the speech-conscious users of /hw/ in England use it wherever the spelling has *wh*; but those who 'naturally' retain historical /hw/ in Scotland, Ireland, and North America, have a somewhat more complicated relationship between sound and spelling. The word *whelk* is reportedly /wɛlk/, not /hwɛlk/, in Scotland (Jones 1956: 380); but *weasel* has /hw/ in much of central and eastern Scotland (Mather & Speitel 1975: vol. 2, map 1).

Like other cases of /h/, the cluster /hw/ is sensitive to stress. Words such as *which, when, why* are often unstressed, and then pronounced with plain /w/ by those who would use /hw/ for the same word in stressed position.

Speech-conscious people who do not 'naturally' use /hw/ often produce hypercorrections when they attempt to incorporate /hw/ into their accent. A British television newsreader has been noticed saying things like /ˈhwɛəhaʊs/ for *warehouse*. (Most of her colleagues make no attempt to use /hw/. They incur no stigmatization for this.)

In North America /hw/ is still a widespread usage, with a consistent distinction between *whine* and *wine, where* and *ware*. But Glide Cluster Reduction is clearly on the increase, particularly in large cities. The Linguistic Atlas shows plain /w/ in *whip* and *wheelbarrow* in three areas: a large area around New York, including not only metropolitan New York City itself but also Albany, Philadelphia, Harrisburg, and Baltimore; and two much smaller coastal areas in Massachussetts–Maine and South Carolina–Georgia, including the ports of Boston, Portland, Charleston, and Savannah. This geographical distribution suggests that in the United States Glide Cluster Reduction, like non-rhoticity, represents an innovation imported from England via the seaports which before the advent of air travel were the places in closest contact with Europe and its influences. On the other hand it is clear that by now it has spread well away from the east coast. I have been struck by /w/ for /hw/ in the speech of Californians, not least in words of Spanish origin, as /ˈmɛrəˈwɑnə/ *marijuana, the San* /wɑˈkin/ (*Joaquin*) *Valley*.

Many Americans consider the use of /w/ for /hw/ slipshod and erroneous. To quote one drama-oriented work on phonetics, 'this simplification is commonplace throughout the country and can be heard wherever thoughtlessness and laziness pervade speech patterns' (Blunt 1967: 30).

It might be expected that what applies to /hw/ also applies to /hj/. But this is not the case: RP retains historical /hj/ in words such as *huge, human, hew* (with a realization which may be either the two-segment sequence [hj] or else a single segment [ç]). In England, the omission of /h/ in these words is on a par with ordinary prevocalic H Dropping (3.4.1 below). The word *humour* is a special case, since it is a French word which when first borrowed had no /h/ (like *hour, honest*, etc.). Although the spelling pronunciation /ˈhjuːmə/ has now become the predominant RP form, /ˈjuːmə/ remains as an old-fashioned and increasingly rare alternative.

In America, Glide Cluster Reduction of /hj/ is apparently quite widespread in working-class speech, and not unknown in cultivated speech (Bronstein 1960: 124). In the word *humor*, Kenyon & Knott (1953) suggest the possibility of a different treatment according to meaning, with /ju-/ in 'sense of humor', 'mood', and for the verb, but /hju-/ in other senses. *PEAS*, on the other hand, calls /ju-/ 'the prevalent pronunciation' (178), and it is certainly true that, as McDavid (1952) says, 'it is far more widely current in standard speech in the United States than in England'.

3.2.5 Suffix vowels

Another innovation which has affected RP since the Great Divide (and has hence also, to a varying extent, affected other British accents and those of the southern hemisphere) concerns disyllabic suffixes in words of four or more syllables.

Words ending in -*ary*, such as *secretary, necessary, momentary,* used to have, and still do have in GenAm, a strong penultimate vowel (GenAm /'sɛkrətɛrɪ/, /'nɛsəsɛrɪ/ etc.; these penultimate syllables may also have a non-accentual stress, thus /'sɛkrə,tɛrɪ/ etc.) In RP the penultimate vowel is normally weakened, and may be entirely elided (RP /'sekrətrɪ/, /'nesɪsrɪ ~ 'nesəs(ə)rɪ/; but near-RP often preserves a strong vowel). The earliest evidence for the weakening of these vowels in England dates from the end of the seventeenth century (Dobson 1968: §1). Other suffixes involved are -*ory*, as in *category* (GenAm /'kætəgɔrɪ ~ -gorɪ/, RP /'kætɪg(ə)rɪ/), *reformatory, lavatory, regulatory, conciliatory; -mony,* as in *testimony* (GenAm /'tɛstəmonɪ/, RP /'testɪmənɪ/), *alimony, ceremony, matrimony; -borough, -boro, -burgh,* as in *Scarborough* (GenAm /'skɑrbɜro/, RP /'skɑːb(ə)rə/), *Edinburgh, Peterboro; -berry, -bury,* as in *strawberry* (GenAm /'strɔbɛrɪ/, RP /'strɔːb(ə)rɪ/), *Newbury, Waterbury;* also such words as *dysentery* (GenAm /'dɪsn̩tɛrɪ/, RP /'dɪsn̩trɪ/).

In the word *primarily,* the traditional RP form is /'praɪm(ə)rɪlɪ/. GenAm usage is somewhat varied, since trisyllabic words in -*ary,* such as *primary* and *library,* often have the vowel weakened in the suffix, and this is extended to the adverb form in -*arily.* But there has also developed an emphatic variant in GenAm, /praɪ'mɛrəli/, and this variant has within my lifetime caught on in Britain too, giving a new and quite anomalous RP form /praɪ'merəlɪ/.

In some quadrisyllabic words RP has reduced the number of successive weak syllables by shifting the stress from the first syllable to the second: thus *corollary* (GenAm /'kɔrəlɛrɪ/, RP /kə'rɒlərɪ/), *capillary* (GenAm /'kæpəlɛrɪ/, RP /kə'pɪlərɪ/). Compare, though, *coronary,* where all accents keep the stress on the first syllable (GenAm /'kɔrənɛrɪ/, RP /'kɒrən(ə)rɪ/). In *laboratory* the older RP form /'læb(ə)rət(ə)rɪ/ (GenAm /'læbrətori/etc.) has now been displaced by the stress-shifted /lə'bɒrət(ə)rɪ/, although its abbreviation remains /læb/ *lab.*

The suffixes *-ile* and *-ization* exhibit just the contrary behaviour. In England they have /aɪ/, thus *missile* /ˈmɪsaɪl/, *docile* /ˈdəʊsaɪl/, *hostile* /ˈhɒstaɪl/, *organization* /ˈɔːɡənaɪˈzeɪʃn̩/ *mechanization* /ˈmekənaɪˈzeɪʃn̩/. In American speech the suffix vowel is usually weakened, thus GenAm /ˈmɪsl̩/, /ˈdɑsl̩/, /ˈhɑstl̩/, /ˈɔrɡənəˈzeɪʃən/, /ˈmɛkənəˈzeɪʃn̩/.

3.2.6 BATH and CLOTH

In the mid-eighteenth century we tentatively left the precursor of RP with [aː] in PALM and [aːr] in START, but [æː], phonemically perhaps still /æ/, in BATH (3.1.13 above). By the twentieth century all three lexical sets had /ɑː/, i.e. a vowel which is not only long but also (relatively) back. The details and timing of the changes involved are not altogether clear. Presumably, though, two stages are involved: the phonemic split of TRAP and BATH, and the backing of BATH–PALM–START from [aː] to [ɑː].

The **TRAP–BATH Split** became implicitly established once it was clear that lexical diffusion meant that some lexical items previously said with [a ~ æ] now had a long vowel ([æː ~ aː], later to become [ɑː]), while others, although involving an identical phonological environment, retained the short vowel. Thus nowadays in RP, in the environment __s #, we have /ɑː/ in *pass, glass, grass, class, brass*, but /æ/ in *gas, lass, morass, amass, mass* (in physics), *cuirass, crass*, and *bass* (fish, fibre, or beer), and usually also in *mass* (eucharist) and *ass*. GenAm, however, with no corresponding TRAP–BATH Split, keeps the same vowel in all such words. In other relevant phonetic environments similarly inconsistent developments characterize RP and other 'broad-BATH' accents, as examplified in (155).

(155)	Current RP /ɑː/	Current RP /æ/
__f #	*staff, laugh, giraffe, calf, half*	*gaff, gaffe, chiffchaff*
__fC	*craft, shaft* etc., *after, laughter*	*Taft*
__θ #	*path, bath*	*math(s), hath, strath*
__st	*last, past, mast* etc., *master, disaster, nasty* etc.	*hast, bast, enthusiast, aster, Astor, raster, Rasta(farian)*
__sp #	*clasp, grasp, rasp, gasp*	*asp*
__sk	*ask, flask, mask* etc., *basket, casket*	*Aske, casque, gasket, Ascot, mascot*
__sl̩	*castle*	*tassel, hassle, vassal*
__sn̩	*fasten*	*Masson*

__ns	*dance, chance, France* etc., *answer, chancel* etc.	*manse, romance, expanse, cancer, cancel, fancy* etc.
__nt	*grant, slant, aunt* etc., *advantage, chanter* etc.	*rant, ant, cant, extant, banter, canter, antic* etc.
__n(t)ʃ	*branch, blanch* etc., *stanchion*	*mansion, expansion, scansion*
__nd	*demand, command, remand, slander, commando* etc.	*stand, grand, hand* etc., *gander, panda, glissando* etc.
__mpl	*example, sample*	*ample, trample*

It is noteworthy that many Australians use short /æ/, rather than their long /aː/ of START, in all BATH words which have the vowel followed by a nasal (i.e. the last five lines of (155), (59b) of 2.2.7 above). Thus they say /staːf, paːθ, laːst/ etc., but /dæns, grænt, əgˈzæmpl̩/. So do Leeward Islanders. Other Australians and West Indians have the long START vowel in all the BATH words, as do New Zealanders and South Africans. This may well be because in eighteenth-century south-east England these *dance*-type words were still fluctuating between short and long vowel; or indeed they may still generally have had a short vowel, and have gone over to the long vowel only later. (The issue is complicated by the fact that *dance* had a diphthong /aʊ/ in Middle English, as did several other BATH words; what needs to be explained with them is really the short /æ/ of GenAm and various other accents. I am assuming that they had joined *bath* etc. before the great divide.)

The TRAP–BATH Split thus represents the ossification of a half-completed sound change, which seems to have come to a stop well before completing its lexical diffusion through the vocabulary which met the structural description of the lengthening rule. In 3.1.9 we stated this structural description as merely vowel plus voiceless fricative, while noting that vowels before /ʃ/ were unaffected. The *dance*-type words suggest that the other relevant environment was nasal plus voiceless consonant; but here we see that *sample* and *example* are the only __mp words affected, while there are no __ŋk words affected at all (RP /æ/ in *damp, bank, ankle*). On the other hand, several __nd words do have lengthening in the environment of a nasal plus a **voiced** consonant; but in this they are unique (RP /æ/ in *amber, anvil, flange, anger*). The inconsistency of this change has had the effect of increasing the functional load of the /æ/ vs. /ɑː/ opposition in broad-BATH accents.

In RP and the south-east of England, the earlier [aː] of

BATH—PALM—START has undergone a change of quality, becoming the relatively back [ɑ+ː]. This START **Backing** probably happened early in the nineteenth century. Many English provincial accents retain a front [aː]; this applies both to broad-BATH accents, which have [aː] in all three lexical sets, and to flat-BATH accents, which have [aː] only in PALM and START. (Examples of the latter are the urban accents of Liverpool and Leeds.) But other provincial accents have back [ɑː] (e.g. Stoke-on-Trent). The geographical spread of START Backing is neither well described nor historically explained. In the southern hemisphere, START Backing is notable for the fact that South African English has undergone it, but Australian and New Zealand English not.

As we saw in 3.1.9, Pre-Fricative Lengthening extended to [ɒ] in early Modern English, giving a long [ɒː] in the CLOTH words. Then R Dropping left *cloth* a perfect rhyme of *north*: [klɒːθ, nɒːθ]. Since then, the NORTH—THOUGHT vowel has got steadily less open in RP, passing through the now old-fashioned [ɔː] to the current nearly half-close [o̞ː]. It would be expected that CLOTH would share this quality adjustment, to yield current [klo̞ːθ] etc.; but in fact this pronunciation is restricted to older U-RP and older working-class south-of-England speech. Mainstream RP, and accents of England in general, now have the /ɒ/ of LOT in CLOTH words. What must have happened, for reasons that are by no means clear, is that the short vowel which persisted in the north of England in CLOTH (just as in BATH) succeeded in regaining lost ground in the south and RP. The change in fashion as far as RP is concerned was a twentieth-century development: Sweet (1888: §807) assumes /ɔː/ in CLOTH as the norm (while noting /ɒ/ as 'still common'), while Wyld (1921: §245) gives /ɔː/, 'though not among all speakers'. At the time of writing (1980) the use of /ɔː/ in CLOTH is perceived as a laughable archaism of 'affected' or aristocratic U-RP. The period of fluctuation or sociolinguistic variation in CLOTH words in England is thus now drawing to an end, with /ɒ/ re-established as not only standard but nearly universal. The Pre-Fricative Lengthening innovation has succeeded in BATH but failed in CLOTH.

3.2.7 The FORCE Mergers

It was only when R Dropping became usual that English grammarians seem to have become aware of the opener quality of FORCE

as compared to GOAT. As long as the /r/ remained, the [ɔə] which
resulted from Breaking and Pre-Schwa Laxing (3.2.1 above) was no
more than an allophonic variant of /oː/. With the loss of /r/, /ɔə/
became established as a distinct phoneme, particularly since in all
other environments early Modern English /oː/ became diphthongal
(3.1.12 above): *coat* and *court, stow* and *store* were now minimal pairs
for /ou/ vs. /ɔə/.

R Dropping had already led to a merger of THOUGHT and NORTH,
so that *caught* and *short* rhymed as [-ɒːt] (3.2.2 above). This vowel
became less open, i.e. [ɔː], by the nineteenth century; since then it
has merged with the phonetically similar [ɔə] resulting from earlier
/oːr/, so that nowadays RP *sport, short,* and *caught* all rhyme, with
/-ɔːt/. Thus FORCE has merged with NORTH, which had already
merged with THOUGHT. We refer to the merger of FORCE and NORTH
as the **First FORCE Merger**. It results essentially from the
Monophthonging of [ɔə] (3.2.1) to give [ɔː]. These developments are
tabulated in (156).

(156)	THOUGHT	NORTH	FORCE
	(*caught, flaw*)	(*short, Thor*)	(*sport, floor*)
Input (early Modern English)	ɒː	ɒr	oːr
Pre-R Lengthening	–	ɒːr	–
Pre-R Breaking and Laxing	–	–	ɔər
Quality adjustment (ɒː → ɔː)	ɔː	ɔːr	–
R Dropping	–	ɔː	ɔə
First FORCE Merger			
(Monophthonging)	–	–	ɔː
Output (current RP etc.)	ɔː	ɔː	ɔː

The First FORCE Merger was not complete in RP until the current
century, though by now pairs such as *for–four, horse–hoarse,
warn–worn* are normally entirely homophonous in RP, as also
generally in the south of England, in the southern hemisphere, and
increasingly everywhere else. On the evidence of the *English
Pronouncing Dictionary* (*EPD*), the opposition persisted longest in
word-final position: in the last edition to be edited by Jones himself
(the twelfth, 1963), /ɔə/ is included as a (less usual) alternative to /ɔː/
in all FORCE words where the vowel is final (e.g. *store, four, core,
door*), but usually not in FORCE words where there is a following
consonant (e.g. *force, forge, afford, torn, story*). No NORTH or
THOUGHT words are given with /ɔə/. Exceptionally, certain FORCE
words where there is a following consonant are given /ɔə/ as an

alternative: they include *sword* and those spelt *our* or *oar* (*court, board, coarse, hoarse*). One is driven to ask whether the spelling might not have had some influence upon Jones, who did not himself make the distinction consistently. (Or of course the spelling may have exerted some influence upon speech-conscious Englishmen in general, encouraging them to retain the opposition only where it was reinforced by the orthography, e.g. *horse* vs. *hoarse*, but not otherwise, e.g. *short* vs. *sport, fork* vs. *pork, corn* vs. *torn*.)

As from Gimson's *Introduction* (first edition 1962) phoneticians describing RP have abandoned all lingering mention of /ɔə/ as a phonemically distinct entity. The First FORCE Merger is completed – except in some provincial, Celtic, West Indian, and American accents.

London speech has tended to generalize the diphthong [ɔə] in word-final position, but [ɔː] preconsonantally. This makes *flaw* and *floor* homophonous as [flɔə] (compare RP, both [flɔː]).

The FORCE set includes words of two distinct Middle English origins, /oːr/ (e.g. *coarse*) and /uːr/ (e.g. *course*; the Great Vowel Shift often failed with /uːr/). In the seventeenth century there was apparently a great deal of fluctuation in FORCE words between [oː] and [uː], with [oː] prevailing generally by the eighteenth century (and hence current RP /ɔː/ via Breaking and Laxing). The close vowel won out, however, in *boor, poor*, and *moor* (possibly owing to the preceding labial). The /uːr/ in these words was phonologically identical with the /uːr/ which had arisen in words such as *cure, pure* as the falling diphthong [ĭu] gave way to a rising [ĭuː] (3.1.10 above): *poor* and *pure* now rhymed as /puːr/, /pjuːr/. Through Breaking and Laxing this /uːr/ developed into [ʊər], then through R Dropping to the current /ʊə/. Certain other words are believed to have been attracted to the CURE set through the influence of spelling pronunciation (e.g. *amour, gourd*); others are recent loan-words (e.g. *tour*; compare also the *Ruhr*, RP /rʊə/). New spelling pronunciations of this kind may yet arise: my father, a clergyman, regularly distinguished *mourning* from *morning* (which after the First FORCE Merger would regularly be homophonous) by consciously insisting on pronouncing the former with /ʊə/: Dobson (1968: §209) calls this, no doubt correctly, 'rare and artificial and generally confined to theatrical and clerical pronunciation'.

Any such efforts will be rendered vacuous through a further

development which is now under way, the **Second FORCE Merger**.
(= CURE Lowering), whereby the /ʊə/ of CURE undergoes a lowering, sometimes via intermediate stages such as [oə] and [ɔə], to [ɔ:],
which is identical phonetically with the /ɔ:/ of FORCE–NORTH–
THOUGHT. Thus *sure* comes to be a homophone of *shore* and *Shaw*;
poor falls in with *pore, pour*, and *paw. Your* and *you're*, attracted to
the CURE category through the influence of the close vowel in *you*,
become homophones of *yore* and *yaw*. See further vol. 2, 4.1.5.

3.2.8 The realization of GOAT

Long Mid Diphthonging (3.1.12 above) gave GOAT the realization
[oʊ]. While it remains a back monophthong or narrow diphthong in
American English (with some exceptions), the starting-point of the
diphthong used in current RP, the south of England, and the
southern hemisphere is now not back but central, i.e. [ɜʊ] or, with
Diphthong Shift, [ʌʊ]. Hence the phonemic notation /əʊ/ introduced by Gimson (1962). We might refer to this development as
GOAT **Advancement**; it has presumably been current since at least
the nineteenth century, although [ɜʊ] has only quite recently (since
the Second World War?) ousted [oʊ], or perhaps rather [öʊ], as the
ideal image of a 'correct' or 'beautiful' RP GOAT diphthong. Some
forms of RP have a further advanced variant, [ëʊ]. Others retain
some rounding, having a rounded mid central vocoid as the first
element of a diphthong [ɵʊ]. The second element tends to be very
weak, which makes the distinction between [əʊ] (GOAT) and [ɜ:]
(NURSE) a small one, sometimes potentially neutralizable. Then *own*
may be mistaken for *earn* and vice versa. This is particularly likely
before /l/ (*goal–girl*), where RP characteristically lacks the pre-/l/
allophone [ɒʊ] of many other accents. On the other hand the possibility of maintaining a degree of closing-diphthong glide in GOAT,
but without lip action, gives a variant [ɜɪ] which is very similar to
some varieties of FACE. It remains to be seen whether the functional
load of the oppositions involved (GOAT vs. NURSE, GOAT vs. FACE) is
so great that these prospective mergers will be avoided, or whether
they will nevertheless take place, thus bringing about important
systemic realignments.

The *SED* shows [ʌʊ] for GOAT in Essex, Suffolk, and Hert-
fordshire, as well as London; everywhere else is recorded as having

a monophthong or diphthong with back rounded starting-point (*LAE* map Ph137, *nose*). The *SED* materials contain no mention of the [ɜʊ] type of RP.

In the United States the [ɜʊ] type (or its rounded equivalent, [ɵʊ]) is particularly associated with three regions of the country: the Philadelphia area, the Pittsburgh area, and in north-eastern North Carolina (*PEAS* map 20). Presumably these constitute independent indigenous innovations unconnected with British GOAT Advancement. According to Bronstein (1960: 168–9), the use of [ɜʊ] is on the increase in the United States, although 'persons who use this form in speaking studiously avoid it in singing'.

3.2.9 Smoothing

In RP and some other accents, when diphthongs of part-systems B and C occur in a prevocalic environment, there exists the possibility of a monophthongal realization. Thus /eɪ/ in *chaos* may be pronounced [eː], thus ['keːɒs]. This is an optional realization rule; there is also the possibility of ['keɪɒs], with the ordinary diphthongal realization of the FACE vowel.

We may refer to this monophthonging process as **Smoothing**. The quality of the monophthong which results from the Smoothing of a diphthong is that of the starting-point of the underlying diphthong. Thus it gives RP /eɪ/ the realization [eː], /əʊ/ a quality ranging from [öː] through [ɜː] to a centralized [eː], and /aɪ, aʊ/ realizations ranging from front [aː] to centralized-back [ɑː]. Not everyone extends Smoothing to /ɔɪ/, but for those who do /ɔɪ/ takes the form [ɔː]. Examples: *player* ['pleːə], *saying* ['seːɪŋ], *mower* ['mɜːə], *going* ['gɜːɪŋ], *science* ['saːəns], *trying* ['traːɪŋ], *coward* ['kɑːəd], *ploughing* ['plɑːɪŋ]; for some, *buoyant* ['bɔːənt], *annoying* [ə'nɔːɪŋ].

Smoothing applies particularly readily to /aɪ/ and /aʊ/ in the environment of a following /ə/. As well as historically disyllabic words like *science* and *coward* above, there are the words like *fire* and *tower* which owe their present underlying disyllabicity to Breaking and Syllabicity Gain (3.2.1 above). The option of Syllabicity Loss (making [ə] non-syllabic after a vowel) gives such words a monosyllabic variant; and this remains true when Smoothing applies. Hence *fire* may be phonetically ['faɪə] (two syllables), [faɪ̯ə] (one syllable, triphthongal, by Syllabicity Loss), ['faːə] (two syllables, by

Smoothing), or [faɜ̆] (one syllable, diphthongal, by Syllabicity Loss and Smoothing). Although the distinction between monosyllabic and disyllabic variants may be difficult or indeed impossible for the hearer to perceive, it seems to be valid for the speaker; poets have long exploited these options. Syllabicity loss is particularly usual in cases where the /aɪ, aʊ/ is unstressed, such as *empire, sapphire, safflower* (all normally disyllabic); so also *scientific, hierarchic* (three syllables).

The centring diphthongs derived from underlying /aɪə/ and /aʊə/ respectively may or may not be identical. A common possibility in RP is a fronter starting-point in [faə] *fire* than in [tɑə] *tower*. Cockney speakers, on the other hand, regularly have a back starting-point in [fɑə ~ fɒə] *fire*, a front one in [tæə] *tower*. Some speakers have new homophones by smoothing /aɪə/ and /aʊə/ to identical qualities, e.g. *tire–tower* [tɑə], *shire–shower* [ʃɑə], *hired–Howard* [hɑəd].

Yet another optional process now comes into play. The centring diphthongs derived from /aɪə, aʊə/ may become monophthongal, with qualities ranging from [aː] to [ɑː]. Whereas Smoothing is restricted to the environment of a following vowel, this **Monophthonging** is context-free. Hence *fire* has the fifth realizational possibility, [faː]. while *tower* may be [tɑː], homophonous with *tar*. Those who merge *tire* and *tower* may or may not make both homophonous with *tar*; many do. Similarly, *shire, shower*, and *Shah* can merge as [ʃɑː], *hired, Howard*, and *hard* as [hɑːd]. Other speakers have *tar* distinct from *tire–tower*, or *tire* distinct from *tower–tar*.

The link between [aː ~ ɑː] and its putative underlying representations /aɪə, aʊə/ is now so complex that one is not surprised to find evidence of restructuring. This may be seen in spelling mistakes such as *sar* for *sour*, which shows that phonetic [ɑː] is reinterpreted as the realization of START, /ɑː/.

As someone who has an [aː] in words like *fire* which is much fronter than the realization of /ɑː/ (START–BATH–PALM), I am aware that I use [aː] in a number of words where there is no historical justification for an /aɪə/ analysis. They include *reservoir* ['rezəvwaː] *soirée* ['swaːreɪ], *moiré* ['mwaːreɪ], and *savoir-faire* ['sævwaː'fɛə]. All are French loan-words, though *reservoir* is a word I knew long before I started to learn French. *EPD* offers only /ɑː/ (and sometimes /ɒ, ɔː/) in these words. Although they may be no more than a

personal idiosyncrasy, they led me to infer phonemic status for my
/aə/ (Wells 1962).

Returning to the disyllabic, Smoothed forms such as ['faːə],
['saːəns], ['traːɪŋ], ['kɑːəd], ['gɜːɪŋ], ['mɜːə], etc., it is noteworthy that
R Insertion is not a possibility in these words. We conclude that
Smoothing is ordered after R Insertion.

Smoothing can apply across word boundaries where one word
ends in one of the relevant diphthongs and the next word begins
with a vowel. Thus we have *way out* [weː aʊt], *they eat* [ðeː iːt], *how
odd* [hɑː ɒd], *my aunt* [maː ɑːnt], *go off* [gɜː ɒf], *so early* [sɜː ɜːlɪ] (in this
last example it is not in my opinion necessarily the case that 'some
movement towards [ʊ] and lip-rounding normally takes place', as
Gimson claims (1980: 141); but Smoothing remains optional, and if
the option is not exercised there will remain some gesture towards
[ʊ]).

In RP Smoothing can also apply to /iː/ and /uː/. It has the
phonetic effect of laxing them to [ɪ] and [ʊ:] respectively. (This can
be interpreted as evidence in favour of analysing FLEECE and GOOSE
as underlyingly diphthongal, /ɪi, ʊu/; Smoothing then has its usual
effect of producing a monophthong with the phonetic quality of the
starting-point of the underlying diphthong.) Examples include
Thea ['θɪːə], *seeing* ['sɪːɪŋ], *fluent* ['flʊːənt], *doing* ['dʊːɪŋ]; across word
boundaries, note for instance ['tʊː ə'klɒk], ['θɜːɪ ə'klɒk].

Syllabicity Loss can then make disyllabic [ɪə, ʊ:ə] into monosyllabic [ɪ̃ə, ʊ̃ə], which are identical in realization with NEAR and CURE
respectively. Hence *freer* (comparative of *free*) may be a perfect
rhyme of *dear*, and *truer* of *sure*; *theory* may rhyme with *dreary*, and
brewery with *jury*; *don't be a fool* may have [bɪə] exactly like *beer*, and
I can't do a thing may have [dʊə] exactly like *dour*.

Some speakers have optional Syllabicity Loss with weak [ɪ], too.
Then *ruin* and *doing* become monosyllabic, with a diphthong [ʊ̃ɪ];
poet and *going* similarly have [ɜ̃ɪ] (old-fashioned [oĭ]).

Neither the social nor the geographical spread of Smoothing has
been much investigated. As Gimson correctly remarks (1980: 140)
shire–shower–Shah homophony is 'criticized as an affectation and
also as a Cockney vulgarism, but widely heard amongst educated
RP speakers'. Smoothing (with Syllabicity Loss) in *player* and
snowing likewise seems to be shared by all social classes in London
(RP [pleə, snɜɪŋ]; Cockney [plʌə, snʌɪn]). Trudgill (1974a: 159–66)

has analysed the slightly different scope of Smoothing in the local accent of Norwich ([plæː, snɒːn]). Smoothing of /iː/ and /uː/ is perhaps socially more restricted, though characteristic of both extremes of the social scale: on the one hand, I have sometimes found people called *Ian* or *Stuart* reacting to my pronunciation of their name as [ɪən], [stjʊət] as 'affected', but on the other hand Cockney has [traːn] *trying*, [grʌːən] *growing*, [dɔːt] *do at* (all from Beaken 1971), while Norwich has [sɛːn] *seeing* and [bɔːn] *booing*.

In looking at dialectological evidence, we must obviously discount cases where PRICE, MOUTH, etc., are monophthongal in preconsonantal or final environments. With that proviso, *SED* shows Smoothing in *fire* only in a small area centred on London and reaching up into Cambridgeshire (*LAE* map Ph112), in *flour* only in Norfolk (map Ph155), and in *throwing* nowhere (*SED* viii.7.7). At the turn of the century, Wright's discussion of *fire* (1905: §179) contains no hint of Smoothing, though in 1914 Shaw has Eliza Doolittle saying 'flahrz' for *flowers*. It seems reasonable to conclude that Smoothing of /ai/ and /au/ originated in London and/or East Anglia towards the end of the nineteenth century; but whether it spread up the social scale into RP or down from it I do not know. At the present day it is certainly found in broad Cockney as well as in U-RP. (I have the impression that it is more prevalent at the two ends of the social scale than in between.)

The first phonetician to give detailed attention to Smoothing in RP seems to have been Daniel Jones. In the first edition of his *Pronunciation of English* he drew attention to the pronunciation of *fire* as [faː], commenting that this phenomenon was 'especially frequent in unstressed syllables, e.g. *irate*' (1909: §126). By the first edition of *EPD* (1917), *chaos* is given an entry which in our notation implies ['keɒs] alongside ['keɪɒs]; and similarly in many other cases. Jones 1954 is largely devoted to this topic.

The phenomenon has sometimes been referred to as 'levelling' (so Jones 1956: §414). But this term usually implies something rather different. I did for a time think of calling it 'correption' (mindful of the Latin grammarians' phrase *vocalis ante vocalem corripitur*), but have now decided to propose Smoothing as a more generally acceptable term.

In the United States, the neutralization of the opposition between /ai/ and /ɑ/ in the environment of a following /r/ is not uncommon. This 'characteristic feature of Midland speech' (*PEAS*: 122) has the effect of making *fire* and *far* homophonous, which is one of the possible effects of RP-style Smoothing; but it does not apply, as Smoothing does, in prevocalic environments. In the non-rhotic south, where /aɪ/ is often monophthongal [aː] or barely diphthongal, [aə], the distinction between *tied* and *tired* tends to be neutralizable, since both may be [taːəd]; but again this is rather a different phenomenon from Smoothing.

We conclude that Smoothing is as yet a purely English development. Gimson may well be right in his claim (1980: 140) that 'this monophthongization of /aɪə/ and /aʊə/ and their coalescence with /ɑː/ is likely to be one of the most striking sound changes affecting southern British English in the twentieth century'.

3.3 Some American innovations

In this section we consider phonological developments in the history of GenAm which took effect after the separation from Britain. Some of these developments apply to all North American accents; others were more restricted in their effects. They have in common that they do not generally speaking apply to British accents or those of the West Indies or southern hemisphere. They may thus constitute innovations upon American soil. It is wise, though, not to be too categorical in claiming them as indigenous American innovations, since most of the developments discussed in this section can be found somewhere or other in local accents of England. It is clear that GenAm is in fact a rather conservative accent when compared with RP.

Two further American developments, currently still in progress, are discussed not here but in vol. 3, 6.1: they are the merger of /ɑ/ and /ɔ/ and the splitting of /æ/.

3.3.1 Vowels before /r/

We have followed Kenyon & Knott (1953), Thomas (1958), Bronstein (1960) and many other scholars in assuming that the correct phonemicization of NEAR words in GenAm is with /ɪr/, e.g.

beard /bɪrd/, *beer* /bɪr/. It is clear, though, that for most Americans (not those with eastern or southern accents) there is a neutralization of certain paired vowels in the environment of a following /r/: in the case of NEAR, the vowel before the /r/ reflects a neutralization of the opposition /i/ (FLEECE) vs. /ɪ/ (KIT). The grounds for preferring to identify it with /ɪ/ rather than with /i/ are twofold: first, its phonetic quality, which is comparable with the often rather diphthongal [ɪə] /ɪ/ of *bid*, and secondly the fact that in such an accent *spear it* is a likely homophone of *spirit*, both being /'spɪrɪt/, while *nearer* and *mirror* rhyme in /-ɪrər/.

On similar grounds we write GenAm SQUARE words with /ɛr/ and CURE words with /ʊr/. For the majority who do not distinguish FORCE from NORTH, the merged vowel in both sets is appropriately written /ɔr/. (See further vol. 3, 6.1.5.)

If we compare the current GenAm pronunciation of such words with the early Modern English of 3.1.13 above, the relationship appears very straightforward, as shown in (157).

(157)	NEAR (*beard, beer, weary*)	SQUARE (*scarce, bare, Mary*)	FORCE (*forge, four, glory*)	CURE (*poor, during*)
Input (early Modern English)	iːr	eːr	ɔːr	uːr
GenAm	ɪr	ɛr	ɔr	ʊr

We can derive the GenAm vowels by applying a simple rule of Laxing, which lowers and centralizes tense (long) vowels in the environment of a following /r/. (Compare the Laxing rule of 3.2.1 above, which operated in the environment of a following schwa.) Thus we might assume that in the history of GenAm phonology there is a rule of the form (158).

(158)   V → [-tense] / __r

Although this simple hypothesis fits the present-day facts, the truth seems to have been rather more complicated. As we saw in 3.2.1, Pre-R Breaking, as an allophonic rule at least, is datable to the sixteenth century; it is mentioned by Gil in 1619 for a large number of words. Pre-Schwa Laxing, too, is likely to have been taken to America by the earliest settlers, since it is datable to the late sixteenth or early seventeenth century (Dobson 1968: §203–9). Thus the structural description for the posited rule (158) could not have been met (at least at the realizational level). Rather, the special characteristic of GenAm in this connection is the subsequent addition to Breaking and Laxing of a third rule, **Pre-R Schwa Deletion**, whereby non-syllabic [ə] disappeared between a vowel and a following /r/. Thus three successive developments took place (159–161).

(159) $Ø → \tilde{ə} / [-low, +long V]\_r$ Breaking

(160) $V → [\text{-tense}] / \_\tilde{ə}$ Laxing

(161) $\tilde{ə} → Ø / V\_r$ Schwa Deletion

It is (161) which is responsible for the fact that in GenAm *nearer* rhymes with *mirror* and *sharing* with *herring*. (There is, however, a problem here, since all GenAm vowels may often have some degree of non-significant [ə] glide, particularly in the environment of a following liquid – in *mirror* as much as in *nearer*, in *herring* as much as in *sharing*. Perhaps instead of (161) we should widen (159) to apply to all V _r environments.) Rather than (157), we have derivations as (162).

(162)	NEAR	SQUARE	FORCE	CURE
Input (early Modern English)	iːr	eːr	ɔːr	uːr
by (159)	iːər	eːər	ɔːər	uːər
by (160)	ɪər	ɛər	ɔər	ʊər
by (161)	ɪr	ɛr	ɔr	ʊr

The last line of (162) corresponds to contemporary GenAm. The result is the same as if only (158) had been added, but the route is more complicated. Once this result had been achieved, a restructuring no doubt took place: there is no reason to impute to present-day speakers of GenAm any knowledge of the historical difference between *herring* and *sharing*, *Mary* and *merry*.

We have already noted (3.1.8) the Second NURSE Merger in GenAm, which leads to the rhyming of *furry–hurry, stir it–turret*. Combined with the developments just outlined, the result is a considerable reduction in the subsystem of vowels contrasting in the environment of a following /r/.

Many Americans have /ær/ rather than /ɛr/ in SQUARE. Some even have an opposition between the two possibilities (as in

Kenyon's own pronunciation, 1958: §362, with /ær/ in *precarious* and *fairy*, /ɛr/ in *barbarian, Sarah*). Increasingly, however, the opposition between /æ/ and /ɛ/ is lost in the environment of a following /r/. This gives an identical sequence (identifiable on phonetic grounds as /ɛr/ rather than as /ær/) not only in SQUARE words and in words such as *herald, very, merry* (RP etc /er/), but also in words such as *narrow, charity, marry* (RP etc /ær/). This gives three-way homophony in sets such as *merry–marry–Mary, Kerry–carry–Carey*, something found nowhere outside North America.

There are certain words in which RP has /ɪr/ where the usual GenAm pronunciation is not /ɪr/ but /ɜr/. Examples are *squirrel* and *syrup*. These forms may well have been brought over from England; they appear to be of considerable antiquity (Dobson 1968: §213).

3.3.2 LOT Unrounding; loss of distinctive length

The vowel of LOT was rounded in Middle English; it has remained rounded in RP and the southern hemisphere, as well as in most British accents. In North America, on the other hand, only a minority use a rounded vowel; the majority, including the speakers of GenAm, have an unrounded [ɑ] (phonetically ranging from back to centralized front). We may refer to this development as LOT **Unrounding**. Scholars differ as to whether it is in fact an independent innovation on American soil. Some see it rather as 'a survival of the pronunciation that was current in Britain at the time of colonization' (Hanks 1979: xxvi). Others, e.g. Lass (1976: 139), argue that it is an indigenous American development, dating probably from the late seventeenth or early eighteenth century. Since [ɑ] in LOT is so relatively uncommon in present-day British speech, I incline to agree. Apart from North America, though, LOT Unrounding is also characteristic of the accents of southern Ireland and most of the West Indies.

The unrounding of LOT while retaining its distinctiveness vis-à-vis TRAP must not be confused with a merger of LOT and TRAP as [a] which is known as a sixteenth- and seventeenth-century vulgarism (Dobson 1968: §87). It was this earlier merger which, originating as early as the thirteenth century and seeping into standard speech in a few lexical items, is responsible for the by-forms *strap* alongside *strop* and *by Gad* alongside *by God*. But actual merger of LOT and TRAP is quite unknown in North America (and nowadays found only in certain popular West Indian accents).

The merger which did occur in the history of GenAm (though not by any means for all American accents) is exemplified by the pair *bother–father*, which is GenAm rhyme as /ˈbɑðər, ˈfɑðər/ (compare RP /ˈbɒðə/ but /ˈfɑːðə/). This implies the **loss of distinctive length** in open vowels, since the PALM–START set, long in other accents, is merged with the LOT set, short in other accents.

Although it is convenient to write the resultant vowel, GenAm /ɑ/, without length marks, the result of the merger is phonetically usually a rather long vowel, as is immediately audible if one compares RP /ˈbɒðə/ with GenAm /ˈbɑðər/ [ˈbɑːðɚ]. The phonetic development is thus essentially one of lengthening open vowels, as is clear also from the comparison of GenAm and RP /æ/ in words such as *manner, ladder*. It so happens that the lengthening of TRAP had no systemic consequences, while the lengthening of LOT, because of its unrounding, did.

This tendency to lengthen traditionally short vowels is sufficient justification for the non-use of length marks in transcription of GenAm. All vowel contrasts are now ones of quality rather than length. Even the merging of vowels before /r/ through Pre-R Schwa Deletion (3.3.1 above) fits this pattern: the vowels in pairs such as *merry* and *Mary* in accents which distinguish them often differ mainly in duration rather than in quality; GenAm, by abandoning length contrasts, naturally lost the distinction.

Some Americans retain a length contrast only in a very restricted range of environments. It is not unusual to have a distinction before nasals only, so that *Tom* and *con* have short [ɑ], while *calm* and *Kahn* have a longer [ɑː]; but the same speaker would rhyme *bother* and *father* and have *dolly* and *Dali* as homophones. (There are of course relatively few environments in which PALM and LOT contrast, even at the best of times; most common PALM words are vowel-final, e.g. *bra*, while LOT is always checked.)

The lengthened vowel of CLOTH words was not affected by LOT Unrounding. In the environments illustrated by *cloth* itself and by *strong* the earlier short [ɒ] had been lengthened (3.1.9 above); this lengthened vowel remained rounded. Later, like other vowels, it lost its distinctive length. It can be seen that logically the two developments must have occurred in that order. The fact that LOT Unrounding preceded loss of distinctive length explains why the lengthened former allophone of /ɒ/ became phonemically distinct in GenAm (merging at some stage with the long /ɔ/ of THOUGHT) while the inherited lengthened allophone of /æ/ in BATH did not. In tabular form, we have successive GenAm developments as in (163).

(163)	*trap*	*bath*	*lot*	*cloth*	*thought*
Inherited form (with Pre-					
Fricative Lengthening)	træp	bæːθ	lɒt	klɒːθ	θɔːt
LOT Unrounding	–	–	lɑt	–	–
Loss of distinctive length	–	bæθ	–	klɒθ	θɔt
CLOTH–THOUGHT Merger	–	–	–	klɔθ	–
Output	/træp/	/bæθ/	/lɑt/	/klɔθ/	/θɔt/

3.3.3 Later Yod Dropping

In 3.1.10 above we discussed Early Yod Dropping, the loss of /j/ from /juː/ after palatals, /r/, and clusters with /l/. In GenAm this process has been extended so that /j/ tends to be absent after all coronal consonants. It remains after labials and velars (*beauty*, *cute*).

The environments in which **Later Yod Dropping** has eliminated /j/ from historical /ju/ (or, where there is a following /r/, from /jʊ/) are: /t__/ *tune, student, attitude*; /d__/ *duke, reduce, during*; /n__/ *new, numerous, avenue*; /θ__/ *enthusiasm, Thule*; /s__/ *suit, assume, pseudonym*; /z__/ *presume, resume*; /l__/ *lewd, allude, solution*. In these environments GenAm predominantly has plain /u/, thus, /tun, duk, nu/ etc. Some easterners and southerners, however, have either /ju/ or the diphthong /ɪu/, and GenAm usage is not entirely uniform.

The discussion so far relates to strong syllables: either stressed syllables (*tune, new*) or syllables where there is no possibility of vowel reduction and where some would identify a secondary (some, a tertiary) degree of stress (*attitude, avenue*). In the case of weak syllables, the complete elimination of the palatal is less widespread; but here GenAm shows a marked tendency towards **Yod Coalescence**. Thus GenAm *situate* is /ˈsɪtʃueɪt ~ ˈsɪtʃəweɪt/, with an affricate /tʃ/ corresponding to the /tj/ of RP /ˈsɪtjʊeɪt/ (in England the /tʃ/ pronunciation is felt to be rather vulgar, whereas

American dictionaries prescribe it unhesitatingly). So also with the voiced affricate /dʒ/, where RP has /dj/, as in *education*, GenAm /ˈɛdʒəˈkeɪʃən/ (compare RP /ˈedjʊˈkeɪʃn̩/). In America *issue* typically has /ʃ/, /ˈɪʃʊ/ etc., whereas in RP the pronunciation with /sj/, /ˈɪsjuː/, is at least as generally heard. In each of these cases an alveolar consonant has coalesced with the following palatal semivowel to produce a palato-alveolar. It is my impression that something comparable may happen with /nj/ and /lj/ in American speech, giving [ɲ] or [j] in *annual*, [ʎ] or [j] in *failure*.

The example *education* given above also illustrates another GenAm tendency, namely towards [ə] in weak syllables deriving from /(j)u/. So also *monument*, GenAm /ˈmɑnjəmənt/; in RP /ˈmɒnjəmənt/ is on the whole only a casual-speech variant of /ˈmɒnjʊmənt/. Before, vowels, however, as in *arduous*, /u ~ ʊ/ remains; even those who have what could perhaps be regarded as [ə] in such words have a [w] glide after it.

3.3.4 Tapping and T Voicing

One of the most striking characteristics of American pronunciation to the ears of a non-American is the intervocalic consonant in words such as *atom, better, waiting*. To English people it sounds like /d/ rather than /t/. Phonetically it is usually a rapid tap rather than a more deliberate plosive; it is also frequently voiced. But it is an oversimplification just to call it [d].

The process of **Tapping** optionally affects both /t/ and /d/ in GenAm, giving them a tap realization, [ɾ̥] and [ɾ] respectively. It operates in certain syllable-final prevocalic environments, both word-internally and across word boundaries: thus *atom* [ˈæɾəm], *getting* [ˈgɛɾɪŋ], *get it in* [ˈgɛɾɪɾ ˈɪn]; *ready* [ˈɹɛɾi], *reading* [ˈɹiɾɪŋ], *bad egg* [ˈbæɾ ˈɛg]. A necessary condition is that the preceding segment be a sonorant (vowel, liquid, or nasal); the following segment must not be a consonant (other than syllabic [l]). We can formulate the rule as (164):

(164) Alveolar Stop → Tap / Sonorant — $\begin{Bmatrix} V \\ || \end{Bmatrix}$

Thus we may have *party* [ˈpɑɹɾi], *builder* [ˈbɪlɾɚ], *dental* [ˈdɛ̃ɾl̩]. Usually, though, [ɾ̥] represents only a theoretical, half-way stage, since the output tap ends up voiced.

Scholars are in some disagreement over the appropriate classification and transcription of what I have called a tap and written [ɾ]. Recent American discussion of the phenomenon has popularized the term 'flapping'; but if we follow Abercrombie (1967: 49) in distinguishing between taps (one-tap-trills) and flaps (ballistic movements), then the medial consonant in GenAm *atom* is a tap, not a flap. It remains true, however, that it is not identical with the [ɾ] allophone of Spanish /r/, which has a somewhat different configuration of the front of the tongue (see x-ray tracings in Monnot & Freeman 1972). This leads Kenyon to reject the view that 'voiced t' is a tap, since 'to the author's ear the two are quite distinct' (1958: §163). Bronstein (1960), on the other hand, regards them as 'almost identical'; Bloomfield (1933: 100) calls 'voiced t' a 'tongue-flip'. Some, furthermore, describe it as fortis (e.g. Trager & Smith 1951: 32), others as lenis (e.g. Bronstein 1960: 73). As far as notation is concerned, the voiced tap as a realization of /t/ is often written [t̬]; but Chomsky (1964: 74) writes [D], while Wise (1957: 123) is content with [d]. *LAUM* distinguishes [t̬] from [ɾ], and finds the second twice as common as the first in the word *attic*, but [t̬] commoner than [ɾ] in *thirty* (*LAUM*: 322).

When the intervocalic tap realization of /t/ undergoes the second process, that of T Voicing (165), the result may be the neutralization of the opposition between /t/ and /d/. This makes *atom* and *Adam* homophonous, ['ærəm]; likewise *bitter* and *bidder*, ['bɪɾɚ], and *waiting* and *wading* ['weɪɪŋ], *parity* and *parody*, ['pæɹəɾi]. Oswald (1943) demonstrated that American listeners could not consistently hear a difference when tested on sentences such as *The injured lamb was bleating/bleeding*.

(165)   [tap] → [+ voice] / __ V

This, then, is the basis for the British impression that Americans pronounce /d/ instead of /t/. Such a claim is commonly denied by the phonetically naive; and T Voicing is widely regarded by the speech-conscious as undesirable. A typical view is that expressed by Thomas (1958: 48), when he opines that

the principal shortcoming among native speakers is an excessive weakening of the sound ... [t] may then change to a weakly articulated [d], [*or*] to a variety of [r] produced by a short tap of the tip of the tongue against the gum ridge.... Though opinions differ as to what is standard and what is substandard in this type of variation, the weakened allophones of [t] frequently

heard in such words as *little, better*,... can usually be somewhat streng-
thened without laying the speaker open to the charge of artificiality.

The typical RP form, involving a voiceless alveolar plosive for /t/
in such words, is often perceived by Americans as artificial, prissy,
or effeminate.

It is possible to have T Voicing without the neutralization of the
opposition between /t/ and /d/. In this case /t/ has the intervocalic
realization [ɾ], while /d/ is [d]; the difference between them is then
primarily one of rate of articulation, i.e. a difference in the duration
of the alveolar contact. This is the kind of pronunciation described
by Kenyon, who writes (1958: §163) 'voiced *t* is not the same as *d*.
and does not belong to the *d* phoneme, since Americans do not
confuse such words as *latter–ladder* or *putting–pudding*'. Trager &
Smith (1951), too, assume without question that 'voiced fortis [t]'
belongs to the phoneme /t/ and is distinct from the [d] of /d/.

This view was first challenged by Oswald (1943), with his dem-
onstration that /d/ is also affected and that the /t/–/d/ opposition
can be neutralized as a consequence. Ten years later, Lehmann
(1953) was reporting hypercorrections in Texan speech (e.g. ['rɛtɪ]
as a careful pronunciation of *ready*), as well as 'graphic evidence' in
the form of *t-d* spelling mistakes in the writings of University of
Texas students. In 1966 McDavid recognized that 'neutralization
of the contrast between intervocalic /-t-/ and /-d-/, as in *latter* and
ladder,... is an innovation that seems to be spreading, especially
among the younger and better educated speakers'. If this perception is accurate, we are indeed dealing with an American innovation
and a fairly recent one. There is, on the other hand, a possible
British source in the west of England, where the *SED* records [d] in
butter throughout the south-western counties: see *LAE* map Ph239.
Another source could be Ulster.

T Voicing is sometimes to be observed in southern-hemisphere
English (Australians assure me, though, that it is only younger
speakers there who do it), and also in certain casual styles in British
accents ranging from RP to Cockney. It is not altogether clear
whether these non-American cases of T Voicing represent the
diffusion of an American innovation, or independent innovations
in several different places. I suspect the former, and see T Voicing
as the first distinctively American phonetic innovation likely to
spread in time to all accents of English.

As pointed out by Joos (1942) and elaborated upon by Chomsky (1964: 82–3), T Voicing gives rise to an interesting phonological problem in certain accents (notably those of Canada and parts of the north, east, and south of the United States). These are accents in which the PRICE vowel has positional allophones conditioned by the voicing or otherwise of the following consonant, e.g. [ʌɪ] before a voiceless consonant, [aˑɪ] elsewhere. But before voiced /t/ the allophone used is that appropriate to a following voiceless consonant (even though the consonant is actually voiced), which means that pairs such as *writer* and *rider* do not fall together: they remain distinct, e.g. as [ˈɹʌɪɾɚ] and [ˈɹaˑɪɾɚ] respectively. Thus what is underlyingly a consonantal distinction, /t/ in *writer* vs. /d/ in *rider*, is realized phonetically as a vowel distinction, [ʌɪ] vs. [aˑɪ]. This analysis depends crucially upon the admissibility of rule ordering in phonology, since in order to achieve the correct result the rule assigning appropriate realizations to /aɪ/ must precede the rule of T Voicing (1.2.13 above).

In GenAm T Voicing applies not only intervocalically but also between a vowel and a following syllabic lateral, as in *battle* [bæɾɫ]. Here the phonetic result is a laterally released tap. There is also the possibility of a tap with lateral approach, as in *guilty* [ˈgɪɫɾi]. Another variant is used by some Americans when the preceding consonant is /r/, namely a retroflex flap, [ɽ], thus *party* [pɑɹɽi], *dirty* [dɝɽi]; this is the only environment in which a genuine flap, as opposed to a tap, is to be encountered.

Although T Voicing may apply before a syllabic lateral, it does not apply before a syllabic nasal. In words such as *button* Americans keep a voiceless /t/, realized either as a nasally released alveolar [tᴺ] or as a glottal [ʔ]. In words such as *sentence*, where English people usually have an orally exploded [t] plus [ən], thus [ˈsentəns], many Americans use [ʔ] plus [n̩]; when this is combined with a nasalized vowel as a realization of vowel plus /n/, the resultant [ˈsɛ̃ʔn̩ts] can be difficult for non-Americans to recognize correctly.

I am not sure whether a tap with a nasal approach is a genuine possibility in a word such as *hunting*, although Trager & Smith (1951: 32) speak of this word having a 'flap-release short nasal'. More usual, it seems to me, is [ˈhʌ̃ɾɪŋ], in which the /n/ is again realized as nasality during the vowel. Although I find it exceedingly difficult to discriminate between *winter* and *winner* in casual American pronunciation, there appears to be at least the theoretical possibility of ['wɪɾ̃ɚ] *winter* vs. ['wɪnɚ] *winner*. If Stampe is right in claiming (1972: 55) that Tapping also applies to /n/ in the same environments as it applies to /t/ and /d/, with an output which is a nasalized tap [ɾ̃], then the contrast may be between ['wɪɾ̃ɚ] and ['wɪɾ̃ɚ]. There is little doubt that this subtle distinction may be completely lost.

Actually, there is clearly geographical variation in North America with respect to treatment of /nt/ in *winter*, *hunting*, etc. Southerners tend to have in their phonology a rule simply deleting /t/ in this environment, (166); this turns /'wɪntɚ/ into ['wɪnɚ], which is then a potential input for an N Tapping rule.

(166)   t → Ø / 'Vn __ V

Northerners, on the other hand, particularly those from the east coast, may preserve a firm distinction between *winter* and *winner*. The first may be ['wɪɾ̃ɚ], as against ['wɪnɚ] for the second (Trager 1942: 146, specifically states that [ɾ̃] and [n] are in contrast in his speech). Or the first may be ['wɪnɾɚ], having a nasal [n] with tap release as the soft palate cuts off nasal escape fractionally before the tongue tip leaves the alveolar ridge. Or the first may even have a British-style [nt], thus ['wɪntɚ].

3.4 Some further British innovations

In this section we consider some further sound changes which have spread reasonably widely in the English-speaking world. H Dropping and Diphthong Shift must have become established in England (though not in RP) by the beginning of the nineteenth century, since they seem to have been taken to the southern hemisphere by settlers; they are not, however, found in the New World, so presumably postdate the colonization of North America in the seventeenth and eighteenth centuries. The same may be true of L Vocalization and of *Happy* Tensing, though here the patterns are more complicated and the facts more difficult to establish. T Glottalling in intervocalic environments is a more recent development in Britain, as attested by its absence from accents of English elsewhere. All these developments are characteristics of popular speech in the south-east of England, but not of RP in the traditional sense.

3.4.1 H Dropping

Initially in words such as *hit, hammer, happy, hedge,* standard accents have /h/, which is realized as [h] – conventionally referred to as a voiceless glottal fricative, but more accurately described as a range of voiceless approximants varying with the quality of the following vowel. This /h/ contrasts with zero (which may sometimes include the realization [ʔ]), as shown by minimal pairs such as *hedge* vs. *edge, heat* vs. *eat, hall* vs. *all.* The phoneme /h/ also occurs intervocalically (though still syllable-initially), as in *ahead, rehearse, behind, to heat*; here it is sometimes realized as [ɦ], the 'voiced glottal fricative' more accurately described as comprising a range of breathy-voiced vocoids.

In the working-class accents of most of England, **H Dropping** prevails. That is to say, the [h] of standard accents is absent: words such as *hit, hammer, happy, hedge,* begin with a vowel (or sometimes [ʔ]).

There seem in principle to be two possible synchronic phonological accounts of H Dropping. In one view, perhaps the obvious one, we claim that there is simply no /h/ in the phoneme system. It follows that *hedge* and *edge, heat* and *eat, hall* and *all,* are perfect homophones with identical phonological representations in the lexicon. The phone [h] occurs, if at all, only as a variable marker of emphasis (like initial [ʔ]). This means that both *hedge* and *edge* may on occasion be pronounced [hɛdʒ], although both are usually [ɛdʒ]. Historically speaking, this state of affairs results essentially from a sound change deleting /h/ (167), perhaps with the addition of a rule (168) which variably adds [h] before an initial vowel as a mark of emphasis.

(167) h → Ø

(168) Ø → h / __ V / [+emphasis]

In the other possible view, we maintain that /h/ remains in the phoneme system, but acquires an optional zero realization. This means that *hedge* and *edge* are phonologically distinct in the speaker's mental lexicon, as /hɛdʒ/ and /ɛdʒ/ respectively; but /hɛdʒ/ may sometimes be realized as [ɛdʒ] (or [ʔɛdʒ]) rather than as [hɛdʒ]. In this case, *edge* would be expected never to be pronounced [hɛdʒ]. There may be other consequences: several words in English have alternating forms sensitive to the vowel vs. consonant character of the initial segment of the following word, and even an underlying /h/ with zero phonetic realization may be able to trigger the preconsonantal variant. Thus for example we may have [ə 'ɛdʒ] *a hedge* but [ən 'ɛdʒ] *an edge*; or *your edge* with linking /r/ and *your hedge* without it. This seems to be a correct account of the usage of some working-class Londoners. On the other hand there are plenty who do say, for example, [ʌʊvər 'ɪə] *over here*, or *Wolverhampton* [wʊlvər'æmptən].

Perhaps the most realistic view combines elements of both the above. In the basic phonological system acquired in childhood there is no /h/. But social pressures from teachers and others, supported by the effects of literacy, lead to the partial and inconsistent addition of /h/ to the phoneme inventory, often with some uncertainty as to whether or not it is appropriate in some given word.

H Dropping does appear to be the single most powerful pronunciation shibboleth in England. A London school teacher tells me he has only to look sternly at any child who drops an /h/, and that child will say the word again, this time correctly. The correlation between H Dropping and social factors has been confirmed by sociolinguistic research. Among London schoolchildren, Hudson & Holloway (1977) found that middle-class boys dropped only 14 percent of possible /h/s, while working-class boys dropped 81 percent. In Norwich, a city in whose rural hinterland /h/ is still to some extent preserved, Trudgill (1974a: 131) found that in casual speech the percentage of /h/ dropped ranged from 6 for the middle middle class through 14 for the lower middle class and 40 for the upper working class to 59 for the middle working class and 61 for the lower working class.

There are certain complications here. In standard accents the pronouns *he, him, her, his* (and sometimes *who*), together with the auxiliaries *has, have, had*, regularly lack [h] if neither stressed nor postpausal. Thus RP *tell him* ['tɛlɪm] must not be counted as an instance of H Dropping in the sense discussed above. Nevertheless, it is my impression that some middle-class speakers, perhaps in a genteel anxiety not to do something so vulgar as dropping an /h/, tend to insist on giving even these unstressed pronouns and auxiliaries [h], thus ['telhɪm]. The near-RP [-həm] in *Birmingham* and *Nottingham* (RP /'bɜːmɪŋəm/, /'nɒtɪŋəm/) has a similar explanation.

In words such as *historic, hysteria*, the traditional RP principle of no [h] in unstressed syllables gave the old-fashioned standard pronunciations [ɪˈstɒrɪk], [ɪˈstɪərɪə]. It was natural to pronounce, and write, *an* rather than *a* in the phrase *an historic event*. Nowadays such words are usually pronounced with a restored [h], but the literary convention persists (to an extent) of writing *an*, and even of pronouncing it, before the following *h* ([h]).

There are several instances of words adopted into English via French from Latin where the /h/ now customary in standard accents reflects no more than a spelling pronunciation. Thus *habit, heritage, host*, and *Humphrey* (amongst others) are known to have been /h/-less in the early Modern English period (Dobson 1968: §426 n. 3). In *hour, heir, honest, honour* and their derivatives the /h/-less pronunciation has persisted in spite of the spelling. In *herb*, GenAm /ɜrb/ reflects an earlier form than RP /hɜːb/, which has /h/ from the spelling. In *humble*, the earlier /h/-less form is still found in the American south. In *hotel*, the form with spelling-derived /h/ has largely displaced the earlier /h/-less form (though /əʊˈtel/ remains in U-RP, together with *an hotel*).

In nouns, verbs, and adjectives, and leaving aside special cases such as we have just been considering, H Dropping has been known in popular London speech since at least the eighteenth century. (It was obviously very well established by Dickens's day!) Explicit condemnation of H Dropping is first found at the close of the eighteenth century (Strang 1970: 81). The fact that H Dropping is unknown in North America strongly suggests that it arose in England only well after the American colonies were founded. Australians, on the other hand, tend to drop /h/ just like the English, as we should expect from their settlement history.

Historical details of the spread of H Dropping through England are lacking. In 1905 Wright wrote (§357), 'initial *h* has remained before vowels in ... Sc. Irel. Nhb. and perhaps also in portions of

n. Dur and n. Cum. In the remaining parts of Eng. it has disappeared.' More than half a century later, the *SED* researches demonstrated that Wright may have been somewhat overstating the case, since there are pockets of /h/ in the south of England (relic areas). But H Dropping does not seem to have gained more territory since Wright's day.

On the other side of the Atlantic, some Jamaicans, Bahamians, and Guyanese exhibit H Dropping. Others do not. It is not known whether this West Indian H Dropping represents the importation of a popular British speech habit, or whether it is an independent local innovation.

The fact that Northumbrians, Scots, Irish, Americans, and Barbadians do not incline to H Dropping is sufficient proof, if proof were needed, that there is no truth in the popular English view that H Dropping is a product of laziness and original sin. Or are there no lazy Americans?

3.4.2 Diphthong Shift

When the Reverend A. J. D. D'Orsey, Professor of Public Reading at King's College in the University of London, pointed out that in popular London speech 'such words as *paper, shape, train* are pronounced *piper, shipe, trine*' and went on to hold the teachers of English responsible in that 'the very first letter of the alphabet [was] thus wrongly taught' (quoted by Matthews 1938: 63), his understanding of the way linguistic changes are propagated and of the relationship between orthography and pronunciation may have been faulty; but his observation was basically accurate. Cockney, and also the local accents of much of the south of England and the midlands, together with those of Australia and New Zealand, exhibit a set of phonetic changes almost as fundamental as the Great Vowel Shift of half a millenium ago. This is the **Diphthong Shift**.

In schematic and drastically simplified form, the Diphthong Shift can be diagrammed as (169).

(169)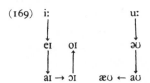

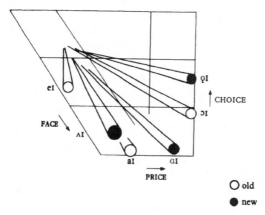

Fig. 7   The Diphthong Shift in part-system B

Thus FLEECE shifts from [iː] to [eɪ],or more commonly actually [əi]; FACE shifts from [eɪ] to [aɪ], or sometimes just to [ʌɪ] (where the symbol [ʌ] denotes a central half-open vowel); PRICE shifts from [aɪ] to [ɔɪ] or sometimes just to [ɑɪ] or [ɒɪ]; CHOICE moves up from [ɔɪ] to [oɪ]. There is thus a rearrangement among the members of part-system B. Similarly, in part-system C, GOOSE shifts from [uː] to [əʊ], though usually with the competing possibility of [ʉː]; GOAT moves from earlier [oʊ] or [əʊ] to [ʌʊ], [œʊ], or even as far as [aʊ]; MOUTH shifts forwards to [æʊ ~ æə ~ ɛʊ]. To an outsider it does indeed seem as if *paper* is pronounced 'piper', *tie* 'toy', and *no* 'now'.

It is not known when the Diphthong Shift arose. Probably it originated in London; presumably it was well under way by the first half of the nineteenth century, so that early settlers took it to Australia. Since Long Mid Diphthonging (3.1.12 above) must logically have preceded it, and in RP is dated to the beginning of the nineteenth century, we can infer that Long Mid Diphthonging operated in popular speech well before it did in cultivated speech.

3.4.3 *Happy* Tensing

What we have called the *happy* vowel – the final vowel in words such as *happy*, *lucky*, *coffee* – was between the seventeenth century and 1950 regularly analysed by phoneticians as [ɪ] and implicitly assigned to the KIT phoneme. Latterly, though, there has been an increasing tendency throughout the English-speaking world to use a closer quality, [i(:)], and for speakers to feel intuitively that *happy* belongs with FLEECE rather than with KIT.

Where and when the [i] pronunciation arose is not certain. It has probably been in use in provincial and vulgar speech for centuries (though Wright 1905, for example, makes absolutely no mention of it). It is the customary form in southern-hemisphere accents, which suggests that it was already prevalent in the local accents of southeast England by the early nineteenth century. Kenyon (1958: §253; first edition, 1924) speaks of 'a tendency in the younger generation of the North and West [of the United States]' to use /i/; by 1960 Bronstein is writing (147) that 'most speakers use ... /i/'. RP has always traditionally been described as having /ɪ/, but by 1962 Gimson comments (§7.10) that '/ɪ/ is increasingly replaced in the speech of the younger generations by a short variety of /iː/'.

It is clear, therefore, that a trend towards what we may refer to as *Happy* **Tensing** is currently in operation both in Britain and the United States.

3.4.4 L Vocalization

The RP allophonic rule for /l/ provides for the clear allophone (with a frontish tamber) in the environment of a following vowel, but the dark allophone (with back tamber) elsewhere, i.e. before a consonant or in final position. Thus [l] occurs in *let, look, valley*, and [ɫ] in *milk, bulb,* and (prepausal) *feel, fall, middle.* Of the semivowels, /j/ is treated like a vowel (clear [l] in *million*), but /w/ as a consonant (dark [ɫ] in *always*). Ignoring this slight complication, we can formulate the rule as (170), which treats the clear allophone as basic.

$$(170) \quad l \rightarrow ɫ \, / \, — \left\{ \begin{array}{c} \| \\ \#_0 \, C \end{array} \right\}$$

This rule generally takes no account of word boundaries: thus *feel upset, fall off* have clear [l], and it is only when prepausal or when followed by a word beginning with a consonant that *feel* and *fall* have [ɫ].

The development we call **L Vocalization** converts [ɫ] into a non-syllabic back vocoid, [ɣ], or its rounded equivalent, [o]. (The precise quality varies. We could equally well write [o] or [ʊ].) Thus *milk* comes to be pronounced [mɪɒ̆k], *shelf* [ʃɛɒ̆f], and *bulb* [bʌɒ̆b]. Prepausal *feel* becomes [fiːɵ̆] (etc.; there may also be special developments in the preceding vowel), *fall* [fɔːɵ̆]. Syllabic dark [ɫ] becomes syllabic [o] (etc.), thus *middle* ['mɪdo]. Instead of (170) we have (171).

$$(171) \quad l \rightarrow o \; / \; - \left\{ \begin{array}{l} \| \\ \#_0 \; C \end{array} \right\}$$

L Vocalization has potentially massive implications for the reorganization of the vowel system, comparable in its magnitude to the effects of R Dropping. Just as it was R Dropping which assured phonemic status for the diphthongs /ɪə, ɛə, ɔə, ʊə/, so L Vocalization offers the prospect of eventual phonemic status for new diphthongs such as /ɪʊ/ (*milk*), /ɛʊ/ (*shelf*), etc. (Note the formal similarily between (170) and (146′) of 3.2.2 above.) It will also, incidentally, simplify the foreign learner's task: most will find ['mɪdo] a good deal easier than the laterally released [d] plus dark [ɫ] of ['mɪdɫ].

This development seems to be a recent one. There have been droppings or vocalizations of /l/ in various environments in the earlier history of English (*walk, calm*) and of traditional-dialects (*owd* for *old*, etc.). But the precise development now under discussion is probably less than a century old in London. For all his orthographic contortions in his Cockney characters' speech, Shaw leaves Eliza Doolittle with *l* in 'gel, spawl' (*girl, spoil*); even Drinkwater in *Captain Brassbound's Conversion* (1900) is allowed *call* and *little* (Shaw could easily have invented something like *caw, li'oo* to represent the current Cockney pronunciation). The *LAE* shows *uncle* and *weasel* with [u] in a stretch of the south of England from Sussex to Essex. Jones seems again to be the first to describe the phenomenon accurately (1956: §298; first edition 1909), attributing it to 'London dialectal speech'.

From its putative origins in the local accent of London and the surrounding counties, L Vocalization is now beginning to seep into RP. It seems likely that it will become entirely standard in English over the course of the next century.

A different kind of L Vocalization is found in the American south (generally as an optional realization rule). It changes nonprevocalic /l/ into a velar lateral (vol. 3, 6.5.9). This may well be a historically unconnected development.

3.4.5 Glottalization

The voiceless plosives /p, t, k/, and also the affricate /tʃ/, are in England often preceded in certain syllable-final environments by a glottal stop [ʔ]. Either this is a new, twentieth-century, phenomenon, or else no phonetician had previously noticed it. Because the [ʔ] is inserted before the oral closure is effected, and thus masks the approach phase of the oral plosive, it is referred to as **Preglottalization,** or Glottal Reinforcement.

The precise details of the environments favouring Preglottalization are intricate and variable. The following conditions appear to apply: (i) it occurs only when /p, t, k, tʃ/ are in syllable-final position (including in certain syllable-final clusters); (ii) it occurs only when /p, t, k, tʃ/ are preceded by a vowel, a liquid, or a nasal. Subject to these conditions, consider the cases set out in (173) below. The expression 'true C' (true consonant) covers obstruents and nasals, but not liquids or semivowels. 'L' stands for non-syllabic liquids, 'S' for semivowels. 'Word-internal' includes cases where a clitic (such as *it*) is attached. The effect of Preglottalization can be formulated as (172).

(172)   Ø → ʔ / V (L or nasal) __ [Voiceless Plosive]

(173)		/p/	/t/	/k/
(a)	__ # true C	*stop talking*	*quite good*	*look down*
(b)	__ # L or S	*stop worrying*	*quite likely*	*look worried*
(c)	__ # V	*stop eating*	*quite easy*	*look up*
(d)	__ pause	*Stop!*	*Quite!*	*Look!*
(e)	__ true C	*stopped, capsule*	*nights, curtsey*	*looks, picture*
(f)	__ L or S	*hopeless*	*mattress*	*equal*
(g)	__ [m, n̩, ŋ]	(*happen*)	*button*	(*bacon*)
(h)	__ V or [l̩]	*happy, apple, stop it*	*butter, bottle, get 'im*	*ticket, buckle, lick it*

(For case (g) to be relevant, underlying /ən/ must have coalesced to [n̩] by Syllabic Consonant Formation; for *happen* and *bacon*, moreover, [n̩] must have become bilabial or velar respectively through Progressive Assimilation.)

In RP, Preglottalization may apply to any of cases (a, b, d, e, f). Some speakers do not have it at all; others have it only in (a, b, e) (where it is difficult to perceive). Strangely, no social value appears to attach to Preglottalization in the environments where it is very clearly audible, namely (d) and (f): English people do not have strong feelings about which is more elegant of ['hɔʊpləs, 'hɔʊʔpləs], ['mætrəs, 'mæʔtrəs], ['iːkwəl, 'iːʔkwəl].

The affricate /tʃ/ is more widely preglottalized, including in the environment corresponding to (h) of (173) (*teacher*, ['tiːʔtʃə], *watch it* ['wɒʔtʃɪt]).

Preglottalization is not particularly associated with the south of England rather than the north. Indeed, my subjective impression is that in environment (d) it is at least as common in northern accents as in southern (thus [stɒʔp, kwaɪʔt, lʊʔk]). An emphatic articulation of the glottal component will readily convert this into an ejective, thus [stɒp', kwaɪt', lʊk']; both northerners and southerners may be found who use these forms under appropriate stylistic conditions.

Another possibility is the use of a glottal stop which masks the release stage of the oral plosive. This is not easily distinguished perceptually from complete replacement of the oral articulation by [ʔ]. In the local accents of London, Glasgow, Edinburgh, in many rural accents of the south of England and East Anglia, and increasingly in urban accents everywhere in England, such **Glottalling** is now to be observed for /t/ in all the environments mentioned in (173). Sometimes it applies to /p/ and /k/ as well, though here there appears always to be the potential of some kind of labial or velar gesture respectively to distinguish /p/ and /k/ from /t/ (where no alveolar gesture is necessary). T Glottalling is well-known as a Cockneyism in words such as ['bʌʔə], ['bɒʔo]. These forms are sharply stigmatized; but T Glottalling in environments (a, b, e) must be considered to fall within current mainstream RP. Some younger RP speakers even use plain [ʔ] for /t/ in environment (c).

I know of no systematic investigation of Preglottalization and Glottalling in American speech; but T Glottalling is clearly to be observed in the speech of some Americans in environments (a, b, g).

The *LAE* shows [ʔ] for /t/ only in a small area around London and in East Anglia (map Ph239). Wright (1905: §287) recognizes it only in 'west-mid Scotland, Lothian, and Edinburgh', and then only before /ə/ plus a liquid (*kettle*, *water*). But by 1909 Jones, in the first edition of his *Pronunciation of English*, writes 'In Scotland and London *t* is often replaced by the glottal plosive ʔ', giving the London example [ɑaiŋgɔʔwan] *I haven't got one*. The very widespread dissemination of [ʔ] for /t/ at the present day suggests, therefore, that Glottalling must have spread very fast in the course of the present century.

3.4.6 The -*ing* variable

We have already noted the sociolinguistic variability of the ending
-*ing*, in which the final nasal may be either velar or alveolar (1.1.5,
.6, .8). Although this variability is neither exclusively British nor a
recent innovation, we discuss it in this section of chapter 3 for lack
of anywhere better.

In a word such as *running* the form ['rʌnɪŋ] is on the whole
associated with higher social class and more formal speech, ['rʌnɪn
~ 'rʌnən] with lower social class and less formal speech. The
special spelling *runnin'* is sometimes used to show the [n] form.
There is a phonetic variant [n̩] alongside [ən] where Syllabic
Consonant Formation allows, thus ['raɪdn̩] *riding* etc.; this means
that *eating* and *eaten* may be homophonous, ['iːʔn̩] etc. Less
common phonetic variants include [iŋ] and [əŋ].

The -*ing* in question is not only the verbal ending (*calling, trying,
stopping*), but also the -*ing* of nouns such as *ceiling, morning, shil-
ling, pudding*, and of adjectives such as *cunning*, which can hardly
be called a separate morpheme, at least from a synchronic point of
view. Names such as *Hastings, Buckingham, Headingley* also exhibit
the alternation. But words such as *string, fling, redwing* never have
[-n]: that is, the alternation is restricted to weak syllables.

It is probably not correct to regard [n] for [ŋ] in -*ing* as an
innovation (as implied by Ekwall 1975: §125). Both alveolar and
velar forms are to be found in early Middle English: they were at
one time distinct, -*inde* forming the participle and -*ing(e)* the
verbal noun (Strang 1970: 238). Although the spelling -*ing* became
established for both, the pronunciation with [n] appears to have
been very much more widespread in educated speech at one time
than it is today. The fashionable pronunciation in eighteenth-
century England was [-ɪn], and this remains in English folk-
memory as the U-RP stereotype of *huntin', shootin' and fishin'*.
Wyld (1936: 289) regards [-ɪŋ] as an innovation, indeed a spelling
pronunciation, which arose in the 1820s.

At the present day it seems that almost every English-speaking
community exhibits a social or stylistic alternation between the two
possibilities, the form with the velar nasal being 'high' and that with
the alveolar 'low'. But there is evidently geographical variation in
respect of the point in social or stylistic stratification at which the

changeover occurs. In Birmingham, England, it appears that the velar form extends well down into working-class speech, while in Birmingham, Alabama, the alveolar form extends well up into middle-class or educated speech. It is safe, though, to make the generalization that where there is an English-speaking working class at least some speakers have [-n]. The one native-English-speaking territory where everyone uses [-ŋ] is South Africa: and the South African working class does not have English as its first language.

Hypercorrection gives rise to would-be elegant pronunciations such as ['tʃɪkɪŋ] *chicken*, ['gɑːdɪŋ] *garden* (= *guarding*), *a braz*[ɪŋ] *hussy*, *Badmi*[ŋ]*ton*.

Sources and further reading

Other works which attempt a similar geographical coverage to the three volumes of *Accents of English* include Bähr 1974; Blunt 1967; Wächtler 1977; Wise 1957. The only one of these on which I have drawn is Bähr, and that very sparingly.

1.1 Accent, dialect: Abercrombie 1967: ch. 2; Hill 1958; Trudgill 1974b Geographical variation: see particularly Bloomfield 1933: ch. 19; Trudgill 1974c; Bailey 1973b; Chambers & Trudgill 1980. Class, sex, ethnicity, age, styles: Labov 1966, 1972a; Trudgill 1974b; Hudson 1980. 'Labov-hypercorrection': particularly Labov 1972a: ch. 5. Stereotypes, images: Trudgill 1972; Giles & Powesland 1975.

1.2 Good recent surveys of phonological theory include Hyman 1975; Sommerstein 1977; see also Jones 1962; Pike 1947. Polylectal phonology: Bailey 1973a.

1.3 Trubetzkoy 1931; O'Connor 1973: ch. 6. Intonation: O'Connor & Arnold 1973; Crystal 1969; Smith & Wilson 1979: ch. 7–8. Voice quality: Catford 1964; Laver 1980.

1.4 Historical linguistics: Bynon 1977. Overt/covert prestige: Trudgill 1972. Spread: Bailey 1973a, 1973b; Chambers & Trudgill 1980.

2. Original. A rival typology: *PEAS*: ch. 1.

3.1, 3.2 I have relied principally on Dobson 1968 (to 1700); Ekwall 1975; Gimson 1980; also Lass 1976; Strang 1970; and older treatments such as Sweet 1888; Wyld 1921, 1936. R Insertion: Johanssen 1973.

3.4 Glottalization: Andrésen 1968; Christophersen 1952; Gimson 1980; Higginbottom 1964; O'Connor 1952; Roach 1973.

References

Abberton, E. 1973. Review of Ondráčková, *The physiological activity of the speech organs*. *Journal of the International Phonetic Association* 3.2.98–100

Abercrombie, D. 1964. Syllable quantity and enclitics in English. In Abercrombie *et al.* 1964: 216–22. Reprinted in Abercrombie 1965: 26–34

Abercrombie, D. 1965. *Studies in phonetics and linguistics*. London: Longman

Abercrombie, D. 1967. *Elements of general phonetics*. Edinburgh University Press

Abercrombie, D., Fry, D. B., MacCarthy, P. A. D., Scott, N. C. & Trim, J. L. M. (eds.) 1964. *In honour of Daniel Jones*. London: Longman

Allen, H. B. 1976. *The linguistic atlas of the Upper Midwest (LAUM)*. Vol. 3. Minneapolis: University of Minnesota Press

Andrésen, B. S. 1968. *Pre-glottalization in English Standard Pronunciation*. Oslo: Norwegian Universities Press

Bähr, D. 1974. *Standard English und seine geographischen Varianten*. Munich: Wilhelm Fink

Bailey, C.-J. N. 1973a. *Variation and linguistic theory*. Arlington, Va.: Center for Applied Linguistics

Bailey, C.-J. N. 1973b. The patterning of language variation. In Bailey & Robinson 1973: 156–86

Bailey, R. W. & Robinson, J. L. 1973. *Varieties of present-day English*. New York: Macmillan

Beaken, M. A. 1971. A study of phonological development in a primary school population of East London. PhD thesis, University of London

Bertz, S. 1975. Der Dubliner Stadtdialekt. Eine synchronische Beschreibung der Struktur und Variabilität des heutigen Dubliner Englischen. I. Phonologie. Doctoral dissertation, University of Freiburg i. Br.

Bickerton, D. 1972. The structure of polylectal grammars. In Shuy 1972: 17–42

Bickerton, D. 1973. The nature of a creole continuum. *Language* 49. 640–69

Bickerton, D. 1975. *Dynamics of a creole system*. Cambridge University Press

Bloomfield, L. 1933. *Language.* New York: Henry Holt & Co. Inc.

Blunt, J. 1967. *Stage dialects.* San Francisco: Chandler Pub. Co.

Bronstein, A. J. 1960. *The pronunciation of American English.* New York: Appleton-Century-Crofts

Bynon, T. 1977. *Historical linguistics.* Cambridge University Press

Catford, J. C. 1964. Phonation types: the classification of some laryngeal components of speech production. In Abercrombie *et al.* 1964: 26–37

Chambers, J. K. & Trudgill, P. 1980. *Dialectology.* Cambridge University Press

Chomsky, N. 1964. *Current issues in linguistic theory.* The Hague: Mouton

Chomsky, N. & Halle, M. 1968. *The sound pattern of English (SPE).* New York: Harper & Row

Christophersen, P. 1952. The glottal stop in English. *English Studies* 33.156–63

Crystal, D. 1969. *Prosodic systems and intonation in English.* Cambridge University Press

Dillard, J. (ed.) 1975. *Perspectives on Black English.* The Hague: Mouton

Dobson, E. J. 1968. *English pronunciation 1500–1700.* Vol. 2, *Phonology.* Second edn. Oxford University Press (First edn 1957)

Ekwall, E. 1975. *A history of Modern English sounds and morphology.* Translated and edited by Alan Ward. Oxford: Blackwell (Original title 1914, fourth edn 1965: *Historische neuenglische Laut- und Formenlehre.* Berlin: Walter de Gruyter)

EPD = Jones 1963; Gimson 1977

Fischer, J. L. 1958. Social influences on the choice of a linguistic variant. *Word* 14.47–56

Giles, H. 1970. Evaluative reaction to accents. *Educational Review* 23. 211–27

Giles, H. 1971. Patterns of evaluation in reaction to RP, South Welsh and Somerset accented speech. *British Journal of Social and Clinical Psychology* 10.3.280–1

Giles, H., Bourhis, R., Trudgill, P. & Lewis, A. 1974. The imposed norm hypothesis: a validation. *Quarterly Journal of Speech* 60.4.405–10

Giles, H. & Powesland, P. F. 1975. *Speech style and social evaluation.* London: Academic Press

Gimson, A. C. 1977. *English pronouncing dictionary (EPD).* Originally compiled by Daniel Jones. Fourteenth edn. London: Dent (Twelfth edn: see Jones 1963)

Gimson, A. C. 1980. *An introduction to the pronunciation of English.* Third edn. London: Edward Arnold (First edn 1962; second edn 1970)

Hanks, P. (ed.) 1979. *Collins dictionary of the English language.* London: Collins

Higginbottom, E. 1964. Glottal reinforcement in English. *Transactions of the Philological Society*

Hill, A. A. 1940. Early loss of [r] before dentals. *Publications of the Modern Language Association* 55.308–321. Reprinted in Williamson & Burke, 1971: 87–100

Hill, G. B. (ed.) 1934. *Boswell's Life of Johnson*. Revised by L. F. Powell. Oxford: Clarendon Press

Hill, T. 1958. Institutional Linguistics. *Orbis* 7.2.441–55

Honikman, B., 1964. Articulatory settings. In Abercrombie *et al.* 1964: 73–84

Hudson, R. A. 1980. *Sociolinguistics*. Cambridge University Press

Hudson, R. A. & Holloway, A. F. 1977. Variation in London English. Mimeo., Dept. of Phonetics and Linguistics, University College London

Hyman, L. 1975. *Phonology: theory and analysis*. New York: Holt, Rinehart & Winston

Jarman, E. & Cruttenden, A. 1976. Belfast intonation and the myth of the fall. *Journal of the International Phonetic Association* 6.1.4–12

Jernudd, B. 1969. A listener experiment: variants of Australian English. *Kivung* 2.1.19–29

Johanssen, S. 1973. Linking and intrusive /r/ in English: a case for a more concrete phonology. *Studia linguistica* 53–68

Jones, D. 1954. Falling and rising diphthongs in Southern English. *Miscellanea Phonetica* II.1–12

Jones, D. 1956. *The pronunciation of English*. Fourth edn. Cambridge University Press (First edn 1909)

Jones, D. 1962. *The phoneme: its nature and use*. Second edn. Cambridge: Heffer

Jones, D. 1963. *English pronouncing dictionary*. Twelfth edn. London: Dent (First edn 1917)

Joos, M. 1942. A phonological dilemma in Canadian English. *Language* 18.141–4

Jordan, R. 1934. *Handbuch der mittelenglischen Grammatik*. Revised by H. Ch. Matthes. Heidelberg: Carl Winter

Kenyon, J. S. 1958. *American pronunciation*. Tenth edn. Ann Arbor, Michigan: George Wahr (First edn 1924)

Kenyon, J. S. & Knott, T. A. 1953. *A pronouncing dictionary of American English*. Springfield, Mass.: Merriam

Knowles, G. O. 1974. Scouse: the urban dialect of Liverpool. PhD thesis, University of Leeds

Knowles, G. O. 1978. The nature of phonological variables in Scouse. In Trudgill 1978: 80–90

Kurath, H. & McDavid, R. I., Jr 1961. *The pronunciation of English in the Atlantic states (PEAS)*. Ann Arbor: University of Michigan Press

Labov, W. 1966. *The social stratification of English in New York City*.

Washington, D. C.: Center for Applied Linguistics

Labov, W. 1969. Contraction, deletion, and inherent variability of the English copula. *Language* 45.4.715–62. Reprinted with modifications in Labov 1972b: 65–129

Labov, W. 1972a. *Sociolinguistic patterns*. Philadelphia: University of Pennsylvania Press (British edn 1978. Oxford: Blackwell)

Labov, W. 1972b. *Language in the inner city*. Studies in the Black English Vernacular. Philadelphia: University of Pennsylvania Press (British edn 1977. Oxford: Blackwell)

LAE = Orton *et al.* 1978

Lakoff, R. T. 1975. *Language and woman's place*. New York: Harper & Row

Lass, R. 1976. *English phonology and phonological theory*. Cambridge University Press

LAUM = Allen 1976

Laver, J. 1968. Voice quality and indexical information. *British Journal of Disorders of Communication* 3.43–54. Reprinted in Laver & Hutcheson 1972

Laver, J. 1980. *The phonetic description of voice quality*. Cambridge University Press

Laver, J. & Hutcheson, S. 1972. *Communication in face to face interaction*. Harmondsworth: Penguin

Lediard, J. 1977. The sounds of the dialect of Canton, a suburb of Cardiff. Appendix A in D. Parry (ed.), *The Survey of Anglo-Welsh dialects*. Vol. 1, *The South-East*. Swansea: David Parry, University College

Lehmann, W. P. 1953. A note on the change of American English /t/. *American Speech* 28.4.271–5

Le Page, R. B. 1977. De-creolization and re-creolization: a preliminary report on the sociolinguistic survey of multilingual communities stage II: St Lucia. *York Papers in Linguistics* 7.107–28

Luelsdorff, P. A. 1975. Dialectology in generative grammar. In Dillard 1975: 74–85

McDavid, R. I., Jr 1952. *H* before semi-vowels in the eastern United States. *Language* 28.41–62. Reprinted in McDavid 1979: 185–98

McDavid, R. I., Jr 1966. Review of Thomas 1958 and Bronstein 1960. *Language* 42.149–55. Reprinted in McDavid 1979: 381–4

McDavid, R. I., Jr 1979. *Dialects in culture: essays in general dialectology*. Edited by W. A. Kretzschmar, Jr. University of Alabama Press

Mather, J. Y. & Speitel, H.-H. 1975. *The linguistic atlas of Scotland*. Scots section. London: Croom Helm

Matthews, W. 1938. *Cockney past and present*. Reprinted 1972 with new preface. London: Routledge & Kegan Paul

Monnot, M. & Freeman, M. 1972. A comparison of Spanish single tap /r/ with American /t/ and /d/ in post-stress intervocalic position. In A. Valdman (ed.), *Papers in linguistics and phonetics to the memory of*

Pierre Delattre. The Hague: Mouton

O'Connor, J. D. 1952. RP and the reinforcing glottal stop. *English Studies* 33.214–18

O'Connor, J. D. 1973. *Phonetics*. Harmondsworth: Penguin

O'Connor, J. D. & Arnold, G. F. 1973. *Intonation of colloquial English*. Second edn. London: Longman

Orton, H., *et al.* (ed.) 1962–71. *Survey of English dialects (SED)*. Introduction; Basic material (four volumes). Leeds: Arnold

Orton, H., Sanderson, S. & Widdowson, J. 1978. *The linguistic atlas of England (LAE)*. London: Croom Helm (American edition 1977. Atlantic Highlands, N. J.: Humanities Press)

Oswald, V. A., Jr 1943. 'Voiced T' – a misnomer. *American Speech* 18.18–25

PEAS = Kurath & McDavid 1961

Pike, K. L. 1947. *Phonemics*. Ann Arbor: University of Michigan Press

Pilch, H. 1976. *Empirical linguistics*. Munich: Francke

Prator, C. H., Jr & Robinett, B. W. 1972. *Manual of American English pronunciation*. Third edn. New York: Holt, Rinehart & Winston

Ramsaran, S. M. 1978. Phonetic and phonological correlates of style in English: a preliminary investigation. PhD thesis, University of London

Reed, C. E. 1967. *Dialects of American English*. Cleveland, Ohio: World Pub. Co. Second printing 1973: University of Massachusetts Press

Reid, I. 1977. *Social class differences in Britain: a sourcebook*. London: Open Books

Roach, P. 1973. Glottalization of English /p/, /t/, /k/ and /tʃ/: a reexamination. *Journal of the International Phonetic Association* 3.1.10–21

Schirmunski, V. 1930. Sprachgeschichte und Siedlungsmundarten. *GRM* 18.118

Schmidt, J. 1872. *Die Verwandtschaftsverhältnisse der indogermanischen Sprachen*. Weimar: Hermann Böhlau

SED = Orton *et al.* 1961–72

Sheridan, T. 1762. *A course of lectures on elocution*. Reprinted 1968, Menston: Scholar Press

Shuy, R. W. (ed.) 1972. *Sociolinguistics: current trends and prospects*. Washington: Georgetown University Press

Sivertsen, E. 1960. *Cockney phonology*. Oslo University Press

Smith, N. V. & Wilson, D. 1979. *Modern linguistics. The results of Chomsky's revolution*. Harmondsworth: Penguin

Sommerstein, A. 1977. *Modern phonology*. London: Edward Arnold

SPE = Chomsky & Halle 1968

Speitel, H.-H. 1968. Some studies in the dialect of Midlothian. PhD thesis, University of Edinburgh

Sprague de Camp, L. 1971. Arse and ass. *Journal of the International Phonetic Association* 1.2.79–80

Stampe, D. 1972. How I spent my summer vacation. Unpub. PhD diss.,

Ohio State University
Strang, B. M. H. 1970. *A history of English*. London: Methuen
Sweet, H. 1888. *A history of English sounds*. Oxford: Henry Frowde
Thomas, C. K. 1958. *Phonetics of American English*. New York: Ronald
Trager, G. L. 1942. The phoneme 't': a study in theory and method. *American Speech* 17.3.144–8
Trager, G. L. & Smith, H. L., Jr 1951. *An outline of English structure*. Washington, D.C.: American Council of Learned Societies ˙
Tripp, C. A. 1975. *The homosexual matrix*. New York: McGraw-Hill (British edn 1977. London: Quartet)
Trubetzkoy, N. S. 1931. Phonologie et géographie linguistique. *Travaux du Cercle Linguistique de Prague* 4.228–34
Trudgill, P. J. 1972. Sex, covert prestige and linguistic change in the urban British English of Norwich. *Language in Society* 1.179–95
Trudgill, P. J. 1974a. *The social differentiation of English in Norwich*. Cambridge University Press
Trudgill, P. 1974b. *Sociolinguistics: an introduction*. Harmondsworth: Penguin Books
Trudgill, P. 1974c. Linguistic change and diffusion: description and explanation in sociolinguistic dialect geography. *Language in Society* 2.215–46
Trudgill, P. (ed.) 1978. *Sociolinguistic patterns in British English*. London: Edward Arnold
Trudgill, P. J. & Foxcroft, T. 1978. On the sociolinguistics of vocalic merger: transfer and approximation in East Anglia. In Trudgill 1978: 69–79
Wächtler, K. 1977. *Geographie und Stratifikation der englischen Sprache*. Düsseldorf: Bagel, and Munich: Francke
Wakelin, M. F. 1972. *English dialects: an introduction*. London: Athlone Press
Wells, J. C. 1962. A specimen of British English. *Maître Phonétique* 117.2–5
Wells, J. C. 1970. Local accents in England and Wales. *Journal of Linguistics* 6.231–52
Wells, J. C. 1973. *Jamaican pronunciation in London*. Oxford: Blackwell
Wells, J. C. & Colson, G. 1971. *Practical phonetics*. London: Pitman
Williamson, J. V. & Burke, V. M. 1971. *A various language: perspectives on American dialects*. New York: Holt, Rinehart & Winston
Wise, C. M. 1957. *Applied phonetics*. Englewood Cliffs, N. J.: Prentice-Hall
Wolfram, W. A. 1969. *A sociolinguistic description of Detroit Negro speech*. Washington, D.C.: Center for Applied Linguistics
Wright, J. 1905. *The English dialect grammar*. Oxford: Henry Frowde
Wyld, H. C. 1921. *A short history of English*. London: John Murray (First edn 1914)
Wyld, H. C. 1936. *A history of modern colloquial English*. Oxford: Blackwell (First edn 1920)

Index

Made in the USA
Lexington, KY
17 October 2016